THE GUIDE TO
ARTS & CRAFTS
WORKSHOPS

Other *ShawGuides*:

- *The Guide to Cooking Schools*
- *The Guide to Writers Conferences*
- *The Guide to Photography Workshops*

If *ShawGuides* are not available at your local bookseller, you can order directly from us. Include the book's title with a check or money order for $16.95 (includes shipping and handling) and mail to:

Shaw Associates
625 Biltmore Way, Dept. 1406A
Coral Gables, FL 33134

FIRST EDITION

THE GUIDE TO ARTS & CRAFTS WORKSHOPS

SHAW ASSOCIATES, Publishers
625 Biltmore Way, Suite 1406
Coral Gables, Florida 33134
(305) 446-8888

Please note that the information herein has been obtained from
the listed schools, organizations, and individuals and is subject
to change. The editors and publisher accept no responsibility
for inaccuracies. Sponsors should be contacted prior to sending money and/or making travel plans.

Library of Congress Catalog Card Number 89-61937
ISBN 0-945834-05-5

Printed by R. R. Donnelley & Sons Company

INTRODUCTION

The Guide to Arts & Crafts Workshops is the first comprehensive source of information about short-term intensive programs for creative people of all ages. Designed for all of you who are interested in the arts and crafts, whether you are a beginner exploring a new hobby or career or an experienced artist or craftsperson seeking to improve your expertise, the Guide will help you find the programs that fit your interests, schedule, and budget.

The programs listed in *The Guide* cover a wide range of subjects in arts — drawing, painting, and sculpting — and crafts that relate to fiber, metal, wood, glass, ceramics, and precious gems — as well as decorative, folk, and native arts and crafts — and practical crafts such as boat and house building. All programs are taught by professional artists and craftspeople, most of whom have either won awards or exhibited their work and some of whom are considered leaders in their fields. While programs range in length from one day to several weeks, they all adhere to the intensive "workshop" format — meeting daily rather than once or twice weekly — and many programs are geared toward taking you from start to finish on at least one project.

Section I — Arts & Crafts Workshops — contains detailed descriptions of workshops offered by 237 sponsors, including arts and crafts centers and organizations, schools and colleges, and individual artists and craftspeople. Each listing contains such specific details as dates, type and scope of instruction, number of students per instructor or workshop, topics, daily schedule, faculty credentials, teaching methods, costs and payment and refund policies, facilities, accommodations, location and nearby attractions, special activities, and contact. Included also are a sampling of the titles offered as well as in-depth descriptions of some programs.

Section II — Residencies and Retreats — is for experienced, self-motivated artists and craftspeople who desire a distraction-free working environment so that they can focus solely on their projects for a period of a few weeks to a few months. Some are open only to those who have achieved a measure of success while others welcome dedicated artists of all levels. Residencies usually require a commitment to teaching and assistance with work at the facility in exchange for studio and living space. In addition to the contact address and telephone, each listing contains information about living and working quarters, admission requirements and application procedures, and costs. Because retreats depend upon public and private funding and have limited resources available for mailing expenses, they ask that inquiries be accompanied by a self-addressed, stamped envelope.

Section III — Appendix — contains three indexes to assist you in finding workshops suited to your particular needs: a Geographic Index of workshops in 43 states and 28 countries, which will direct you to programs that are convenient to your location or travel plans; a Specialty Index, which will help you find programs in your area of interest or expertise; and an index of Workshops for Young People, which directs you to programs that will nurture your children's artistic talents.

The content of *The Guide* is based on factual information obtained from questionnaires, brochures, catalogs, and personal interviews with workshop sponsors. Each listing was sent to the sponsor for verification prior to publication. The length of a listing depends largely on the amount of information provided by the sponsor and is not intended to reflect the merit of its faculty or curriculum. The workshops are not endorsed by the publisher nor do sponsors pay for their listings. Although every effort has been made to ensure accuracy, changes do occur. Workshop sponsors request that you call or write for a free current workshop schedule or catalog in order to confirm dates, costs, and programs before sending money or making travel plans.

We thank the workshop sponsors and the retreat directors for their cooperation and assistance. Readers are invited to let us know about their workshop experiences and to submit names and addresses of sponsors and/or sources of additional listings. Comments and suggestions are also welcome.

We wish you success in your creative endeavors.

The Editor

CONTENTS

I

ARTS & CRAFTS WORKSHOPS

ACAPULCO ART WORKSHOPS
Acapulco, Mexico
One-week workshops from October-April

These winter vacation painting workshops offer artists of all levels of ability the opportunity to study with accomplished instructors in a tropical setting. Each workshop is limited to 17 students, who arrive on Sunday, receive four hours of instruction daily from Monday through Friday, and depart on Saturday. Some workshops are conducted almost entirely in the studio while landscape workshops feature excursions to non-tourist, picturesque sites. Each instructor determines the format and schedule for the week. A variety of painting styles and media are offered, including pastel, oil, acrylic, watercolor, and collage.

Specialties: Painting in a variety of media.

Faculty: Includes transparent watercolor painter Marge Alderson; Don Andrews, author of *Interpreting the Figure in Watercolor*; Al Brouillette, author of *The Evolving Picture*; Bob Gerbracht, a graduate of the Yale School of Fine Arts who has exhibited in the U.S. and abroad; and Barbara Nechis, author of *Watercolor, The Creative Experience*, and a faculty member of Parsons School of Design.

Costs, Accommodations: The cost, which includes room and board, is $550 for the student, $400 for a nonparticipant spouse or guest. A $100 deposit secures reservation with balance due on arrival. Those who cancel at least 30 days prior receive a $75 refund. Oceanfront accommodations are provided on the private estate of Mexican artist Nora Beteta and meals are served family style on one of the verandahs overlooking the pool and ocean.

Location: The estate is situated across the bay from Roqueta Island, near the Caletilla beach in Acapulco.

Contact: Johanna Morrell, Av. Caletilla No. 62, Acapulco, Gro. Mexico 39390; (52) 748 33860.

ADAMY'S WORKSHOPS
Larchmont, New York and other locations
One to five-day workshops

A sculptor and teacher since 1968, George E. Adamy offers three sculpting workshops that stress the use of industrial materials he has developed for durability, lightness, and unlimited size. One-day workshops held in his home run for six hours and are limited to four students and on-location workshops are by special arrangement. Workshop topics are concrete system, in which students learn to cast, mold, model, and apply a special cement mixture directly to armatures; cast paper, for casting and directly building three-dimensional objects of any size or color; and molding humans and objects, in which students learn a half-dozen techniques for molding the human body, plants, machinery, and sculptures.

Specialties: Sculpting using industrial materials.

Faculty: George Adamy, who formerly taught at SUNY College-Purchase, has taught many workshops and is listed in *Who's Who in American Art*. His work is in the collections of the Mayo Clinic, the White Plains Hospital Medical Center, and the State of Connecticut School at Silvermine.

Costs: The one-day workshop fee is $250 for up to four students. On-location workshops and courses are $250 per day plus travel, lodging, and materials.

Location: The studio is 22 miles from mid-town New York City and five miles from White Plains.

Contact: George E. Adamy, 19 Elkan Rd., Larchmont, NY 10538; (914) 834-6276.

ADELE BISHOP CERTIFIED STENCIL SEMINARS
St. Louis, Missouri; Waukesha, Wisconsin; Manchester, Vermont
Three-day seminars year-round

The Adele Bishop National Certification Seminars, established in 1980, cover the various aspects of stenciling, from preparing stencils to completion of stenciled projects. Three to five Friday to Sunday seminars are held annually at each of the three locations, with each class usually limited to ten to twelve students of all levels, who are taught by two instructors. Sessions begin at 9 am and end at 5 pm on Friday, 6 pm on Saturday, and 4 pm on Sunday and homework assignments prepare students for the next day's lesson. The course covers the use of Adele Bishop's specially designed stenciling materials and cutting tools; the fundamentals of design, layout, pattern, and color selection; basic to advanced techniques, including hands-on wall stenciling practice; business aspects of a teaching and/or stenciling career; and at least three take-home projects in the areas of floorcloth, fabric, and woodenware stenciling. On completion of the seminar, students receive the Certified Stenciler Certificate and qualify to apply for the Certified Teacher Certificate.

Specialties: Stenciling.

Faculty: Each class is instructed by at least one Master Teacher, who is assisted by an Adele Bishop Certified Teacher. Master Teachers include Zilda McKinstry and Kathie Marron-Wall, Jeanie Benson, and Louise Spheeris.

Costs, Accommodations: Seminar cost, which covers all materials, projects, and luncheons, is $350. A $75 deposit must accompany registration with balance due 30 days prior. Cancellations more than 29 days prior receive full refund, from 15 to 29 days prior refund is $225, no refund thereafter. Lodging and transportation information is provided by the instructor at each location.

Location: Information about specific locations is available from Jeanie Benson (314) 822-7412 (St. Louis, Missouri); Louis Spheeris (414) 646-8050 (Waukesha, Wisconsin); Kathie Marron-Wall *or* Zilda McKinstry (802) 867-5915 (Manchester, Vermont).

Contact: Adele Bishop Seminars, P.O. Box 3349, Kinston, NC 28502-3349; (800) 334-4186 *or* (919) 527-4186.

ADULT INSTITUTES IN THE ARTS (AIA)
Oklahoma Arts Institute
Quartz Mountain State Park, Oklahoma
One weekend in mid-October

Established in 1976 as a nonprofit institution dedicated to providing summer workshops for artistically gifted teenagers, the Oklahoma Arts Institute began offering a series of four October weekend workshops for adult artists and writers in 1983. Each three-day (Thursday noon to Sunday noon) workshop is devoted to one of four disciplines — visual arts, theatre, writing, or photography — with five courses offered during each weekend. Each course is led by a noted expert and limited to 25 professionals and serious amateurs who desire an intensive class and study environment in which to develop their skills. Typical course titles include Watercolor (Carolyn Brady), a series of discussions, studio sessions, and demonstrations that stress image rather than technique and focus on the history of watercolor painting, its characteristics, and new ways to use the medium; Sculpture (Suzanne Klotz), in which each participant builds a free-standing or hanging piece from meaningful "junk" brought from home; Monotype (Tom Berg), a hands-on workshop devoted to the basic techniques and translating the student's style of painting into this medium; and Art History/Criticism (Gerrit Henry) a survey of American landscape painting. Other weekend activities include chamber music concerts, panel discussions, and lectures by visiting artists. One graduate credit hour is available from the College of Fine Arts, University of Oklahoma.

Specialties: Visual arts.

Faculty: In addition to the above, has included papermakers Timothy Barrett and Kathryn Clark, painters Don Nice, Juan Gonzalez, Don Eddy and Peter Plagens, illustrator Alan E. Cober, sculptors Richard Hunt and Norman Laliberté, ceramist Paul Soldner, and screenprinter Dan Kiacz.

Costs, Accommodations: Fee for each workshop is $325, which includes double occupancy lodging, meals, and a $25 processing fee. Single supplement is $75. A 50% deposit must accompany application; enrollment deadline is August 15 and a $10 late fee is charged after this date. Cancellations at least five days prior to workshop receive a full refund less $25 fee. Accommodations are in Quartz Mountain State Lodge rooms, cabins, or duplexes. Scholarships are available for Oklahoma public school educators.

Location, Facilities: Quartz Mountain State Park is situated in the Great Plains country of southwestern Oklahoma, off Highway 44, ten miles south of Lone Wolf and 20 miles north of Altus. Lodge facilities include studio pavilions and a new library and amphitheatre.

Contact: Oklahoma Arts Institute, Adult Institutes in the Arts, P.O. Box 18154, Oklahoma City, OK 73154; (405) 842-0890.

ADVANCED LAMPWORKING SEMINAR
Northstar Glassworks
Camp Colton, Oregon
One-week workshop in October

This intensive glass blowing workshop, sponsored by Northstar Glassworks each year since 1987, is designed for experienced and professional glass blowers, although beginners are accepted if space is available. Instruction covers the techniques of how to shape and apply color to hollow-blown forms on the end of a glass blowpipe; building up a "gather"; making a neck, foot, and stopper; and coloration and blow hose techniques. Students make containers, vases, goblets, scent bottles, beads, marbles, and paperweights. The focus is on hands-on experience and aesthetics with relevant discussions of glass chemistry and physics.

Specialties: Glass blowing.

Faculty: Paul Trautman produces his own line of lamp-blown art glass and is also a neon sculptor, scientific glass blower, and colored glass maker.

Costs, Accommodations: The fee, which includes lodging, meals, and materials, is $625. A $100 deposit reserves a space with balance due four weeks prior. Enrollment closes eight weeks prior. Double occupancy rooms are provided in the student cottages and meals are served in Riverfalls Lodge, a rustic building situated between two creeks.

Location, Facilities: Colton is located 35 miles southeast of Portland, between Estacada and Molalla on Hwy. 211. The camp covers 56 acres of woods, ponds, and streams and the student cottages are built around a fishing lake. The old Dining Hall contains two well-equipped studios, a meeting room/lounge, and a student store. A third studio, furnished with hot glass working equipment, is located deep in the woods.

Contact: Northstar Glassworks, 9060 SW Sunstead Ln., Portland, OR 97225; (503) 292-6780.

ADVENTURES IN WATERCOLOR
Indian Nations International
Locations include Texas, Arizona, and Guatamala
Ten-day workshops

Incorporated in 1988, Indian Nations International sponsors three or four watercolor workshops a year at scenic locales, each limited to approximately 25 artists of all levels. Special efforts are made to accommodate handicapped persons, on the basis of prior consultation.

Specialties: Watercolor.

Faculty: John Carter was appointed "State Artist of Texas" by the Texas House of Representatives in 1981. A Signature Member of the Southwestern Watercolor Society, he has taught painting for more than 18 years, won awards in a variety of media, and is represented in private and public collections. Larry Weston, who specializes in landscapes of the Southwest, is represented in galleries and private collections and is president of the Southwestern Watercolor Society and associate member of the American Watercolor Society. Milford Zornes, who is represented in the collections of the Metropolitan Museum of Art in New York, the Los Angeles County Museum, and the White House, is a member of the American Watercolor Society and California Watercolor Society.

Costs, Accommodations: The cost, which includes local transportation, hotel, and some meals, ranges from $900 to $1,000. A $100 deposit must accompany registration approximately five weeks prior. Cancellations are granted a full refund less hotel cancellation costs, if applicable. Participants are lodged at the Chisos Mountain Lodge in Big Bend National Park, Texas, and at the Thunderbird Lodge at the mouth of Canyon de Chelly in Arizona.

Location: The Guatamala workshop features painting opportunities in colonial towns and villages, the archeological site at Tikal, Guatamala City, Antigua, Panajachel, and Chichicastenago. The Texas workshop is held in Big Bend National Park, which offers 1,100-square-miles of desert and mountain wilderness along the Rio Grande. Canyon de Chelly National Monument, Arizona, situated on the 16-million-acre Navajo Reservation, contains the ruins of the Anasazi cliff dwellers.

Contact: Indian Nations International, 730 Asp, #211, Norman, OK 73069; (405) 321-5380.

THE AEGEAN CENTER FOR THE FINE ARTS (ACFA)
Paros, Cyclades, Greece and Pistoia, Tuscany, Italy

Eight-week sessions in April/May and June/July; nine-week Italy-Greece Session from September-November

Founded in 1966 by award-winning painter Brett Taylor, The Aegean Center for the Fine Arts offers small, individualized eight-week courses in printmaking, sculpture, painting and drawing, creative writing, photography, history of the arts, and Greek literature. Course enrollment is limited to 15 students per five instructors and self-motivation and self-discipline are emphasized. The Printmaking course explores all aspects of the intaglio and block process and the separate printmaking studio provides for such techniques as application of hard and soft grounds and aquatint, scraping and burnishing, drypoint engraving, color inks, monoprints, collographs, and mounting and storage. Painting and Drawing, which is conducted mostly outdoors, covers a variety of techniques and materials with emphasis on life drawing, however each student is free to work on landscape, portrait, still life, abstract, or more experimental ideas. Sculpture, which involves the use of various tools, techniques, and materials, stresses evolving ideas with clay models and hands-on work with the unique white marble of the island of Paros. Students have the opportunity to visit the ancient quarries to obtain material for carving. Additional Center activities include gallery exhibits, poetry and prose readings, slide lectures, and musical evenings.

The Italy-Greece Session, first offered in September-November, 1990, is open to ten students, who spend the first three weeks in Pistoia, where they study art history, tour historical and artistic sites, and gather images and ideas. The last six weeks are spent at the Center in Paros, where they develop ideas and images in the studio.

Specialties: Drawing, painting, printmaking, sculpture, photography.

Faculty: Alice Meyer-Wallace, a freelance illustrator and scholarship recipient from *Scholastic Magazine*, Roma (RISD), and Yale Summer School, has exhibited since 1964. Jane C. Morris, a professional artist and teacher since 1979 and former manager of a fine arts foundry casting bronze, has exhibited in the U.S. and Greece.

Costs, Accommodations: The eight-week course fee is $1,000 plus $45 lab fee. Nearby accommodations (rooms, efficiencies, hotels) range from $12 to $50 per day. The Italy-Greece Session tuition is $3,000 (registration deadline July 1), which includes room, board, and travel in Italy and room and lab fees in Greece. Round-trip travel from the U.S. is not included. Both programs require a nonrefundable $25 application fee and balance is due on acceptance. An 80% refund is granted cancellations at least 60 days prior to arrival; 50% between 30 and 60 days prior; no refund thereafter.

Location, Facilities: The Center is in a 230-year-old Venetian structure in the main port town of Paros, one of the Cycladic Islands in the Aegean Sea, approximately 100 miles from Athens. Facilities include a darkroom and studio space. The Italy portion of the Italy-Greece Sessions is in a 16th century villa in the Tuscan countryside above Pistoia, 20 miles west of Florence, which is included in field trips along with Sienna, Lucca, and Pisa.

Contact: The Aegean Center for the Fine Arts, Paros 844 00 Cyclades, Greece; Fax (30) 28422449 *or* Suite 155, 3650 Silverside Rd., Wilmington, DE 19810.

AIRBRUSH WORKSHOPS
New York City, Tampa, Boston, Washington, D.C., and Orange, CT
Three-day workshops year-round

Airbrush artist Stephen D. Rubelmann offers a three-day hands-on workshop for anyone desiring basic airbrush skills. Each workshop is limited to six participants and is scheduled from 9 am to 5 pm each day. The first day covers airbrush principles, including construction, how it works, materials used, maintenance, and how to set up an airbrush station. Students begin airbrush practice sessions. The second day concludes the practice sessions and starts frisketing, silhouetting, and airbrushing on a photo project. The third day is devoted to a photo retouching project in black and white, finishing with a color project using paints and dyes.

Specialties: Airbrush.

Faculty: Stephen D. Rubelmann is author of *The Encyclopedia of the Airbrush*, Volumes I, II, and III. He has been an artist, illustrator, retoucher, designer, art director, and set designer and has managed studios and company art departments.

Costs: The workshop fee of $500 includes the three volumes of *The Encyclopedia of the Airbrush*, a Paasche V1 Airbrush, other equipment, discounts on future purchases, and free follow-up advice and information. A $10 deposit must accompany registration with balance due ten days prior. Deposit is refunded if cancellation is received at least ten days prior. Credit card (VISA, MasterCard) payment accepted. A $25 discount is granted the second and additional persons from the same company who register at the same time.

Location: Workshops in major cities are usually scheduled the second Friday-Sunday of the month. Companies and private groups can schedule workshops at their convenience.

Contact: Airbrush Workshops, P.O. Box 623, Orange, CT 06477; (203) 795-0565.

AL BROUILLETTE, A.N.A.-A.W.S.
Locations in the U.S., Canada, and Mexico
Four-day workshops

Since 1972, Al Brouillette has taught watercolor and acrylic workshops under the sponsorship of state, regional, and national art organizations. Classes are limited to 15 to 25 intermediate to advanced students and emphasize the translation of the subject and the design of the painting.

Specialties: Watercolor and acrylic painting.

Faculty: Al Brouillette has received Gold Medals of Honor from the American Watercolor Society, the Rockport Art Association, and the Southwestern Watercolor Society and awards from the National Academy of Design, the National Watercolor Society, and the Southern Watercolor Society. He has been invited to jury for acceptance and awards for state, regional and national exhibitions and his work has appeared in such publications as *The Artist's Magazine*, *American Artist* magazine, and *Southwestern Art Magazine*.

Costs, Accommodations: Costs and refund policies vary, depending on sponsoring organization, location, housing, and meals.

Location: Includes art centers, art societies, and conference rooms in motels and hotels in cities in the U.S., Canada, and Mexico. Most public facilities are handicapped accessible.

Contact (for schedule): Al Brouillette, 1300 Sunset Ct., Arlington, TX 76013; (817) 261-8723.

THE ALAN BAXTER POTTERY WORKSHOP
The White House
Somersham, Ipswich, Suffolk, England
Five-day residential courses year-round

Since 1980, Alan Baxter has offered residential ceramic/pottery courses for students of all ages and levels. Designed to develop creative ideas through demonstrations, one-on-one instruction, and practical application, the courses cover the techniques and skills of working with clay, including preparation, throwing, turning, pinching, coiling, slabbing, liquid clays, and firing according to the needs and desires of the students. Each program begins with a Sunday evening get together and meal and classes meet daily from 9:30 am to 4:30 pm, Monday to Friday, with the studios open to students until 9:30 pm. Any pieces desired to be kept and not completed by week's end will be finished by the instructors according to the students' direction. A formal certificate of attendance is available to all who successfully complete the course.

Specialties: Pottery/ceramics.

Faculty: Alan Baxter trained in ceramics/pottery at London's Central School of Art and Design and has worked in his own studios as a freelance artist since 1969. He founded the East Anglican Potters Association in 1982 and his work has been exhibited in England and West Germany.

Costs, Accommodations: Cost of the five-day course, including meals and lodging, is £170. A camping facilities option, which includes lunches, is available for a fee of £120. A nonrefundable, transferable £40 deposit must accompany application with balance due four weeks prior. Cancellations more than four weeks prior forfeit deposit and thereafter the fee balance, less a £50 fee, is refunded unless space can be filled. Extended accommodation for Friday evening, which includes dinner and Saturday breakfast, is offered at an additional cost of £20. Bookings of three or more persons receive a 10% discount, which includes a per person allowance of up to six pieces or eleven pounds of completed ceramics. Accommodations are at the White House Studio Workshop and, if necessary, at neighboring private homes or secluded campsites.

Location, Facilities: The house and workshops, in the rural agricultural village of Somersham, are close to the 14th century locales of Ipswich, Lavenham, and Kersey and approximately one hour from London by train. Transportation to and from the Ipswich railway and bus station is provided at no charge, and pickup from Felixstowe Port and Harwich Port are available for an additional £10. The studios, housed within old Suffolk buildings, are equipped with seven small and large electric throwing wheels, a continental momentum wheel, a large traditional kick wheel, four kilns, a baby raku kiln, and a small salt kiln.

Contact: The Alan Baxter Pottery Workshop, The White House, Somersham, Ipswich, Suffolk, IP8 4QA, England; (44) 0473 831256.

ALFRED C. CHADBOURN OIL & ACRYLIC WORKSHOP
New Orleans, Louisiana
Four-day April workshop

Since 1980, Alfred Chadbourn has conducted workshops that are designed to stimulate a more creative and provocative approach to painting, encouraging students to take liberties with nature, experiment, exaggerate colors, and transform scenes into more dynamic statements. This four-day workshop, scheduled from 9:30 am to 3:30 pm daily and limited to 20 artists of all levels, includes demonstrations, individual instruction, and critiques. Students paint on location for the landscape portion of the course and inside for still life.

Specialties: Painting.

Faculty: Alfred C. Chadbourn, an elected member of National Academy, studied at the Chouinard Arts Institute, the Academie de La Grande Chaumiere, and L'Ecole Des Beaux Arts. He is author of *A Direct Approach to Painting* and *Painting With a Fresh Eye* and his paintings are in such major museums as the Chicago Art Institute, Corcoran Gallery, Boston Museum of Fine Arts, Los Angeles County Museum, and National Academy of Design.

Costs, Accommodations: Course fee is $180. A $90 deposit must accompany registration with balance due eight weeks prior. Participants arrange their own lodging at area hotels or bed & breakfasts; daily rates range from $25 to $65.

Contact: Georgia Taylor, 8809 Tanglewild Pl., New Orleans, LA 70123; (504) 737-5281.

AMERICAN CRAFT MUSEUM
New York, New York
One-day workshops

Established as The Museum of Contemporary Crafts in 1956 and renamed in 1979, the nonprofit American Craft Museum offers free demonstrations and hands-on workshops that relate to current exhibitions. Typical sessions include quilting and confectionary art.

Specialties: A variety of crafts.

Faculty: The workshops are taught by exhibiting artists and professionals.

Location: The museum is situated in mid-town Manhattan on the ground floor of the E.F. Hutton Building, which was built in 1986.

Contact: American Craft Museum, 40 W. 53rd St., New York, NY 10019; (212) 956-3535.

AMERICAN WOODCARVING SCHOOL
Wayne, New Jersey
Five-day courses in July

Opened in 1974, the American Woodcarving School offers two concentrated five-day (eight hours per day) summer woodcarving courses that are designed to take the student from beginning to advanced work. Basic instruction covers such topics as introductory carving, tool sharpening and maintenance, wood identification, project selection, composition, sketching, styling, use of finishes, and marketing possibilities. The advanced course consists of an open workshop arrangement that allows the student to concentrate on personal projects or problems. On-going three-hour classes in basic and advanced woodcarving are also scheduled on Monday and Thursday evenings and Wednesday and Saturday mornings. A study and workshop in custom carving, minimum 15 hours per week, is also offered for the career-oriented student. The school is accredited by the Veterans Administration of New Jersey for the education of disabled veterans who qualify.

Specialties: Woodcarving.

Faculty: Founder/director Michael DeNike, a graduate of the National Academy of Design, received awards and commissions in church sculpture and public buildings and is listed in *Who's Who in American Art*.

Costs, Accommodations: Course fee, which must be paid in advance, is $350 per week. Lodging can be arranged at local motels or in private homes and campsites are available.

Location: The school is located in northern New Jersey, near Paterson and Pompton Lakes.

Contact: Michael DeNike, American Woodcarving School, 21 Pompton Plains Crossroad, Wayne, NJ 07470; (201) 835-8555.

ANAGAMA WOODFIRE WORKSHOPS
Belvidere, New Jersey
Ten-day workshops and two-day seminars in summer and fall

Ceramist Peter Callas began firing anagama wood kilns in 1976 and established his present facility in Belvidere in 1987. His workshop, which is limited to six to eight students of all levels, includes a ten-day firing cycle that concludes with a two-day clay seminar by Peter Voulkos. The firing cycle includes stacking, firing, cooling, and unloading and participants are asked to bring five cubic feet of dry greenware or bisque, unglazed, cone 10 stoneware, and/or porcelain. During the five or six-day firing, daily shifts fire the kiln and participate in other activities such as swimming and barbecues. Peter Callas presents slide shows and informal talks on all aspects of wood firing and clay and wheels are available. The two-day concluding clay seminar features afternoon demonstrations followed by a preview and sale of the anagama results with comments by Peter Voulkos.

Specialties: Ceramics fired in the anagama wood kiln.

Faculty: Ceramists Peter Callas and Peter Voulkos have collaborated on projects. Peter Callas has exhibited in shows in Philadelphia, Little Rock, New York, Detroit, and Chicago. His work is in the collections of the Gotoh Art Museum in Tokyo and the Western Electric Corporation in New York.

Costs, Accommodations: The cost of the ten-day workshop is $350, which includes 5 cubic feet of kiln space. The two-day seminar is $80 and kiln space is available at $30 per foot. A 50% deposit must accompany registration at least two weeks in advance with balance due on arrival. A full refund is granted cancellations at least one week prior. A list of nearby accommodations is provided or participants can camp in the pine forest for $7 per day.

Location, Facilities: The workshop facility, situated on three acres, consists of an 18th century 1,700-square-foot barn renovated for studio use, an 18-foot long tunnel anagama kiln (300 cubic foot capacity), a swimming pool, and a trout stream. Yard games include croquet, volleyball, badminton, and horseshoes. Belvidere is in northwest New Jersey, eight miles from Delaware Water Gap, 70 miles from New York City, and 80 miles from Philadelphia. Area sports include golf, canoeing, and riding.

Contact: Peter Callas, RD #2, Box 213, Belvidere, NJ 07823; (201) 475-8907.

ANDERSON RANCH ARTS CENTER
Snowmass Village, Colorado
Two, five, and ten-day workshops from May-September

This interdisciplinary visual arts center, founded in 1966 by ceramist Paul Soldner, offers almost 80 intensive workshops in woodworking and furniture design, painting and drawing, ceramics, photography and interdisciplinary and critical studies, as well as a Studio Residency Program for emerging and recognized artists. Most participants are experienced or professional artists and craftsmen, however programs are available for both the novice and intermediate student, as well as one and two-week sessions for children and teenagers.

Sessions typically meet from 9 am to 5 pm, Monday through Friday, average 12 participants per instructor and assistant, and are designed to encourage personal interaction, individual development, and excellence in technical skills. Many workshops begin early in the morning and extend late into the evening, with demonstrations, slide lectures, hands-on practice, and individual critique a part of the daily schedule. Other activities include a Sunday evening movie and a Tuesday evening potluck dinner followed by a guest slide lecture. A Photography Forum is held on Thursday evenings and a Ceramics Forum every other Friday noon and faculty slide lectures are presented throughout the summer. Group shows of visiting and resident faculty, open to the public, are exhibited as an extension of the workshop experience. College credit is available through Colorado Mountain College and most universities.

The workshops are taught by a distinguished faculty and most of them relate to the instructor's specialty or particular area of expertise. Typical titles include Rustic Furniture (Daniel Mack), Furniture (Sam Maloof), A Personal Approach (James Krenov), Running A Business (Thomas Moser), Soldner's Turf (Paul Soldner), Tableware and the Occasion (Akio Takamori), Clay Constructions (Anne Currier), Finding Form and Inspiration (Chris Bertoni), Drawing: Pushing Your Own Limits (Irv Tepper), and The Joy of Drawing the Figure (Robert Kushner). Interdisciplinary workshops involve participants in exploration of different media and critical workshops examine the nature of criticism and its role in contemporary art. The children's and teenagers' workshops are scheduled 2 1/2 hours daily, four or five days a week. Topics include sculpture, clay, visual design, art, printmaking, and photography.

Specialties: Woodworking, furniture design, ceramics, painting, drawing, and photography.

Faculty: In addition to the above, has included multi-media artist Sas Colby, woodworkers Tage Frid, Peter Korn, and Alan Peters, furniture designers Robert DeFuccio and Hy Zelkowitz, woodcarver Nora Hall, ceramists Doug Casebeer, Chris Staley, Dorothy Hafner, Brad Miller, Ron Nagle, and Ken Price.

Costs, Accommodations: Workshop tuition is $150 to $175 for a two-day workshop, $225 to $325 for five days, and $350 to $475 for ten days. Lab fee ranges from $30 to $100 and children's workshops range from $85 to $120. Application must be accompanied by a $200 deposit and nonrefundable $30 registration fee, which is payable by VISA or MasterCard. Full refund is granted cancellations more than 30 days prior; no refunds thereafter. On-campus housing with meals is available for $235 per week, double occupancy. A $100 housing deposit must accompany registration, with balance due 30 days prior. Tuition grants of $250 are awarded yearly to three furniture designer/makers and four ceramists. Applicants must submit five to eight slides, a description of the work, a resume, and a statement of career goals. Application deadline is April 15 and notification is by May 1. Four scholarships are offered to children in the Roaring Fork Valley.

Location, Facilities: The ranch, a mixture of historic log cabins and barns, modern studio facilities, and new buildings, is located in the mountain resort of Snowmass Village, ten miles west of Aspen and 200 miles west of Denver. Facilities include a well equipped ceramics studio and woodshop, which is open 24 hours a day. Local cultural activities include the Aspen Music Festival, Ballet/Aspen, the International Design Conference, the Aspen Art Museum, and the Snowmass Repertory Theater.

Contact: Anderson Ranch Arts Center, P.O. Box 5598, Snowmass Village, CO 81615; (303) 923-3181.

ANN HYDE INSTITUTE OF DESIGN SUMMER WORKSHOP
Winter Park, Colorado
Two-week sessions in July and August

The Ann Hyde Institute of Design in Denver offers three identical two-week summer sessions in design and sewing, with concentration on the art of haute couture. Open to anyone who loves to sew, from the home seamstress to the professional dressmaker, the sessions are conducted in a lecture/lab format providing both theory and hands-on experience. The first week is devoted to individual color and figure analysis, making the master pattern, and learning basic couture sewing and finishing techniques. During the second week, students are taught how to use the basic pattern to make any design or to alter any commercial pattern. Individual fit is stressed throughout the course, as well as integration of fit with personalized design. Evenings are reserved for fashion and business seminars presented by guest experts and weekend activities include an optional Saturday bus trip to Georgetown and a Sunday brunch near Winter Park. The Institute offers graduate, undergraduate, and continuing education credit from Colorado State University and 30 DPUs from the American Home Economics Association.

Specialties: Haute couture sewing.

Faculty: Ann Hyde is a graduate of the Cours Spêcial Supérieur, Ecole Supérieure de la Couture, Chambre Syndicale de la Couture, in Paris, holds an MA in education and counseling from Syracuse University, and is a member of the International Fashion Group.

Costs, Accommodations: Tuition is $1,250, which includes basic pattern and professional dressmaking drafting equipment. Full or half payment must accompany registration with balance due 30 days prior. Cancellations at least 30 days prior receive an 80% refund. Shared lodging (two bedroom, private bath) in the Beaver Village condominiums is $840 per session, which includes continental breakfasts and lunches, five dinners, airport transportation, and planned excursions.

Location, Facilities: The workshop is held in the Beaver Village condominium clubhouse, which is equipped with sewing machines, notions, and fabrics. Winter Park is situated at an elevation of 9,000 feet 64 miles west of Denver. Summer recreational activities include hiking, golf, tennis, horseback riding, and white water rafting.

Contact: Ann Hyde Institute of Design, P.O. Box 61271, Denver, CO 80206; (303) 355-1655.

ARCTIC EXPERIENCE FOR FIBERISTS
AND SACHS HARBOUR MUSKOX TOUR
Holman Eskimo Co-op and Down North
Northwest Territories, Canada

Two or three one-week summer tours

These two Arctic workshop/tours are taught by Wendy Chambers, proprietor of Down North, a fiber business specializing in qiviuq, the under down of the wild muskox. The programs offer participants the opportunity to experience the Arctic and receive instruction in spinning and dyeing qiviuq.

Arctic Experience for Fiberists, sponsored by the Holman Eskimo Co-op and held once the end of June or beginning of July each year since 1986, is limited to ten individuals with an interest in fiber arts and some knowledge of spinning, knitting, or weaving. Participants live in Holman, an Arctic community, and learn to work with qiviuq in a five-day workshop. Lichens growing nearby are gathered, identified, and used to dye wool and qiviuq by fermentation, boiling water, and photochemical oxidation. The particular characteristics of qiviuq, a cashmere-like down that is warmer than wool, are explored through lecture, demonstration, and practical sessions in which students can choose to spin or knit the fiber. The week also includes time for hiking, fishing, and viewing native art production.

The Sachs Harbour Muskox Tour, held during late July/early August since 1989, is limited to four participants with an interest in muskox and qiviuq. The program includes a one-week stay with an Inuvialuit (western Arctic) family who are muskox hunters and craftspeople, as well as camping, hiking, boating, and viewing of muskox in the wild. Participants also receive informal instruction in qiviuq spinning and dyeing.

Specialties: Qiviuq dyeing, weaving, and spinning.

Faculty: Wendy Chambers is proprietor of Down North, a business that manufactures and markets qiviuq blend yarns for knitting and weaving. She has been contracted by the Inuvialuit Development Corporation for product development, has served as a fiber arts judge and her work has appeared in exhibitions. Lena Wolkie is an Inuvialuit with traditional knowledge of Eskimo crafts.

Costs, Accommodations: Tuition for the Arctic Experience is C$475; shared lodging in the Co-op residence or Arctic Char Inn and meals at the Inn are C$910. Students are responsible for booking air transportation from Edmonton, Alberta, to Holman via Northwest Territorial Air, an Air Canada partner. Cost of the Sachs Harbour Muskox Tour is C$1,500. Participants must book their own air transportation via Aklak Air. Deposit, payable by certified check or money order, is C$475 for the Arctic Experience, C$750 for the Sachs Harbour Tour. Full deposit refund, less 10%, is granted written cancellations received at least six weeks prior to departure; no refund thereafter unless space can be filled. Nonparticipants are welcome but space is limited.

Location: Participants in the Arctic Experience live in the central Canadian Arctic community of Holman, a hamlet of 350 people, which is situated on

Victoria Island in Canada's Northwest Territories. The Sachs Harbour Tour commences in Inuvik, Northwest Territories, and participants live with a family in Sachs Harbour, a small hamlet of 150 people on Banks Island.

Contact: Wendy Chambers, Down North, 21 Boxwood Cresc., Whitehorse, Yukon, Y1A 4X8, Canada; (403) 633-2530. Information about the Arctic can be obtained by calling the toll-free Arctic Hotline, (800) 661-0788.

ARROWMONT SCHOOL OF ARTS AND CRAFTS
Gatlinburg, Tennessee
One and two-week courses in March and from June-August

Arrowmont, a visual arts complex open to adults of all ages and abilities, sponsors a wide variety of arts and crafts courses, as well as conferences, seminars, community classes, and Elderhostel sessions. Approximately eight courses are offered during each of eight one and two-week sessions from the beginning of June through mid-August — a total of more than 60 courses each summer. Topics include ceramics, fibers, fabric, wood, drawing, painting, sculpture, enameling, metal design, papermaking, photography, and stained glass. Most courses are open to all levels, however a few are designed specifically for beginners or advanced students. Classes generally meet daily from 9 to 11:30 am and 1 to 4 pm, Monday through Friday, and facilities remain open until midnight. Slide lectures, musical performances, exhibitions, and demonstrations are offered as part of the school's on-going program. In addition, seven courses are offered during each of four week-long sessions in March.

Typical workshop titles include Fiber Techniques for Baskets, which explores knotting, crocheting, and coiling techniques; Bowl and Plate Turning, and Carving, which develops facility with wood tools and techniques; Papermaking — Old Techniques, New Relevance, utilizing modern methods to create unusual paper forms; Painting on Glass, which covers the application of enamels and stains utilizing various techniques; Intuitive Color in Weaving, an intensive study of the intuitive use of color in the woven structure; Forged Metals and Sculptural Forms, exploring the possibilities of forged metals incorporated into other metal work or a new medium; Quilting — Total Immersion, focusing on color expression, design freedom, and production speed; Rattan Wicker Basketry, which covers the design and construction of traditional forms, and Plein-Air Drawing/Painting, which emphasizes editing and controlling the subject matter and light.

Specialties: A variety of topics relating to fiber arts, woodworking, painting and drawing, ceramics, basketry, metal and glass working, papermaking, jewelry making.

Faculty: The more than 50-member faculty of prominent artists and craftsmen has included ceramists Linda Arbuckle, John Chalke, and David Gamble; fiber artists Chad Alice Hagen, Edward Lambert, Patti Lechman, and Clare Verstegen; wood artists Michael O'Donnell, Merryll Saylan, and Alan Stirt; painters Hugh Gibbons, Leonard Koscianski, Don Lake, and Ed Shay; paper artists Donna Koretsky, Margaret Prentice, and Lynn Sures; metalsmiths/goldsmiths John Cogswell, Susan Hamlet, and Leslie Leupp; enamel artists Martha Banyas, and Harold Helwig; and glass artists Paulo Dufour and Gil Reynolds.

Costs, Accommodations: Weekly rates are $150 tuition plus $50 nonrefundable processing fee, and cost of optional room and board package ranges from $120 (dormitory) to $205 (single). A $150 deposit ($250 for those reserving on-campus housing) must accompany application. Credit cards (VISA, MasterCard) accepted. Full refund, less $50 fee, is granted cancellations at least three weeks prior to course with no refunds thereafter. Students may elect to audit or to receive two graduate/undergraduate credit hours per week for an additional $30. A few teaching and working assistantships are available and several scholarships of $175 to $300 are also offered.

Location, Facilities: The Gatlinburg campus, situated on 70 acres of wooded hillside in eastern Tennessee, is located three miles from the entrance to the Great Smoky Mountains National Park and 45 miles from Knoxville McGhee Tyson Airport (students arriving by plane may be met by the school van for an additional base fee). Facilities include cottage-type housing, large and well equipped studios, book and supply store, resource center, a permanent collection of art and craft objects, and an exhibition gallery. Adjacent to the school is the Arrowcraft Shop, Gatlinburg's oldest craft shop, which features works of regional craftsman.

Contact: Arrowmont School of Arts and Crafts, P.O. Box 567, Gatlinburg, TN 37738; (615) 436-5860.

ART BARN
Valparaiso, Indiana
Three to five-day workshops from May-October
This art gallery and nonprofit school offers year-round classes and a Famous Artist Series of about a half dozen workshops annually. Costs range from $175 for a three-day session to $225 for five days. Typical faculty includes Ann Templeton (oil), Mitch Markovitz (pastel), and watercolorists Judi Betts, Neil Kienitz, Catherine Wilson Smith, and Frank Webb.

Contact: Art Barn, 695 N. 400 E., Valparaiso, IN 46383; (219) 462-9009.

ART FARM GALLERY
Lexington, Virginia
Weekend or one-week summer workshops
Established in 1975, Art Farm offers summer workshops in brush painting, calligraphy, and flower arrangement, each limited to 10 beginning to advanced students per instructor. Two sessions, each two hours in length, are scheduled daily.

Specialties: Brush painting, calligraphy, flower arrangement.

Faculty: Owner and instructor Professor I-Hsiung Ju is professor of art and artist-in-residence at Washington & Lee University; Mrs. Chow-Soon Chuang Ju is an artist, writer, and researcher.

Costs, Accommodations: Each two-hour session is $25. Room and board is provided, if desired. Materials are additional. A 50% deposit must accompany registration with balance due on arrival.

Location, Facilities: Art Farm, located two miles north of Lexington, has two brick buildings, one for the gallery and classrooms and one for lodging. The facility is partially equipped for the handicapped. Lexington is the home of Washington & Lee University, Virginia Military Institute, Stonewall Jackson House, and George C. Marshall Library. Nearby scenic locales include the Blue Ridge Mountains, Goshen Pass, Hot Springs, and Luray Caverns.

Contact: Art Farm Gallery, Rt. 5, Box 85, Lexington, VA 24450; (703) 463-7961.

ART INSTITUTE OF BOSTON (AIB)
Continuing Education
Boston, Massachusetts
Five-day intensives in July and August

This nonprofit educational institution, an accredited member of the National Association of Schools of Art and Design, grants a Bachelor of Fine Arts degree and offers day and evening courses and one-week summer intensives in the areas of photography, design, illustration, and fine arts. Typical intensives, which meet from 9:30 am to 4 pm, Monday through Friday, are Watercolor, which begins with in-studio still life work and then proceeds to landscape painting outdoors with demonstrations and daily group critiques; and Landscape Painting, which emphasizes the interaction of colors in nature and includes field trips to scenic locales.

Specialties: Fine arts, illustration, design, photography.

Faculty: AIB faculty members include painters John Bageris, Angelo Fertitta, Nathan Goldstein, Richard King, Alberto Rey, and Maxine Sorokin; fine artist (pastels) Carol Bowen; printmaker Judith Brassard Brown; sculptors Bernadette D'Amore, Mary Kaye, and Andrew McMillan; graphic designers Robert Ebstein, Irene Elios, and Suzanne Perry; and illustrator Jeff Stock.

Costs, Accommodations: The $190 tuition plus $25 registration fee is payable prior to the start of session. Credit card (VISA, MasterCard) registrations accepted. Students who submit written notice of withdrawal before the session starts receive a full tuition refund.

Location: The Art Institute is located just west of Kenmore Square, a short walk from the Kenmore MBTA subway and bus stations.

Contact: Office of Continuing Education, The Art Institute of Boston, 700 Beacon St., Boston, MA 02215; (617) 262-1223.

ART NEW ENGLAND SUMMER WORKSHOPS
Bennington, Vermont
One-week workshops in July and August

Since 1983, Art New England Summer Workshops has offered a three-week summer program consisting of approximately 20 one-week workshops in painting, drawing, sculpture, printmaking, clay, photography, and independent study. Classes are limited to 15 beginning to intermediate adult students, who meet daily from 9 am to 12:30 pm and 1:30 to 3:30 pm and are encouraged to pursue personal goals and develop new skills. Typical workshop titles include Color/Collage, Experimental Drawing, Monoprint, Fresco/Mural Traditions, Pastel, Rakú/Colored Clays, Non-Traditional Water Media, Jewelry as Sculpture, and Oil Stick. Independent Study enables artists who have work in progress to explore and develop their project further in private studio space and receive individual and group critiques each day. Evenings are reserved for lectures and slide presentations by instructors, chamber music concerts, and social activities.

Specialties: Drawing and painting, sculpture, jewelry, clay, printmaking, photography.

Faculty: Instructors, all accomplished artists and craftsmen, have included Miroslav Antic, Harry Bartnick, Stoney Conley, Deborah Cornell, Grant Drumheller, Ruth Fields, Jane E. Goldman, Ana Guerra Hoel, Mela Lyman, Andrew McMillan, Michael Monahan, Christopher Osgood, Florence Putterman, Jo Sandman, James Wilson Rayen, Marc St. Pierre, Anne Smith, Heidi Whitman, Joseph Wood, Makoto Yabe, and Paul Zwietnig-Rotterdam.

Costs, Accommodations: Resident tuition is $585, which includes double occupancy dormitory room and board ($40 extra for single occupancy); nonresident tuition is $380, which includes lunches only. An additional $45 materials/model fee is required for some courses. Slides are requested of those applying for independent study. A $150 nonrefundable deposit must accompany application with balance due by June 1. Cancellations before June 1 receive a full refund minus deposit; cancellations between June 1 and July 30 receive a 50% refund less deposit. Participants receive a one-year subscription to *Art New England* magazine.

Location, Facilities: Art New England Summer Workshops are held on the 550-acre Bennington College campus in the Green Mountains. Facilities include fully equipped studios for drawing, painting, printmaking, ceramics, and sculpture. Tanglewood, Saratoga, Marlboro, Jacob's Pillow, Williamstown, and the Clark Art Museum are nearby.

Contact: Art New England Summer Workshops, 425 Washington St., Brighton, MA 02135; (617) 232-1604.

ART WORKSHOP INTERNATIONAL
Mexico and Italy
Last two weeks in December (Mexico); two to four weeks in July (Italy)

Established in 1975, the Art Workshop International sponsors two annual drawing and painting workshops, each limited to eight students of all levels per instructor. The two-week Christmas workshop, which is conducted at the Instituto Allende, includes daily four-hour morning classes (except Christmas week-end) with critiques and discussions scheduled most evenings from 5 to 6:30 pm. The month-long summer workshop, which is held in Assisi, offers such courses as Painting, Drawing, Color, Collage, and Visual Thinking & Critiques. Students may enroll for two to four weeks. A special program, designed for advanced and professional artists to work independently, is also offered in Italy and culminates in an exhibition sponsored by the Comune di Assisi and the Azienda di Promozione Turistica.

Specialties: Painting and drawing in all media.

Faculty: Edith Isaac-Rose, a graduate of the Chicago Art Institute, has taught painting at Ohio State University, Columbia University, and the Princeton Art Association. Her work has been exhibited in the U.S. and Canada and is in various collections, including the Hirschorn. Bea Kreloff, former head of the Art Department at New York's Fieldston School, attended Pratt Institute, the Brooklyn Museum School, and the Art Students League. She has lectured to art groups in the Northeast and her work has been exhibited in the U.S. and abroad and is in private collections.

Costs, Accommodations: Cost of the two-week Christmas workshop, which includes double room, two meals, airfare, and local transportation, is $1,950. Accommodations are in the Aristos Hotel on the grounds of the Instituto Allende. Cost of the summer workshop, which includes double room, two meals, and gratuities, is $600 to $800 per week. All programs require a $200 deposit with registration and payment in full six weeks prior. A 50% refund is granted cancellations more than one month prior.

Location, Facilities: In San Miguel de Allende, classes are held in the 250-year-old Instituto Allende art school, which consists of several acres of buildings and gardens and was once the colonial palace of the Counts of Canal. Facilities include studios and classrooms, two galleries, lecture hall, and theater. Participants in the month-long program live in Assisi, a medieval town in the heart of Umbria noted for its art treasures. Both locations are easily reached by train or bus from the countries' capital cities.

Contact: Edith Isaac-Rose/Bea Kreloff, 463 West St., 1028H, New York, NY 10014; (212) 691-1159.

ARTISTS BOOK WORKS (ABW)
Chicago, Illinois

One and two-day workshops in spring, summer, and fall

Artists Book Works, a nonprofit organization established in 1983, promotes the art of handmade books through exhibitions, lectures, classes, workshops, studio rental, educational outreach, a slide registry, and a residency program. Approximately 15 workshops are offered from spring through fall, most limited to 6 to 12 students of all levels. Typical workshop titles include Bookmaking For Teachers/Writers/Artists, which explores sequentially developed ideas for the book format and the relationship between words and images; Boxmaking, in which participants construct a two-way, drop-spine folding box; and Non-Silver Approaches to Image Making, Turkish Marbling, Japanese Woodcut, Leatherwork, Headbands, and Limp Vellum Bindings.

ABW sponsors one book residency leading to the production of a limited edition letterpress book, printed on site. The residency includes an honorarium to cover travel, materials, and technical assistance, plus one month's use of the printing and binding facilities. Selection of the artist is by guest jurors.

Specialties: Book arts.

Faculty: Includes local book artists, fine binders and conservators, and such prominent visiting artists as Carol J. Barton, Don Guyot, Keith Smith, Scott McCarney, and Hedi Kyle.

Costs: Tuition ranges from $60 to $125 with an additional materials fee of $5 to $15. Slide registry fee is $5. ABW members receive a 10% discount and full access to facilities. Annual dues begin at $15 for Seniors/Students, $30 for Friends, and $50 for a Family.

Location, Facilities: ABW is a 20-minute drive from downtown Chicago and is served by subway and bus lines. Facilities include a letterpress studio with Vandercook Universal I and Pearl Platten presses and a bookbinding studio with board shears and book, lying, and nipping presses.

Contact: Artists Book Works, 1422 W. Irving Park Rd., Chicago, IL 60613; (312) 348-4469.

ARTISTS AND CRAFTSMEN ASSOCIATED (ACA) WORKSHOPS
Dallas, Texas

Five-day workshops

Founded in 1954, this Dallas-based nonprofit organization dedicated to the preservation, practice, and promotion of representational art sponsors four or five workshops at various times during the year on landscape and portraiture, utilizing such media as oil, pastel, and watercolor. The workshops are open first to ACA members, then to nonmembers if space is available.

The 500-member ACA's objectives are to encourage and promote members' work and to bring members in contact with prominent artists and teachers. Membership benefits include a monthly newsletter, a yearly membership directory, monthly meetings with demonstrations and lectures by guest artists and an awards show, and annual juried and nonjuried shows.

Specialties: Representational art, i.e., landscape and portraiture.

Faculty: Workshops are conducted by such established artists as Delbert Gish, Leonard Wren, Paul Leveille, and Charles Sovek.

Costs, Accommodations: Most workshops are $150. A 25% deposit secures reservation and is refundable for cancellations at least eight weeks prior. Balance is due one week prior. Annual dues range from $20 for associates to $25 for actives (includes voting and annual award show exhibiting privileges), plus a $25 first year initiation fee.

Contact: Janice Hamilton, Workshop Coordinator, Artists and Craftsmen Associated, 2917 Swiss Ave., Dallas, TX 75204; (214) 348-0829.

ARTS AT MENUCHA
Corbett, Oregon
One-week workshops in August

Since 1965, the Creative Arts Community has presented "The Arts at Menucha", a two-week summer resident program consisting of approximately eight workshops each week on a variety of subjects, including arts, crafts, writing, and photography. Limited to eight to ten students of all levels, the workshops encourage creative awareness and development of skills in an atmosphere of personal rapport and group support. Typical titles are Ceramics, which focuses on handbuilding with clay; Printmaking (without a press), emphasizing Japanese woodcut, monotypes, stencil, China-colle, cyanotype, and developing a personal imagery; Maskmaking, in which participants employ facial casting, sculpture in clay, and papier mâché and learn about negative molds and special painting techniques for character and fantasy; Sculpture: Bronze Casting, which includes how to construct and operate a small foundry and concludes with a pour. Other workshops may include Figure Drawing, Painting, and Watercolor.

Specialties: Ceramics, drawing, painting, printmaking, and other topics.

Faculty: Has included Debra Norby, former artist-in-residence for the Oregon School of Arts and Crafts and the Contemporary Crafts Association; Norie Sato, NEA Fellowship recipient; Diane Trapp, resident make-up and wig designer for the Eugene Opera and The Musical Company; former Drake University professor Peter Helzer; and Arvie Smith, recipient of a Marion Butterworth Froman Award.

Costs, Accommodations: Tuition, which includes room and board, is $390 for one week, $695 for both weeks. A $50 nonrefundable deposit must accompany application. Scholarships are available. Students are lodged in dormitory sleeping quarters and homemade meals are taken family style in the main lodge.

Location, Facilities: Menucha, a 96-acre estate overlooking the scenic Columbia River Gorge, is located near Corbett, Oregon, and serves as a retreat and conference center. Several buildings provide lounges, studio spaces, and housing. Facilities include outdoor pool, tennis and volleyball courts, walking and jogging trails, and a rose garden.

Contact: Creative Arts Community, P.O. Box 4958, Portland, OR 97208; (503) 771-4270.

ARTSCAPE PAINTING HOLIDAYS
Southend-on-Sea, Essex, England

Four-day to two-week courses from March-October

Established in 1949 by the nonprofit Workers Travel Association, Artscape Painting Holidays (formerly Galleon Art Holidays) became a division of the privately owned Artists Home Supplies, Ltd., a mail order supplier of artists materials, in 1987. The company offers approximately 60 courses and study tours annually, most limited to 20 students of all levels of ability with a few specifically for either beginning or more competent artists. Topics include portraiture, botanical illustration, and such landscape subjects as impressionist, modern, flowers and plants, lakes and moors, fauna, and greens. Media include watercolor, oil, gouache, pastel, and pencil. The daily schedule usually consists of a morning lecture or studio session with afternoons devoted to individual instruction on location. Evenings are reserved for lectures, demonstrations, or critique and at least one afternoon and evening during the week are usually spent at a nearby place of interest. The course concludes with a party and display of students' work. Selected works produced by students are shown at an annual five-day exhibition, held in November or December in Central London. Two annual five-day study tours — one to Paris (Impressionism and Post-Impressionism) and one to Florence (Renaissance art) — are for practicing artists who wish to study and analyze the works of the masters.

Specialties: Landscape, portraiture, botanical illustration.

Faculty: The 19 instructors, who teach at different locations each year, include Christopher Assheton-Stones, Jill Bays, Sydney Foley, Peter Folkes, Roy Freer, Roger Hallett, Frank Hardy, Catherine Headley, Robin Mackervoy, Neal Meacher, Charles Patrickson, Margaret Petterson, Eric Rowan, John Seabrook, Karen Simmons, Charles Smith, Dennis Syrett, Trevor Tanser, and Colin Verity.

Costs, Accommodations: Costs, which include lodging and may include some or all meals, range from approximately £287 to £992, depending on quality of lodging, number of meals, and length of course. Early booking discounts are granted prior to March 31 and nonparticipant guests receive a discount of £50. A £50 nonrefundable deposit, payable by credit card or bank draft in pounds sterling, secures booking with balance due six weeks prior to departure. Penalty ranges from 30% of course fee for cancellations more than

29 days prior to 100% within 7 days. Participants are lodged in hotels or single study bedrooms of agricultural colleges.

Location: The 28 course locations include Anglesey, Bath, Brackenhurst, Cannington, Cheltenham, Cirencester, Duchy Home Farm, East Horsley, Glynhir, Newton Abbott, Plumpton, Port Isaac, Whitby, Windermere, and Winchester in Great Britain. Overseas locations include Graz, Austria; Bruges, Belgium; Chania, Crete; Paris and Provence, France; Bouley Bay, Jersey; Florence, Gubbio, and Siena, Italy; Guadalupe, Spain; and Morocco in North Africa.

Contact: Artscape Painting Holidays, Units 40 & 41 Temple Farm, Southend-on-Sea, Essex, SS2 5RZ, England; (44) 0702 717900.

ATELIER DE CALVISSON
Calvisson, France

One-week residency workshops from April-October

Established in 1975, the Atelier de Calvisson offers two workshops — one in drawing, painting, watercoloring, and pastels and the other in tapestry and textile creations. The programs are scheduled in one-week increments, from Sunday to Sunday, and are open to artists of all levels. The workshop in drawing, painting, watercolor, and pastels, which emphasizes the development of individual creativity, style, and technique, is limited to about 75 students. Classes are held from 9 am to 1 pm daily with afternoons free for individual pursuits. Work on various subjects usually takes place outdoors although studio space is available to all students, if desired. The workshop in tapestry and textile creations, for which a two-week stay is recommended, is held in the studio from 3 to 7 pm and focuses on the "Gobelins" techniques of tapestry making. A loom is available and wool and cotton may be purchased from the Atelier. The facilities are handicapped accessible.

Specialties: Drawing, painting, watercolor, pastels; tapestry and textile creations.

Faculty: Regis Burckel de Tell, an experienced artist who has taught in Rome and Paris, has participated in various national and international exhibitions.

Costs, Accommodations: Tuition (four hours of daily instruction) is 500 FF per week. A 700 FF deposit must accompany application. Room and board (lunch and dinner) is 1,400 FF per week. Accommodations are private rooms in the artist's residence, a fifteenth century restored house. A central, inner patio serves as the dining area and a breakfast room with kitchenette is available to residents. Nonparticipant spouses or guests are welcome.

Location: Calvisson, an old Mediterranean village surrounded by vineyards and built against wooded hillsides, is 10 miles from Nimes and within a 35-mile radius of such historic centers of Provence as Arles, Avignon, the Cevennes mountains, and the beaches of Camargue. Nimes is 4 1/2 hours from Paris by train and both Nimes and Montpelier are served by air transportation with bus service available between Nimes and Calvisson. Local recreational facilities include a public pool, tennis courts, and a variety of shops.

Contact: Atelier de Calvisson, Grand'rue, 30420 Calvisson, France; (33) 66 01 23 91.

ATELIER NORTH SCHOOL OF CLASSICAL REALISM
Two Harbors, Minnesota

One and two-week workshops from June-September

Atelier North (formerly Art Barn) was opened in 1984 as an extension of Atelier Lack, a private, nonprofit school founded in 1970 by portrait artist Richard Lack, who wanted to re-establish the principles of beauty and craft in painting. The atelier (French for studio-school) follows a disciplined style of instruction that strives to emulate the artistic quality of the work of the French-American Impressionists. In a modified apprentice program, each student is tutored individually and given projects suited to his or her ability and experience.

Most workshops are scheduled from 9 am to noon and 1 to 4 pm, Monday through Friday, and limited to 6 to 8 artists of all levels (students are required to complete a portrait drawing before they can paint) per instructor. Some are also open to young people (minimum age 10). The dozen or so workshops offered each summer cover oils, landscape, seascape, portraiture, drawing and memory, and sculpture. A one-week workshop at sea is planned. Students will live aboard a sailing schooner and go ashore for classes. The final day of each workshop features a get-together and boat ride.

The Atelier North is one of five Ateliers operating in the U.S. and one in Florence, Italy, each founded by Atelier Lack graduates. Graduates spend four years of study to learn the skills needed to pursue a professional career.

Specialties: Landscape, seascape, portraiture, and sculpture in the style of the Old Masters.

Faculty: Atelier founder Richard Lack's work been awarded gold medals in the Grand National Exhibition of the American Artists' Professional League in New York City. He has executed many portrait commissions, including six portraits for the Kennedy family of Hyannisport. The instructors, all of whom have trained in the Ateliers, include Mike Coyle, David Erickson, Stephen Gjertson, Wayne Howell, Fern Koestner, Michael Lahey, Jeff Larson, Myron Lunning, Jim Prohl, Dale Redpath, and Cyd Wicker.

Costs, Accommodations: Landscape workshop tuition is $325 for five days; where a model is used, workshop tuition is $385. A 50% deposit is required with registration and balance is due prior to workshop. Cancellations more than six weeks prior forfeit $50, within six weeks the charge is $100. A list of accommodations and rates is provided.

Location: The Atelier North is 40 miles north of Duluth and 12 miles north of Two Harbors on Lake Superior's scenic North Shore. The nearest airport is in Duluth, where pickup can be arranged for an extra fee. Nearby attractions include hiking trails, marine museums, and a railroad museum and activities include hiking, fishing, boat rides, and golf.

Contact: Atelier North School of Classical Realism, 1066 Highway 61 East, Two Harbors, MN 55616; (218) 834-2059.

ATELIER DU SAFRANIER
Fine Arts on the French Riviera
Antibes, France
One to twelve-week workshops year-round

The Atelier du Safranier offers year-round art and printmaking workshops for individuals of all levels, who may enroll at any time and for any number of weeks. The workshop week begins on Tuesday and ends on Saturday and includes three hours of course work daily plus two hours each day for independent studio time. Students can enroll in either Academy (drawing, painting, watercolor, and outside work) or Printmaking (engraving, etching, monotype, and lithography on stone) or Mixed Work (a combination of both).

Specialties: Drawing, painting, clay sculpture, engraving, etching, monotype, lithography.

Faculty: All instructors have the French National Diploma of Fine Arts.

Costs, Accommodations: Weekly tuition is 900 FF; tuition plus half board is 2,000 FF during April, May, and October (2,300 FF during June, July, and August); single supplement is 380 FF (480 FF); and enrollment fee is 250 FF. A 1,150 FF nonrefundable deposit secures reservation with balance due on arrival. Lodging is provided with nearby families.

Location: The Atelier is in the citadel of old Antibes, on the French Riviera.

Contact: Dominique Prevost, Atelier du Safranier, 2 bis, rue du Cannet, 06600 Vieil Antibes, France; (33) 93 34 53 72, Fax (33) 93 34 72 37.

AUGUSTA HERITAGE CENTER
Davis & Elkins College
Elkins, West Virginia
Weekend to three-week workshops in July and August

Davis & Elkins College, a small, private liberal arts college affiliated with the Presbyterian Church U.S.A., is the home of the Augusta Heritage Center, a nonprofit year-round program dedicated to the promotion and conservation of a wide variety of traditional crafts, music, dances, and customs. The summer workshop program, started in 1973, consists of five one-week sessions from early July to mid-August, offering more than 90 intensive workshops in the folk arts, including in-depth "theme week" classes, which revolve around a specific cultural theme. Most workshops are one week long and open to all levels while a few are geared to those on specific skill levels. To ensure individualized instruction, with each student working on projects suited to his or her level of skill and experience, the student to teacher ratio is a maximum of 12 to 1, less in many classes. Crafts sessions are held simultaneously with extensive offerings on traditional music, dance, and folklore. Each week begins with a Sunday afternoon registration and evening reception, square dance, and jam session. Classes meet Monday through Friday, mornings and afternoons, with craft classes generally scheduled for six to seven hours daily. Evening activities include mini-classes, jam sessions, song swaps, lectures, poetry readings, storytelling concerts, and panel discussions on folk arts and culture.

Craft workshop titles include Basketry, White Oak Basketry, Bobbin Lacemaking, Calligraphy, Folk Carving & Whittling, Folk Painting, Blacksmithing, Log Construction, Paper Marbling, Rug Weaving, Contemporary Quilt Design, Pottery, Quiltmaking, Spinning and Natural Dyeing, Beginning and Intermediate/Advanced Stonemasonry, Stained Glass, Weaving, and Treenware (handmade, functional wooden utensils). Three sessions include Folk Arts for Kids (ages 8 to 13), a one-week workshop that features mountain games, songs, square dancing, storytelling, and crafts. The Musical Instrument Construction workshops, each limited to five to eight students who are familiar with woodworking tools, offer the opportunity to design and build a finely crafted guitar or Appalachian dulcimer from start to finish.

The Center also sponsors a state-wide Folk Arts Apprenticeship Program, which matches master artists with one or more apprentices for a period of several weeks to one year. Master artists should live in West Virginia and apprentices should live within 250 miles of the artist's home or workplace.

Specialties: A variety of folk arts and crafts, including basketry, quilting, papermaking, calligraphy, woodworking, painting, blacksmithing, ceramics, fiber arts, stonemasonry, musical instrument construction.

Faculty: Instructors, who are accomplished folk artists and teachers, include Nancy Crow (quilting), Wayne Henderson (guitar construction), Duke Miecznikowski (stoneware), Susan Elkin (spinning and dyeing), Bill Witzemann (stonemasonry), Olive Goodwin (weaving), R.P. Hale (papermaking and calligraphy), and Doug Elliott (basketry).

Costs, Accommodations: One-week workshop tuition ranges from $210 to $250. A nonrefundable, nontransferable $40 deposit must accompany registration with balance due by June 1. Cancellations at least four weeks prior receive refund less $40, no refunds thereafter; transfer fee is $30. Undergraduate college credit is available. The cost of residence hall room and board (three meals daily in the cafeteria) is $135 for six nights. A nonrefundable $30 deposit must accompany application with balance due by June 1. A list of nearby motels, where special rates are available, bed & breakfasts, and campsites is provided on request.

Location, Facilities: Classes are held throughout the hilly, 170-acre campus of Davis & Elkins College, in facilities that range from an open-air tent to air-conditioned classrooms. Recreational facilities include tennis courts, indoor swimming pool, fitness trail, and Nautilus center. Elkins, a small town located at the edge of the Monongahela National Forest in the mountains of central West Virginia, is three hours from Pittsburgh, four to five hours from Washington, D.C., and nine hours from New York City.

Contact: Augusta Heritage Center, Davis & Elkins College, 100 Sycamore St., Elkins, WV 26241-3996; (304) 636-1903.

AURORA ART WORKSHOP
Aurora, Nebraska

Three-day workshop the second Friday to Sunday in June

This annual workshop, first offered in 1976 and open to artists of all levels, offers a choice of three instructors or an artist's retreat. Sessions are scheduled from 9 am to 4 pm on Friday, Saturday, and Sunday. Students can register for only one instructor and each instructor's class is limited to 20 to 25 participants. Additional activities include a Friday art show and a Saturday night guest performance.

Specialties: Oil, watercolor, and acrylic painting.

Faculty: Changes each year, having included landscape artist Hal Haloun, artist and magician George Kountoupis, and Susan Blackwood, who specializes in paintings of children and animals.

Costs, Accommodations: The $120 fee covers classes, dormitory-style cabin housing, and all meals. The retreat fee, which includes housing, meals, and one critique, is $85. Full payment must accompany reservation and full refund is granted if space can be filled.

Location: Aurora is a small rural town about 20 miles east of Grand Island. The workshop is held in the Nebraska Youth Leadership Development Center, which has an indoor pool, jacuzzi, and outdoor hiking and games.

Contact: Connie McHenry, Registrar, Aurora Art Workshop, 123 W. Fifth St., Grand Island, NE 68801; (308) 384-3092.

B. ALLAN MACKIE SCHOOL OF LOG BUILDING
Prince George, British Columbia, Canada

One to eight-week sessions from March-November

This school for log construction, the first such vocational career course in British Columbian colleges, offers eight sessions for beginning to experienced log builders. Each session begins with an orientation on Sunday at 10 am and instruction begins at 8 am, Monday through Friday, with attendance mandatory. Discussions and video presentations are held in the evenings and students are encouraged to work independently during weekends. Students are advised to enroll in only one session per year.

Beginners and intermediates should enroll first in one of the three or four-week General Sessions, which cover all phases of a log building as well as basic logfitting. The longer sessions allow for more flexibility, hands-on experience, and individual attention. Other sessions include A Constructive Vacation (two weeks), a condensed program that covers basic log building principles, including some double scribes and truss building; Hand Tools and Horses (three weeks), which deals with safety in the woods, building with log decks, and logging with horses; Professional Session (eight weeks) for students who want a complete package of construction techniques, including concrete foundation to lockup stage, doors and windows, stairways and railings, and a wide variety of notches, trusses, and accessories; Advanced Session (five weeks), for highly motivated builders who want to increase work-site efficiency and management techniques; and Teaching Assistance (one week), which prepares log builders to teach others. Candidates may be selected for teaching opportunities at the school or at extension courses.

Specialties: Log building.

Faculty: B. Allan Mackie teaches log building in a variety of locations throughout the world and has taught for the University of Alaska and other schools and colleges. He is author of several books on log building, published by his Log House Publishing Company, Ltd., and utilized in the sessions.

Costs, Accommodations: Tuition ranges from C$300 for a one week session to C$2,150 for eight weeks. A C$100 nonrefundable (if student is accepted) deposit, payable by certified check or money order, must accompany application with nonrefundable balance due at least four weeks prior to session. On campus lodging can be arranged at the orientation session. Students are required to purchase textbooks and their own set of tools.

Contact: B. Allan Mackie School of Log Building, P.O. Box 1925, Prince George, BC, V2L 5E3, Canada; (604) 563-8738.

BALLYNAKILL STUDIOS SUMMER WORKSHOPS
Letterfrack, County Galway, Ireland
One-week workshops from May-September

Since 1989, Ballynakill Studios has offered one-week workshops in landscape painting for artists of all levels. Each session is limited to 12 to 15 participants and runs from Saturday to Saturday, beginning on Saturday evening with orientation and including five full days of painting and instruction in watercolor, pastel, oil, and mixed media and one free day for sightseeing. Two workshops are run consecutively each month during the summer so that participants can enroll in more than one session. On-location classes, with demonstrations of technique, critique, and personal instruction, begin daily at 9:30 am. Studios are also available. The day concludes with dinner and evening relaxation at a lakeside country house. Special activities include a guided nature walk, an archaeology lecture, and an Irish traditional set dancing class.

Specialties: Landscape painting.

Faculty: Painter-sculptor Ann O'Connor-Gordon, founder and director of Ballynakill Studios, studied at the Art Students League of New York and held a studio apprenticeship with sculptor Jose de Creeft. She has exhibited in New York, New Jersey, Massachusetts, and Ireland and her work is in private collections in the U.S., Canada, Australia, Denmark, England, and Ireland. Guest instructors include Terri McMichael Corboy, who has studied with Edgar Whitney and Frank Webb; and Kenneth MacIndoe, who has taught at the Art Students League and received a fellowship from the New Jersey State Council on the Arts.

Costs, Accommodations: Cost, which includes meals, double occupany lodging, and planned activities, is $442 per week. A deposit of $108.50 must accompany registration with full payment due two months prior. Cancellations more than two months prior receive full refund less $105; between one and two months prior, refund is $108.75; no refund thereafter. Students are lodged in bed and breakfast accommodations.

Location: The Ballynakill Studios are situated in the Moyard-Letterfrack area on Ballynakill Bay on the North Coast of Connemara in the West of Ireland, a 90-minute drive from Galway City and approximately six miles from Clifden, the nearest town.

Contact: Ann O'Connor-Gordon, c/o Connemara West, Letterfrack, County Galway, Ireland; (353) 95 41044 *or* Lismore Tours, 106 E. 31st St., New York, NY 10016; (212) 685-0100, (800) 547-6673.

BASKETRY WORKSHOPS
Salisbury, Connecticut
One to four-day workshops in winter, spring, and summer

Since 1984, Carol Hart has taught a series of basketry workshops, each limited to three to eight students of all levels. Approximately 10 to 12 workshops are scheduled each season, mostly one-day sessions that begin at 9:30 am and end at about 3:30 pm. Several types of baskets are taught, including the corn-husk, black ash muffin, twig trivet, Shaker-style cathead, coiled "jewel", English hen, twined Irish sisal, and a variety of vine and wicker topics. In a four-day workshop for ambitious beginners or experienced basketmakers, students pound, sort, shave, and cut black ash logs and use them to weave a pounded black ash splint apple drying or pack basket.

Specialties: Basketry.

Faculty: Carol Hart has studied basketry since 1971 and taught at craft schools and in private homes since 1974. She is author of *Natural Basketry* and has published articles in *Threads* and other magazines.

Costs, Accommodations: Workshop costs range from $45 to $50 per day, which usually includes materials. A $10 registration fee must accompany application with balance due the day of class. Refund is granted cancellations more than two weeks prior. Accommodations may be arranged at area inns, motels, and bed & breakfasts and camping facilities are also available.

Location: Classes are held in the instructor's home or at the local town hall. Salisbury is located in the Southern Berkshires, a resort area.

Contact: Carol Hart, Selleck Hill, Salisbury, CT 06068; (203) 435-9236.

BAULINES CRAFTS GUILD (BCG)
San Francisco Bay Area, California
One and two-day weekend workshops throughout the year

Founded in 1972, the BCG is a nonprofit organization of Northern California craftspeople who are interested in passing on their expertise to students and in developing community appreciation of craftsmanship. The Guild offers a year-round Apprenticeship Program as well as workshops in furniture making and woodworking, textiles, ceramics, glass design, goldsmithing, and papermaking. The workshops, which are geared to the serious hobbyist or aspiring artisan with basic craft skills, are usually limited to ten students and meet for three to five hours each day. Typical furniture and woodworking workshop titles include: The Art of Furniture Making, a slide lecture and discussion covering concept, drawing plans, scale models, wood selection, tool use and maintenance, and finishing; How to Fix Any Mistakes in Woodworking, with a portion of class time devoted to re-sawing solid wood; Veneer Table Tops, which covers slicing, edging, and laminating veneers; and How to Make Router Dovetail Jigs, in which students make their own jigs. Other workshop titles include Dyes From Plants of the Country Side, Computer-Assisted Weaving, and Figurative Ceramic Sculpture.

The Guild's primary focus is its Apprenticeship Program, which requires one Craft Master member to teach one student for a period of three months to a year. Prospective apprentices must submit a resume and portfolio of previous work in order to be considered. BCG's membership categories include Craft Masters, whose qualifications are noted under "Faculty", below, and Associate Members, who wish to foster the crafts tradition and maintain a close connection with craftspeople. BCG's activities include educational forums, tours of Craft Masters' studios, and public exhibitions.

Specialties: Furniture making, woodworking, textiles, ceramics, glass design, goldsmithing, papermaking, home construction, and other crafts.

Faculty: Includes more than 30 Craft Masters, accomplished craftspeople who have fulfilled at least the following requirements: they've earned a living from their craft for at least five years; they have a professional shop or studio; they've received recognition through exhibitions; and they've been sponsored by a Craft Master. Faculty includes furniture makers Garry Knox Bennett and Art Espenet, textile artist Sheila O'Hara, jeweler Joyce Clements, ceramists Beverly Prevost and Dale Roush, glass artists Penelope Comfort Starr and Shaun Weisbach, weaver Ida Grae, goldsmith Carrie Adell, quiltmaker Sonya Lee Barrington, sculptor Tom D'Onofrio, and home builders Roger Peacock and Hugh Winn.

Costs, Accommodations: Most workshops are $35 per day with a 15% discount to seniors and Guild members. Tuition for the Apprenticeship Program is $700 per month plus a $25 nonrefundable application fee.

Location: All workshops and apprenticeships take place in the Craft Masters' studios, which are located throughout the San Francisco Bay Area.

Contact: Baulines Crafts Guild, Schoonmaker Point, Sausalito, CA 94965; (415) 331-8520.

BETHEL COLONY SCHOOL OF THE ARTS
Bethel, Missouri
Weekend and one-week courses in May, June, July, and September

Founded in 1844 as a religious communal society, the historic German village of Bethel offers a variety of courses in the arts and crafts for adults and children of all levels. More than 25 different courses for adults are offered, with subjects that include basketry, stained glass, papermaking, woodworking, fiber arts, painting and drawing, ceramics, printmaking, and book arts. During Family Week, similar courses for children, ages 7 and up, are held at the same time as those for adults. Weekend courses begin at 5 pm Friday and end at 1 pm Sunday; one-week courses begin at 4 pm Sunday and end at 11 am the following Saturday. One hour of undergraduate or graduate credit is available on some courses from the University of Missouri-Columbia.

Specialties: Woodworking, fiber arts, painting, ceramics, printmaking, papermaking.

Faculty: Includes woodworker Larry Ayers, weavers Dan and Flo Mann, artist Debra K. Scoggin, ceramist Sandra Eccles-Walz, and print and papermaker Liane Crawford Smith.

Costs, Accommodations: Tuition (room and board) is $85 ($42) for weekend courses, $165 ($118) for one-week courses (blacksmithing, which includes materials and tools, is $250). College credit is additional. Deadline for application, which must be accompanied by full tuition plus a nonrefundable $25 registration fee, is one month before start of course. Room and board charges are payable on arrival. Written cancellations received at least three weeks prior receive a tuition refund less $50. Men and women sleep in separate rooms in European hostel-type lodging with several beds per room. Camping is also available and the nearest motel is 13 miles away.

Location: Bethel is located on Rte. 15 in northeast Missouri.

Contact: Bethel Colony School of the Arts, P.O. Box 127, Bethel, MO 63434; (816) 284-6493.

BLACKHAWK ARTIST'S WORKSHOP
Black Hawk, Colorado
Weekend and one to ten-week workshops from June-August

Established in 1963 by the nonprofit Blackhawk Mountain School of Art, this ten-week summer program provides the opportunity to work side-by-side with the faculty of artists-in-residence who are prominent professionals in drawing, painting, printmaking, sculpture, and photography. Drawing and painting workshops cover materials and concepts, acrylic, oil, and watercolor; printmaking workshops cover intaglio, lithography, relief, and screenprinting; and sculpture workshop topics include bronze casting, stone, patina, and figure modeling.

Classes meet Monday to Friday, mornings and afternoons. Most classes are designed to take advantage of the landscape as well as studio work. Additional activities include the Outdoors Program, which features sketching, nature hikes, and transportation to scenic painting locations, and the Evening Lecture Series, devoted to music, nature, art, travel, and slide presentations by each resident artist.

Specialties: Drawing, painting, printmaking, sculpture, and photography.

Faculty: Has included Margaret Durant, Jim Foose, Winnie Godfrey, Kay Hofmann, Barbara Jaffee, Bill Joseph, Bob Lockhart, Tom Macauley, Robert Middaugh, Michael Parfenoff, and Michael Reardon.

Costs: The weekly (Sunday through Saturday) cost of $540 double occupancy includes all meals, 24-hour studio access, and outdoor and lecture programs. A $50 nonrefundable deposit must accompany reservation. Credit cards (MasterCard, VISA) accepted.

Location, Facilities: Blackhawk is 45 minutes west of Denver at an elevation of 8,000 feet in Clear Creek Canyon. Facilities include a painting and sculpture studio, outdoor stream-side sculpture area, full printmaking studio with five presses, letterpress and stained glass workshops, and public art gallery. Part of a National Historic District, the old gold-mining town of Black Hawk is adjacent to Central City, which offers a large regional art exhibit, numerous galleries, a summer jazz festival, and the Central City Opera Festival. Nearby activities include golf, fishing, river rafting, and mountaineering.

Contact: Blackhawk Artist's Workshop, P.O. Box 258, Black Hawk, CO 80422; (303) 582-5235 (May 15-Aug. 22) *or* (312) 477-2272.

BROAD BAY INN & GALLERY WATERCOLOR WORKSHOPS
Waldoboro, Maine

Five-day summer workshops

Established in 1984, the Broad Bay Inn & Gallery offers three or four watercolor workshops during the summer that focus on painting the rocky Maine coast. Each workshop is geared specifically to either beginners or intermediate and advanced artists and limited to ten participants. The program begins on Sunday evening with an informal gathering of students and instructor and classes begin the next day at 9 am and are scheduled from 9 am to 4 pm through Friday. Painting is usually done on location and critiques and demonstrations are held in the Gallery. The Gallery art shows, which change every three to four weeks, include watercolors, oil paintings, charcoals, pastels, and sculpture and a small gift shop sells prints, jewelry, and other crafts.

Specialties: Watercolor painting.

Faculty: Beginner workshops are taught by Maude Olsen, an instructor at the Farnsworth Museum and author of *So, You Think You Can't Draw*; and Libby Hopkins, former senior artist for the *Wall Street Journal* and the Educational Testing Service. Intermediate to Advanced workshops are taught by Wini Long, an established watercolor painter who lives and works on the coast of Maine; and Don Dennis, an experienced artist whose works have appeared in *American Artist* magazine.

Costs, Accommodations: Costs range from $175, tuition only, to $575, which includes lodging and two meals at the Inn. A $50 deposit, refundable for cancellations at least one month prior, secures reservation and balance is due two weeks prior. Accommodations (bed and breakfast) are $35 to $60 per night. Several local restaurants are also available.

Location: Waldoboro, on the coast of Maine, is located on Coastal Route 1 north of Brunswick-Bath and south of Thomaston. Attractions and recreational opportunities include a local summer theater, a golf course, the Camden Opera House, Farnsworth Museum, Pemaquid Lighthouse, and Audubon Sanctuary and ferries to Monhegan Island.

Contact: Broad Bay Inn & Gallery, P.O. Box 607, Main St., Waldoboro, ME 04572; (207) 832-6668.

BROOKFIELD CRAFT CENTER (BCC)
Brookfield and South Norwalk, Connecticut

One to six-day workshops year-round

The nonprofit Brookfield Craft Center was founded in 1954 to stimulate interest in handmade objects of good design, to act as a clearing house for information related to handcrafts, and to act as a sales outlet for the encouragement of practicing craftsmen. BCC offers more than 200 workshops a year in basketry, bird carving, boat building, ceramics, decorative arts, design and drawing, fabric and quilting, fibers and weaving, glass, home restoration, jewelry and metalsmithing, paper and book arts, woodworking, photography, business and marketing, and special interest topics such as egg painting and stone cutting. Most workshops are scheduled from 10 am to 4 pm and limited to 10 to 12 students of all levels. Master workshops by visiting artists, four and eight-session courses, and summer classes for children are also offered.

Typical titles include Sculptural Basketmaking, Working & Decorative Decoy Carving, Ceramics on the Wheel, Spray Glazing & Raku Firing, Marbling for Fine Furniture, Calligraphy, Figure Drawing, Creative Clothing Design & Garment Construction, Sashiko Quilting, Tapestry Weaving,

Painting on Glass, Pate de Verre, Hot Glass, Bladesmithing, Jewelry Making Blacksmithing, Principles/Techniques of Gem Setting, Papermaking From Plants, Advanced European Cabinetmaking (for experienced woodworkers), and 18th Century Carving Techniques. During the five and six-day boatbuilding workshops, students build a cedar & canvas canoe, "ultralight" canoe, traditional Norwegian pram, or Adirondack guideboat from start to finish and try it out on Candlewood Lake.

Specialties: A variety of topics, including basketry, bird carving, boat building, ceramics, decorative arts, design and drawing, fiber arts, glass, jewelry and metalsmithing, paper and book arts, woodworking, photography.

Faculty: The more than 50-member changing faculty of accomplished artists, craftsmen, and instructors includes Barbara Allen, Florence Benzer, John Cogswell, Stephen Day, Robert Dodge, Stephen Fellerman, Linda Fisher, William Gundling, Tom Hammang, Jeffry Havill, Gloria Helfgott, Michael Hennessey, Virginia Jones, William Keck, Donald Krueger, Eugene Landon, Bernard Lawrence, Paul Levine, Josh Markel, Tom Matus, and Laura Michaelson.

Costs, Accommodations: Workshop tuition is $75 ($65 for members) for one day, $125 ($115) for two days, $185 ($175) for three days, and $305 ($295) for most five day workshops. Materials are extra. Full nonrefundable tuition, payable by VISA, MasterCard, or American Express, must accompany registration. A few half-tuition scholarships are awarded to students in need. A list of accommodations (hotels, motels, private homes, campsites) is available. Members of the Brookfield Craft Center receive reduced workshop tuition, a subscription to the *Brookfield Quarterly*, and the opportunity to exhibit and sell artwork. Annual dues range from $25 for individual to $250 for patron.

Location: The Brookfield Campus is located on the Still River at the intersection of Routes 7 and 25. The South Norwalk Campus is located in Brookfield Alley in "SoNo", a recently developed Historic Waterfront District known for its diverse cultural arts attractions.

Contact: Brookfield Craft Center, Inc., 286 Whisconier Rd., Brookfield, CT 06804; (203) 775-4526 *or* Brookfield Alley at 127-129 Washington St., S. Norwalk, CT 06854; (203) 853-6155.

BUCHANAN WATERCOLORS, LTD.
Oregon, Washington, Greece

Two to ten-day workshops in U.S., two to four-week workshops in Greece

Since 1978, watercolorist Caroline Buchanan has offered summer workshops for artists of all levels, with some programs designed specifically for beginners and all programs limited to 15 or 16 participants. Her Greek workshops, which range from two to four weeks in duration and are held three or four times from April to September, include sketching, painting and photography as well as art history lectures and cultural excursions. Other programs include a ten-day (or two five-day) workshop(s) in the San Juan Islands off the coast of Washington, five-day "Paint the Coast" of Oregon workshops, and two to five-day workshops at her studio near Corvallis.

Specialties: Watercolor.

Faculty: An art teacher since 1975, Caroline Buchanan received her art history degree with honors from Wellesley College and an MA in teaching art from Western Oregon State College. She also studied with Rex Brandt, Joan Irving, Millard Sheets, and Christopher Schink. Her paintings are in public and private collections, including a 1% for Art Commission at Oregon Institute of Technology.

Costs, Accommodations: Cost for the Greek workshops ranges from $2,500 to $2,900, which includes overseas airfare, lodging, many meals, and planned excursions. Tuition for the San Juan Island workshops is $150 for five days, $225 for ten days; lodging and meals are additional. Tuition for the five-day "Paint the Coast" workshops is $110, not including meals and lodging. Tuition for the workshops at Caroline's studio ranges from $20 for two days to $80 for a five-day workshop. A nonrefundable deposit holds a space.

Contact: Buchanan Watercolors, Ltd., 36976 Soap Creek Rd., Corvallis, OR 97330; (503) 745-5253.

THE BURREN HOLIDAY PAINTING CENTRE
Lisdoonvarna, County Clare, Ireland
Weekend to one-week courses from May-September

Established in 1974, the Painting Centre offers 15 to 20 three to seven-day landscape painting courses during the summer, each limited to 16 adult artists of all levels who paint on location at nearby scenic areas. The courses cover a variety of media, including watercolor, oils, pastel, and gouache. Landscape painting may be supplemented by flower studies, still life, or portraiture, and studio lectures and demonstrations are a part of each week's program. The final night is devoted to an exhibition and critique of the week's work.

Specialties: Landscape painting.

Faculty: All experienced artists and teachers, includes Derek Biddulph, Pat Copperwhite, James English, Jim Flack, Trevor Geoghegan, Mary Golden, Reginald Hobbs, Lorraine Wall, Enda McCann, Patricia O'Breartuin, Shelia Parsons, Desmond Turner, Margaret Watson, and Milford Zornes.

Costs, Accommodations: One-week course cost, including lodging, breakfasts, and dinners, is $315 ($210 without dinners). Payment is by personal check in U.S. dollars or by bank draft in Irish Punts. A $70 deposit secures booking with balance due on arrival. Students are lodged at O'Neills Town Home, an Irish Tourist Board-approved facility situated two minutes from the town center of Lisdoonvarna. Traditional Irish dishes are served for breakfast and dinner. Nonparticipant guests are welcome.

Location: The spa town of Lisdoonvarna is nine miles from the 700-foot-high Cliffs of Moher, four miles from the sea and boats to the Aran Islands, and 35 miles from Shannon Airport. Nearby scenic attractions include weathered limestone rocks, castle ruins, ancient churches, high crosses, inland lakes, dry river valleys, stone walls, megalithic tombs, and traditional thatched cottages.

Contact: Mrs. Christine O'Neill, O'Neills Town Home, Lisdoonvarna, Co. Clare, Ireland; (353) 065-74208.

CALLANWOLDE FINE ARTS CENTER
Atlanta, Georgia

One and two-session workshops year-round

Callanwolde Fine Arts Center, a nonprofit organization dedicated to providing learning and cultural experiences, offers a variety of arts and crafts programs for adults and children, ranging from one-session workshops to ten-week classes. About a half dozen workshops are offered each season, scheduled for one or two morning or evening sessions and limited to 12 to 20 students of all levels. Typical titles include The Phenomenon of Color, an exploration of the physics and psychology of color; Papermaking Demonstration, which emphasizes the use of simple procedures and equipment available at home; Decorative Reed Basket Workshop, which teaches techniques (twining and weaving) to construct a large basket; and Pottery Workshop, a two-day Rakú-firing class that features traditional crackle glazes and dry and gloss copper-flash surfaces. In addition to classes, Callanwolde also presents a variety of cultural activities such as concerts, recitals, dance performances, poetry readings, and drama productions.

Specialties: Basketry, papermaking, pottery-making, and other topics.

Faculty: Includes Laurie Allison, Rick Berman, and Barbara Hughes.

Costs, Accommodations: Workshop fees range from $18 to $48. Full refund, less $10 fee, is granted cancellations more than two days prior; no refund after first class meeting. Motels and hotels are located nearby.

Location: Callanwolde Fine Arts Center, which is handicapped accessible, is a 27,000-square-foot Tudor-style mansion centered about a large courtyard. Built in 1920 as the home of Charles Howard Candler, Coca-Cola founder Asa G. Candler's eldest son, it is listed on the National Register of Historic Places and houses the largest pottery department outside of a university setting. It's located in the Druid Hills section of Atlanta, an area planned by the firm of Frederick Law Olmstead, who designed New York's Central Park.

Contact: Callanwolde Fine Arts Center, 980 Briarcliff Rd. NE, Atlanta, GA 30306; (404) 872-5338.

CALLAWAY SCHOOL OF NEEDLE ARTS
Callaway Gardens
Pine Mountain, Georgia
Five-day sessions in January

Since 1972, Callaway Gardens and the Georgia Chapter of Embroiderers' Guild of America has sponsored the annual Callaway School of Needle Arts, primarily for intermediate to advanced needle artists. The School runs for two consecutive five-day sessions, each consisting of 18 to 20 two and four-day classes devoted to various projects in needle art and sculpture. Class projects, which are designed to teach specific stitches and techniques, may include an Elizabethan Sampler, Magical Houses, Heirloom Dolls, Trellis Flower, and Bouquet in White. Classes are scheduled daily from 8:30 am to noon and from 1:30 pm to 4:30 pm and are limited to 12 to 25 students, depending on room size. During a pre-session four-day course, open to all, participants complete a project using a specific technique, such as Japanese embroidery. Other activities include an opening reception and orientation, a farewell dinner and program, and a judged exhibit open to all attendees.

Specialties: Needle arts.

Faculty: Includes prominent needle artists and teachers Jody Adams, Chottie Alderson, Ilse Altherr, Mary Clubb, Merry Cox, Audrey Francini, Julie Geotsch, Elizabeth Ellsworth, Judy Lehman, Joyce Lukomski, Louise Meier, Darlene O'Steen, Scott Payne, Shay Pendray, Marnie Ritter, Gail Sirna, Judy Souliotis, Jean Taggart, and Caela Conn Tyler.

Costs, Accommodations: The cost, which includes double occupancy room for five nights, all meals, and entrance to Callaway Gardens, is $575 for each school session, $465 for the pre-session course; single supplement $115. Materials are not included. A $195 deposit is required with registration, payable by VISA, MasterCard, or American Express, with balance due on arrival. Full refund is granted cancellations at least 2 1/2 months prior, no refunds thereafter.

Location: Callaway Gardens are operated by the Ida Cason Callaway Foundation, a state chartered, nonprofit horticultural, educational, and scientific organization founded in 1936. They are located on U.S. Hwy. 27 in Pine Mountain, 75 miles south of Atlanta and 30 miles north of Columbus.

Contact: Reservations Dept., Callaway School of Needle Arts, Callaway Gardens, Pine Mountain, GA 31822; (800) 282-8181.

CAMASTRO/PRITCHETT ART INTERNATIONAL, INC.
WATERCOLOR WORKSHOPS
Wales and Cyprus
Two-week workshops from June-October

Since 1987, Rose Camastro-Prichett and her husband, David Pritchett, have offered two-week summer workshops at Capel Ogwen on the North

Wales coast and at the Hotel Minerva on the Isle of Cyprus. Approximately a half-dozen workshops are scheduled during the summer, each consisting of studio and on-location instruction for artists of all levels, with the Wales workshops limited to eight participants and the Cyprus workshops to ten. Students are encouraged to bring nonparticipant spouses and guests for the travel and cultural aspects of the program. Most mornings are devoted to formal instruction or discussion of the technical aspects of the day's painting location with afternoons spent on-location at nearby scenic locales.

Specialties: Watercolor.

Faculty: Rose Camastro-Pritchett received her BFA from Quincy College and MS from Western Illinois University and has taught art for more than 25 years. She has received awards for watercolors, acrylics, weaving, and mixed media on paper and her works are in private, public, and corporate collections in the U.S., Saudi Arabia, Cyprus, Wales, England, Spain, and Australia. David Pritchett received his BSc in education and MA in English from Western Illinois University and studied at Trinity and Keble colleges of Oxford. He has taught junior high school through college level students in the U.S., Nigeria, Wales, and Saudi Arabia.

Costs, Accommodations: The cost, which includes double occupancy lodging, all meals except lunches on-location, and planned excursions (excluding entrance fees), is $1,675 for the Wales workshop, $1,775 for the Cyprus workshop, $200 less for a nonparticipant spouse or guest. A $300 deposit must accompany application with balance due at least two months prior, the final date for full refund. Refund thereafter is subject to a cancellation fee. Lodging for the Wales workshop is provided at Capel Ogwen, a six-bedroom house surrounded by a working farm. The Hotel Minerva, in Cyprus, offers single and double-bedded rooms, most with balconies.

Location: The Wales workshops, which are held from June to August, are based a few minutes drive from the university town of Bangor, on the Menai Straits, with a variety of castles, mountains, agricultural, and seaside villages. Daily excursions visit the walled medieval village of Conway, the Conway River estuary, the mountains at Llanberis, and the Ogwen Valley. The Cyprus workshops, held in September and October, are based in the centrally-located mountain resort village of Pano Platres. Daily excursions visit such villages as Phini, Omodhos, and Troodos; the ancient Roman complex of Curium with its restored amphitheatre; Paphos, on the east coast, and the UNESCO-protected Roman mosaics, medieval harbour, and ancient burial site; monasteries and churches with their revered icons and restored frescoes; and the larger towns of Nicosia and Limassol.

Contact: Camastro/Pritchett Art International, Inc., 41 Hickory Grove, Quincy, IL 62301; (217) 224-4772 or Ask Mr. Foster Travel Center, 1024 Maine St., Quincy, IL 62306; (800) 933-3023 *or* (217) 224-3900.

CAMP COLTON GLASS PROGRAM
Colton, Oregon
Three-day and two-week sessions from May-September

Established in the 1930s by the Colton Lutheran Church as a summer children's camp and retreat, Camp Colton was acquired in 1985 by Boyce and Kathy Lundstrom, who converted it to a home, glass fusing research studio, and center for glass study. Approximately six summer sessions — two for three days and four for two weeks — are offered for glass workers of all levels.

Two-week sessions, which begin on Sunday and end on Saturday, cover fusing, mold making (five varieties), enameling, pate de verre, casting, torch work, and such advanced fusing techniques as stringer and mosaic, inclusions in glass, diamond sawing methods, and free form slumping using wire forms, drop-outs, or air molds. Students choose the projects they want to pursue and work at their own pace, up to 14 hours a day, to design and execute their own work. A tour of the Bullseye Glass Company in Portland is part of the program.

The three-day sessions, which begin on Friday morning and end Sunday afternoon, cover 75% of the information presented in the two-week sessions, including the basics and a survey of advanced fusing techniques, but offer limited opportunities for hands-on work. Individualized instruction can also be arranged.

Specialties: Glass work.

Faculty: Three accomplished glass artists, including Boyce Lundstrom, author of *Advanced Fusing Techniques.*

Costs, Accommodations: Fees are $375 for a three-day session and $1,150 for a two-week session, which includes materials for basic assignments, room, board, and transportation to and from Portland Airport. Students usually spend approximately $75 to $125 on additional materials, which are available at the student store. A 20% discount is granted couples who study in the same session and the cost for a nonparticipant spouse or guest is $125 for three days, $380 for two weeks. A $25 nonrefundable deposit must accompany registration with balance, payable by VISA or MasterCard, due three weeks prior. Applicants with a good background in stained glass or one of the techniques can apply for teaching assistantships and receive up to a $330 reduction in class fees. Double occupancy rooms are arranged in student cottages and meals are served in Riverfalls Lodge, a rustic building situated between two creeks.

Location, Facilities: Colton is located 35 miles southeast of Portland, between Estacada and Molalla on Highway 211. The camp covers 56 acres of woods, ponds, and streams and the student cottages are built around a fishing lake. The old Dining Hall contains two well-equipped studios, a meeting room/lounge, and a student store. A third studio, furnished with hot glass working equipment, is located deep in the woods.

Contact: Kathy Lundstrom, Camp Director, Camp Colton, Colton, OR 97017; (503) 824-3150.

CANDILI RESIDENTIAL POTTERY COURSES
Procopi, Greece
Two-week courses from Easter through October

Begun in Scotland in 1979 and moved to Greece in 1988, these informal pottery courses are offered approximately ten times a year and individually tailored to the specific needs and interests of the students. Courses begin and end on Saturday and each group is limited to eight or nine participants of varying backgrounds, nationalities, and experience, who are taught by two instructors. The course format is designed to encourage students to develop their technical and creative skills through practice, demonstration, and reference to written resource materials. Instruction is given in throwing, handbuilding, and special firing techniques that include wood-firing stoneware, gas and wood-fired raku, and gas, electric, pit, sawdust, and saggar firings. Instructors are on hand for assistance most of the day and for discussions during mealtimes and pottery equipment is available at all times. Excursions to the beach and other places of interest are planned.

Specialties: Pottery.

Faculty: Principal instructor Alan Bain received the equivalent of a First Class Honours degree in ceramics in 1972 from the Glasgow School of Art in Scotland. His assistant is usually a recent ceramics graduate.

Costs, Accommodations: The cost of the two-week program is £375, which includes materials and firing, meals, lodging in single and twin bedded rooms, and excursions. A 25% deposit secures booking and is refundable for cancellations more than two months prior. Balance is due on arrival. Payment is by check or bank money order in sterling or dollar equivalent. The studio and lodging are part of the Candili Craft and Conference Centre in the former outbuildings of the main Estate House, which has two swimming pools and extensive fruit, vegetable, and flower gardens.

Location, Facilities: The village of Procopi, located 2 1/2 hours from Athens, has a population of about 2,500 and is a pilgrimage center of the Shrine of St. John the Russian. Beaches and hot springs are nearby. The studio is equipped with six wheels, extruder, wood-fired raku, Fordham gas, electric, and a fastfire wood-fired kiln.

Contact: Candili Pottery, 34004 Procopi, Evia, Greece; (30) 0227 41298.

CAROLE MYERS WORKSHOPS
Various locations in the U.S. and Mexico
One to seven-day workshops

A painter and teacher for approximately 25 years, Carole Myers offers watercolor and mixed-media/collage workshops under the sponsorship of art groups, organizations, and individuals. Workshops range from one to seven days in length and are limited to 17 to 25 artists of all levels. Following a demonstration, the instructor works with each student individually.

Specialties: Watercolor, mixed-media/collage.

Faculty: Carole Myers, an Associate of the American Watercolor Society, Signature Member of the National Watercolor Society, and signature member of the North Coast Collage Society, studied at the Instituto Allende and Hacienda El Cobano. Her work is in museum, corporate, and private collections and has been shown in juried exhibitions. She is listed in *Who's Who in American Art* and *The New York Art Review*.

Costs: Costs and arrangements are determined by the sponsoring group or institution.

Location: Includes Missouri, New Jersey, Florida, South Carolina, Maryland, Mexico, and others.

Contact (for schedule): Carole Myers, 12870 Ellsinore Dr., Bridgeton, MO 63044; (314) 739-2406.

CARRIAGE HOUSE PAPER
Somerville, Massachusetts

One and two-day workshops year-round; two-week June workshop

Established in 1975 by Elaine Koretsky and Donna Koretsky, Carriage House Handmade Paper Works is involved with research and experimentation in hand papermaking, the design of special papers for printmaking, drawing, calligraphy, and watercolor, and the creation of art works utilizing handmade paper. The studio offers about a half dozen weekend workshops each season with a two-week program, Papermaking in Depth, featured each June. Classes are scheduled from 10 am to 4 pm and are usually limited to 10 students per instructor, with topics ranging from general papermaking, primarily for the beginner, to specialized techniques for those with previous experience.

The one-day general papermaking workshop is directed toward helping the student get started with simple techniques that can be used at home. Instruction covers pulp preparation and sheet forming, lamination, embedding, pulp painting, and collage. Two-day workshops include: Paper As an Art Form, which focuses on two and three-dimensional paper art and sculpture, and From Plants to Paper, in which students create a book of unusual papers from a variety of native and Japanese fibers. The two-week June workshop emphasizes art forms in paper, including manipulation of pulp and paper, pulp painting and spraying, creation of an art work, and completion of a casting project. Evenings are reserved for slide shows and lectures and weekend activities are also planned. The workshop begins with a supper/reception and concludes with an exhibit of participants' work.

Specialties: Papermaking and paper art.

Faculty: Elaine Koretsky, the author or editor of five books and several articles on the historical or technical aspects of papermaking, has been a guest instructor and lecturer at art centers and museums. Donna Koretsky has a background in printmaking, sculpture, calligraphy, and letterpress and her sculptural works are in private collections. Both have done field research in papermaking techniques in Japan, southeast Asia, and Europe. Guest instructors who are prominent in a specific aspect of handmade paper are featured on occasion.

Costs, Accommodations: Tuition for weekend workshops is approximately $50 per day, which includes materials. Cost of the two-week workshop is $460, which includes materials and lunch each weekday. Full payment must accompany registration and is refundable, less a $5 fee, if space can be filled. A list of nearby accommodations is provided.

Location, Facilities: Carriage House Paper at Brickbottom is situated at the northern edge of Boston, a few minutes from the Boston Museum of Science, about three miles from Logan International Airport, and about two miles from downtown Boston. The building is handicapped accessible, with a wheelchair ramp from the outside and an elevator to the second floor, where the 2,000-square-foot studio is located. In addition to a fully-equipped papermaking facility, which is available for rent, the space is occupied by a gallery and showroom/office, where supplies and equipment are offered for sale.

Contact: Carriage House Paper at Brickbottom, 1 Fitchburg St. #C-207, Somerville, MA 02143; (617) 629-2337.

CARRIZO LODGE ART SCHOOL
Ruidoso, New Mexico
Three and five-day workshops from May-September

The Carrizo Lodge Art School, established in 1956, conducts more than 40 three and five-day drawing and painting workshops from the beginning of May until mid-September. Most workshops meet from 9 am to 4 pm daily, Monday through Friday, and three-day sessions are scheduled over a Friday to Sunday or Saturday to Monday. Enrollment is limited to 25 participants and all workshops are open to beginning to advanced students, who are taught by a combination of demonstration, class painting time, and individual help. Instruction covers a range of motifs, including portrait, figure, landscape, seascape, still life, western, florals, wildlife, abstract, animals, and Sumi-e and students paint in a variety of media, including acrylic, watercolor, oil, pastel, charcoal, and mixed media. A few workshops are devoted to such crafts as totem carving, basketry, jewelry making, knife carving, papermaking, and sculpture, and a young artists class is also offered.

Specialties: Drawing and painting and such crafts as sculpture, basketry, and jewelry making.

Faculty: Includes Becky Anthony, Larry Blovits, Betty Braig, Marilynn R. Branham, Louisa Boshardy, Naomi Brotherton, Judith Campbell-Reed, Lita Chavez, Cleda Curtis, Jo Ann Durham, Dwade W. Engle, Josie Fitzgerald, Ken Freeman, Jerry Fugere, Rose Ann Gandy, Ted Goerschner, Ken Hosmer, Jammey Huggins, Susan Jenkins, Barbara A. Jones, Ben Konis, Frankie Lanier, Paula Mallams-Fasken, Georganna Malloff, Mike McCullough, Jo

Mullendore, Harley Murray, Kenneth W. Potter, William J. Reed, Cristina Robbins, Fred Samuelson, Barbara Savage, Robert Schmalzried, Julie Simmons, Catherine Wilson Smith, Joel Smith, Bev Stewart, Loveta Stickland, Betsy Dillard Stroud, Tina Szajko, W.H. Turner, Carol Ann Wells-Baker, Mary Whyte, and James L. Whitlow.

Costs, Accommodations: Tuition is $145 for three days, $190 for five days. Full payment, payable by VISA, MasterCard, or American Express, must accompany registration. A $15 fee is charged cancellations more than three weeks prior; thereafter fee is at discretion of Lodge. Economy lodging ranges from $135 per person for five days in a private bedroom two-bedroom suite to $190 for single or double private accommodations; luxury condominiums are $375 for one or two persons.

Location, Facilities: The Carrizo Lodge, which is handicapped accessible, is situated two miles from Ruidoso in a pine forest next to a mountain stream. Facilities include hot tubs, swimming pool, exercise equipment, and a convenience and package store. Ruidoso is 120 miles northeast of El Paso, 191 miles southeast of Albuquerque. Greyhound Bus Lines offers service from El Paso.

Contact: Carrizo Lodge Art School, P.O. Box 1371-M513, Ruidoso, NM 88345; (505) 257-9131.

CENTER FOR BOOK ARTS
New York, New York
Week-end workshops and one-day seminars

Founded in 1974 to promote and advance the art of the handmade book, the Center for Book Arts sponsors approximately 30 to 40 weekend workshops a year devoted to the various aspects of hand bookmaking, letterpress printing, and papermaking, as well as day-long seminars on related topics. Sessions are usually scheduled from 10 am to 4 pm on Saturday and Sunday and most are open to students of all levels.

Typical bookmaking workshop titles include Fabric Marbling, Photograph Album and Slipcase, Tunnel Book (an accordion of pages bound on two sides and viewed through a central opening), Oriental Bindings, Box Design (boxmaking experience required), Pop-up Paper Structures, Origami (the art of paperfolding and its relationship to bookmaking), Bookbinding For Artists, and Brush Books, an introduction to the use of brush writing in the artist book format. Printing workshops cover such subjects as Platen Press printing and creating Christmas/Hanukah cards and papermaking sessions introduce the student to basic and Japanese Techniques. One-day seminars include the fundamentals of type, basics of book design, typeface design, and preservation of books and prints.

The Center also sponsors on-going evening classes, an exhibitions program, a hand bookbinding and letterpress printing service, workspace and equipment rentals, an annual fair, and a book arts store.

Specialties: Book arts.

Faculty: Includes Sandra Holzman, a professional craftsperson/artist and teacher since 1976, who produces hand-marbled fabric and paper for the interior design trade; Barbara Mauriello, an artist/bookbinder since 1981 and head of the Center's binding services; Carol Barton, a specialist in pop-up and dimensional formats and part of the Virginia Museum's affiliated artist program; Carol Sturm, recipient of the first Pforzheimer Fellowship for Typographical Research and currently head of the Center's printing services; A. Lynn Forgach, a print and paper maker who has taught at the School of Visual Arts and the National Academy of Art; Abe Lerner, an experienced book designer and teacher whose books have appeared in the American Institute of Graphic Arts' "50 Books of the Year" exhibitions; and Susan Swartzburg, a preservation specialist at Rutgers Universities Libraries and author of *Preserving Library Materials*.

Costs: Workshop costs range from $90 ($75 members) to $200 ($185), plus materials fee of $15 to $35. A $20 registration fee must accompany application. One-day seminars are $65 ($50). Full refund is granted cancellations at least 10 days prior. Annual membership dues begin at $35 and include a subscription to the quarterly *Book Arts Review* and reduced rates for all classes and workshop rentals. A work/study program allows students to study tuition-free in exchange for working a pre-set number of hours in the bindery, printshop, library, or administrative offices.

Location, Facilities: The Center is located in New York City's Greenwich Village. Facilities include a fully equipped hand bookbindery, letterpress printshop, and papermill.

Contact: Center for Book Arts, 626 Broadway, New York, NY 10012; (212) 460-9768.

CENTRO DEL BEL LIBRO
Ascona, Southern Switzerland
One-day to two-week courses year-round

The Centro del Bel Libro houses two professional schools: the Professional School for Artisanal Bookbinding and the Professional School for Book Restorers. Both schools are open only to professionals in the field, who must submit a certificate of apprenticeship or business activity and references or a curriculum vitae. Courses are taught in English as well as German if there are non-German-speaking students enrolled and English texts are provided. Class hours are from 8 am until noon and 2 to 5 pm daily. A certificate is awarded on completion of a course.

The artisanal bookbinding courses, which are based on creativity and the knowledge of forms and colors, cover paper, leather, and parchment bindings in a variety of techniques with appropriate slip-cases and boxes; hand gilding, decoration, and inlaying of leather; gold and colored edging processes; and hand-made headbands. Decorative and marbled papers and other kinds of papers are made according to traditional and new methods. The more than 20 courses that comprise the curriculum are scheduled so that they can be taken in sequence as well as individually, and can all be completed within a year.

The book restoration courses include theoretical training in practical chemistry, physics, and biology; the causes of damage and the suitable method of restoration; the history of paper, books, bindings, and style; and practical training in damage analysis, treatment and reconstruction of damaged papers, and how to take apart and reconstruct historical bindings in cardboard, textiles, leather, parchment and wooden-boards. Students can enroll at different times and at different levels or take all courses consecutively and complete the program in six months.

Specialties: Book binding and restoration.

Faculty: Instructors are prominent professionals in the field.

Costs, Accommodations: Tuition begins at sFr.70 for a one-day course. Payment must accompany enrollment and is refundable only if space can be filled. A list of nearby accommodations is provided.

Location, Facilities: Ascona is a tourist resort situated on Lake Maggiore in southern Switzerland. Air taxi service connects Ascona with the international airports of Milan-Linate and Malpensa. Students in the bookbinding courses can utilize the pulp vat, in which hand-made papers with self-designed watermarks can be designed, the extensive library of technical books, and a collection of slides of artistic book creations. Students in the book restoration courses work in the laboratory, which accommodates 10 persons at a time and contains modern equipment for chemical treatment and leafcasting.

Contact: Segretariato Centro del bel libro, Casella Postale 2600, CH-6501 Bellinzona, Switzerland; (41) 92 25 85 55, Fax (41) 92 25 85 95.

CENTRO SPERIMENTALE D'ARTE
Muggio, Switzerland

Five-day workshops from June-October

During the summer and fall, the Centro Sperimentale d'Arte offers approximately a dozen ceramics workshops, each limited to eight to twelve students of all levels. Typical course titles include Handbuilding, an introduction to different surface decorations, working with engobes, clay coloring, and glazing; Columns/The Balance Of Form, which explores the column as a structural format and the technical problems and aesthetics of large scale works; Experimental Ceramics — Art Experiences, a series of practical experiments with each morning devoted to glazes; Exercises In Form, an analysis of forms in terms of elementary structures and their variations; Creating With Plaster Molds, an introduction to the material and its preparation with presentations of various mold techniques; Hand-Traces On Burnt Earth, which deals with creating landscape impressions by combining fiberglass and the ceramic mass into thin sheets that resemble cracked, dried earth; Design and Planning of Ceramic Forms, an introduction to design using a variety of materials and project models; Porcelain and Serigraphy; A Creative Way of Working With Clay; Throwing on The Wheel; Raku; Kiln Construction And Firing; and Forms, Symbols, And Objects.

Specialties: Ceramics.

Faculty: Includes ceramists J. Paul Sires, director of clay works at the Spirit Square Center in Charlotte, N.C.; Gustav Weiss, author of such technical ceramics books as *Neue Keramik*; University of Halle professor Karl Fulle; Dick Lion, professor at the Art Academy in Arnhem, Holland; Fritz Vehring, professor at the University of Art and Music in Bremen; Till Neu, professor of art education at Frankfurt's Wolfgang Goethe University; Emidio Galassi, professor at the Ceramic Academy in Faenza; and Ingrid Mair Zischg, Maria Geszler, David Miller, Wendelin Stahl, Maika Korfmacher, and Friedrich Stachat.

Costs, Accommodations: Cost of each workshop, which includes room, board, and all materials, is sFr.1,050. A sFr.300 deposit must accompany application with balance due ten days prior. Full refund, less sFr.50 fee, is granted cancellations more than three weeks prior; no refunds thereafter.

Location: The Centro is located in the Casa Cantoni-Fontana, an old, elegant manor house in Switzerland's Valle di Muggio, approximately 10 miles northwest of Lake Como.

Contact: Elisabetta Mellier Fontana, Centro Sperimentale d'Arte, CH-6831 Muggio, Valle di Muggio, Switzerland; (41) 091-491462.

CHARLES BAIUNGO WATERCOLOR WORKSHOPS
Stonington, Maine

Three-day workshops from June-September

First offered in 1989 and limited to ten artists of all levels, these Wednesday to Friday workshops emphasize the use of design aesthetics and preliminary studies and how to deal with problems of complex motifs. Following a Tuesday evening get together with slide presentation and discussion, classes meet daily at 8:30 am for a two-hour analysis of the motif and on-site painting demonstration by the instructor. The remainder of the day is devoted to independent painting, sketching, and work with the instructor until 4:30 pm, when the group reconvenes for a critique session. On rainy days, the demonstrations are held in the artist's studio and work stations are provided for participants' use. Approximately six workshops are offered during the summer months.

Specialties: Watercolor.

Faculty: Charles J. Baiungo is an experienced artist.

Costs, Accommodations: Tuition for each session is $95. A $45 deposit must accompany registration with balance due on arrival. A full refund is granted cancellations more than six weeks prior. Accommodations are available at local inns and bed & breakfasts.

Location: Stonington, a scenic island in Penobscot Bay off the Maine coast, is approximately 55 miles from Bangor International Airport. Acadia National Park, Bar Harbor, and the town of Camden are nearby and all offer such activities as sailing, mountain climbing, camping, and boat touring.

Contact: Charles J. Baiungo, P.O. Box 2512, Bangor, ME 04401; (207) 947-2966.

CHAUTAUQUA INSTITUTION
Chautauqua, New York

Five and ten-day sessions in July and August

This educational institution offers a diverse curriculum of more than 100 continuing education courses for adults and young people during its annual nine-week summer program. The Art Center courses, which meet daily from 9 am to noon or from 1 to 4 pm, Monday through Friday, and are limited to six to fifteen students of all levels, cover such subjects as art metals and enameling, ceramics (including dinnerware, teapot creation, and tilemaking), drawing, painting, fibers (including Ikat and hand papermaking), and sculpture. Additional classes in handicrafts and hobbies are typically offered in calligraphy, stenciling, hooked rugs, cross stitch sweaters, quilting, English smocking, knitting, and furniture repair, refinishing, and restoration.

Specialties: Ceramics, drawing and painting, fiber arts, and other topics.

Faculty: Has included metalworkers/enamelists Pamela Lins, Sheri Mendelson, David Siskind; ceramists Diana Gillespie, Paul Wilmoth; artists Al Blaustein, Leslie Burns, Barbara Grossman, Don Kimes, Barbara Rosenthal, Josette Urso, Gina Werfel; fiber artists Libby Kowalski, Carol Townsend; sculptors Barbara Goodstein, Ed Smith; calligrapher Joan Betz; weaver Jane M. Flynn; and needle artists Patricia Henry, Joan Laird, and Elizabeth Lingg.

Costs, Accommodations: The nonrefundable Art Center tuition is approximately $65 per week (15 hours); fees for handicrafts and hobbies range from $30 to $55 per week (five sessions). Students are encouraged to pre-register. An accommodations directory is available on request.

Location: Workshops are held in the intellectual and cultural environment of Chautauqua Institution, a lakeside community in the southwest corner of New York State, midway between Buffalo and Erie and 16 miles north of Jamestown. It is served by motorcoach and by airlines through Chautauqua County Airport at Jamestown and the airports in Buffalo and Erie. Ground transportation to and from airports or bus terminals is available.

Contact: Chautauqua Institution, Dept. A, Box 1098, Chautauqua, NY 14722; (716) 357-6233/6234.

CHINA ADVOCATES
Beijing, China
Four weeks in September and October

This private cultural organization, created to help Americans study in China, sponsors a variety of in-depth programs in painting and sculpture, culture, language, medicine, and the culinary arts. A four-week fall program is offered in Chinese Gongbi Painting at the Academy of Chinese Painting and in Chinese Pottery at the Central Academy of Arts & Design. Both courses hold three-hour morning classes, Monday through Friday, that concentrate on actual painting or pottery-making. Saturdays are reserved for an all-day scenic excursion and Sundays are at leisure. Students are encouraged to practice during free times and are provided with keys to the studios. An optional 11-day tour of China follows the program.

Gongbi Painting, a course devoted to the classical delineation of form through the precise use of line, is divided into two parts — the first two weeks emphasizing portraiture and the final two weeks focusing on birds and flowers. In addition to morning classes, scheduled activities include two afternoon lectures a week, slide shows, videos, demonstrations of seal stone carving and the mounting of Chinese pictures, and visits with artists-in-residence. Chinese Pottery, for the more experienced student, emphasizes hand production and focuses on traditional styles of vases, tea sets, bowls, and other forms. Study also includes the Chinese traditional line and pattern, the history of china and pottery, and an introduction to the importance of gongbi-style and watercolor painting in pottery. Chinese potters ask to be allowed to choose at least one of the students' best work, made while in residence, for display at the school. Students are also requested to bring examples of their work, if possible, to show to the potters.

Specialties: Chinese pottery and gongbi painting.

Faculty: Gongbi painting is taught by two of the Academy of Chinese Painting's most accomplished artists, Professors Pan Jiezi and Gong Wenzhen; pottery classes are taught by experienced potters of the Central Academy of Fine Arts.

Costs, Accommodations: Program fees, which include tuition, airfare, double-occupancy dormitory room, all meals, and weekend excursions, are $2,530 for Chinese Gongbi Painting, $2,380 for Chinese Pottery. A $400 deposit must accompany application with balance due 75 days prior to start of program. Penalty ranges from $200 for cancellations more than 75 days prior to 40% of program cost plus airline cancellation charges less than 15 days prior. Painting students live at the Academy; pottery students are housed on-campus at the Foreign Residence Hall.

Contact: China Advocates, 1635 Irving St., San Francisco, CA 94122; (800) 333-6474 *or* (415) 665-4505.

CINNAMINSON ART WORKSHOPS
Cinnaminson, New Jersey
Three to five-day classes in the spring and fall

Begun in 1987, the Cinnaminson Art Workshops offers five watercolor workshops in the spring and fall. The workshops, which average 20 to 24 participants and run from 9 am to 3 or 4 pm daily, are taught by a different faculty of prominent artists each year. Typical titles include Character Study in Watercolor, Oil, and Pastels, which focuses on techniques to set up the model depending on the medium used; Watercolor Landscape, which emphasizes shapes, value, and color in both a studio and on-location setting; and Floral and Landscape.

Specialties: Watercolor.

Faculty: Typical faculty includes realist painter Burt Silverman, author of *Breaking the Rules of Watercolor* and *Painting People*; Philadelphia-area teacher Jean Uhl Spicer, recipient of the Grumbacher Gold Medal and the Pittsburgh Aqueus' 1986 Patrons Award; Tom Lynch, author of *Magic of Watercolors*; Barbara Nechis, author of *Watercolor, The Creative Experience*; Charles Sovek, Frank Webb, Joan Ashley Rothermel, and Judi Betts.

Cost, Accommodations: Costs range from $200 to $250 per workshop. A $50 deposit must accompany application with balance due four weeks prior. Refund, less $35 fee, is granted cancellations more than six weeks prior; thereafter only if space can be filled. Lodging is available at area motels and private homes (approximately $20 per night including breakfast). There are several restaurants nearby.

Location: Classes are held at the Burlington County Footlighters Playhouse in Cinnaminson, a 20-minute drive from downtown Philadelphia.

Contact: Marie Tranovich, Director, Cinnaminson Art Workshops, 800 Manor Rd., Cinnaminson, NJ 08077; (609) 829-3614.

CLAUDE CRONEY STUDIOS
Cedar Key, Florida
Five-day workshops from February-June and September-November

Established in 1981, Claude Croney Studios offers approximately eight spring and fall on-location painting workshops that are limited to 12 artists who should have basic painting skills. The program begins with a Sunday afternoon reception and classes meet daily at 9 am, Monday through Thursday, for a 2 1/2-hour painting demonstration followed by question and answer period. Students paint on their own until 3 pm, after which individual critiques are held. Fridays are devoted to an open critique of one painting from each student.

Specialties: Watercolor.

Faculty: Claude Croney, an accomplished artist and member of the American Watercolor Society, has taught at the Cape Cod Community College, Falmouth Artists Guild, and Brockton Art Museum and his work is represented in private and museum collections. He is author of *My Way With Watercolor*, *The Watercolor Painting Book*, and *Croney on Watercolor*.

Costs, Accommodations: Workshop fee is $175 and previous attendees may enroll on a daily basis at the rate of $35. A $50 deposit must accompany application with balance due the first day of class. Deposit refund is granted cancellations more than ten days prior. Local accommodations range from $30 to $95 per night, double occupancy.

Location: Cedar Key, located among a group of small islands on Florida's Gulf Coast, is within a half day's drive of Gainesville, Tampa, Orlando, and St. Petersburg.

Contact: Claude Croney Studios, P.O. Box 730, Cedar Key, FL 32625; (904) 543-5883.

THE CLEARING
Ellison Bay, Wisconsin
Five-day to one-week courses from May-October

Built in 1935 by Jens Jensen, a distinguished landscape architect and friend of Frank Lloyd Wright, The Clearing offers a variety of courses for all levels in the arts, nature, and humanities, including watercolor, weaving, and woodcarving. One-week courses begin with supper on Sunday and end with breakfast the following Saturday. Of the more than 40 courses that are offered during the spring, summer, and fall, approximately 15 to 20 are devoted to arts and crafts related topics. Typical course titles include Woodcarving — The Four-Legged Critter, in which students learn to carve an animal of their choice; Beginning Stained Glass, covering both design and techniques for cutting and fitting; Make a Quilt, Make a Memory — Scrap Quilts, a template free approach to traditional quiltmaking on the sewing machine; Navajo Silversmithing, consisting of demonstrations, discussions, and critique of individual projects; Tapestry Weaving, covering design and technique; and Hand Painted China and Jewelry. A five-day Mini Folk School, offered twice in October, features a choice of courses, such as Carve and Paint a Songbird and Lap Quilting.

Specialties: A variety of topics, including painting, weaving, woodcarving.

Faculty: The faculty includes university and college professors and other practicing professionals.

Costs, Accommodations: The one-week course cost, which includes dormitory (twin-bedded) room and all meals except Thursday supper, is approximately $395 ($420). Mini Folk School cost is $250 ($265). A $75 deposit must accompany registration with balance due one month prior. Cancellations at least 20 days prior receive full refund less $25; deposit is forfeited thereafter. Dormitory and double room lodging are in log and stone cabins.

Location: The Clearing is situated in Wisconsin's Door County woods, on Green Bay.

Contact: The Clearing, P.O. Box 65, Ellison Bay, WI 54210; (414) 854-4088.

COLORADO MOUNTAIN COLLEGE
Breckenridge, Colorado
Five and ten-day summer workshops

Colorado Mountain College offers three or four summer fine arts workshops, each meeting four to six hours daily and limited to 15 to 20 students. Typical topics include Landscapes, covering such concepts as composition, line quality, shading, and appropriate use of color; Beginning Watercolor, which explores landscapes and portraits and concentrates on such techniques as washes, wet on wet, dry brush, color mixing, paper preparation, and sketchbook; and Painting Workshop, a multi-media workshop that emphasizes color sense, directness of presentation, and problems of compositions.

Specialties: Painting.

Faculty: Has included Leona Sophocles, formerly assistant director at Denver's St. Charles Gallery, and Edith Palombi, sub-director of the magazine *Viva El Arte,* who has conducted watercolor workshops at Guadalajara's Autonama University.

Costs: Tuition is determined by residency and course credit value (fine arts courses range from 1 to 1 1/2 credits). The rate per credit is $20 for those who live in the district, $40 for those who live in-state, and $140 for those from out-of-state. A nominal materials fee is also charged for some classes. Full refund is granted cancellations at least two days prior to first class and a 75% refund is granted within two days of class.

Location: The college is 85 miles west of Denver, off Interstate 70.

Contact: Colorado Mountain College, Box 2208, Breckenridge, CO 80424; (303) 453-6757.

CONNECTICUT VALLEY CALLIGRAPHERS (CVC)
Farmington, Connecticut
One and two-day workshops

Formed in 1984 to promote and encourage the art of beautiful lettering, the CVC sponsors eight to ten workshops annually, one-day tutorial sessions, two-day programs for beginning and advanced calligraphers interested in a special area of study, and regularly scheduled and special meetings that feature a guest lecturer, displays, and exhibits. Workshops, limited to 15 to 25 students, offer instruction in basic letter forms and a variety of techniques, as well as such applications for calligraphy as watercolor, bookbinding, paper marbling, and illuminating. Typical titles include Creativity and Envelope Art, Upright Copperplate, Gothic for High School Students, Sign Painting, and Beginning Italics.

Specialties: Calligraphy.

Faculty: Includes such area calligraphers as Dick Beasley, Annie Cicale, Jenny Groat, William Hildebrandt, Michael Hughey, Barry Morentz, Anna Pinto, Marcy Robinson, Ellen Sayers, Denys Taipale, Peter Thornton, Sheila Waters, and Eleanor Winters,

Costs, Accommodations: Daily workshop fees are generally $30 ($25 for members) plus materials. Accommodations are available in area inns and hotels. CVC membership dues are $15 annually.

Location: The workshops are usually conducted in the program rooms of area public libraries, which are handicapped accessible, and the Farmington Art Guild. Farmington is within a one-hour drive of Springfield, Massachusetts, and New Haven, Danbury, Litchfield, and Waterbury, Connecticut. Nearby attractions include the Hill-Stead Museum, Farmington Valley Arts Center, Hartford's Wadsworth Atheneum and Noah Webster House, and the Talcott Mountain State Park.

Contact: Workshop Chairpersons, Connecticut Valley Calligraphers, P.O. Box 1122, Farmington, CT 06034.

THE CONNIE AND TOM McCOLLEY BASKETRY SCHOOL
Chloe, West Virginia
Five-day workshops from May-September

Connie and Tom McColley, who began basketmaking in 1974 and developed it into a full-time career by 1978, established The Basketry School to stimulate the creative spirit and provide a center for the basketmaker. A half dozen workshops are scheduled from spring to fall, each limited to 12 students of all levels, who attend classes from Monday through Friday and have studio access 24 hours a day. In each class, students learn the entire process of making a basket from a white oak log; making splints, fashioning handles and rims, weaving the basket, and finishing details. Traditional and contemporary forms are explored and discussed with slide presentations. Other topics include marketing and photographing the work and sources of tools and supplies. Students also have the opportunity to gather and work with honeysuckle, hickory bark, and other natural branch forms.

Specialties: Basketry.

Faculty: The McColleys have taught at Arrowmont in Tennessee and at The Michigan Basketmakers Convention. Their work has been exhibited in The Link, Basketry Exhibit, in California, and in a solo exhibit at the Stiffel Fine Art Center in Wheeling. Their work has appeared in *Fine Woodworking Design Book Three* and other publications.

Costs, Accommodations: Tuition is $225 per workshop plus a one time $25 nonrefundable processing fee. A $100 deposit must accompany application with balance due on arrival. Cancellations more than 20 days prior receive full refund less fee; no refunds thereafter. Cabins are available for $13 per night and the meadow around the School can be used for camping for $10 to $15 per week. Three meals daily are served for $12 per day. A limited number of work/study opportunities are available.

Location: The School is situated in the foothills of the Appalachian Mountains in central West Virginia, eight miles north of Interstate 79 off Route 16. Pick-up at the Charleston Airport, which is 52 miles from Chloe, can be arranged for $25.

Contact: The Basketry School, Route 3, Box 325, Chloe, WV 25235; (304) 655-7429.

CONOVER WORKSHOPS
Parkman, Ohio

Two to five-day summer courses

Since 1978, Conover Woodcraft Specialties, Inc., a company that reproduces a variety of traditional woodworking tools, woodturning lathes, and accessories, has offered approximately 12 summer courses that focus on turning and Windsor chair building. Limited to four to six participants per instructor, the courses emphasize student construction of cameo projects that become a reference notebook of the techniques learned during the week. Hands-on learning is stressed and instructors demonstrate techniques and supervise their immediate application. Some courses are open to all levels while enrollment in others requires wood-turning experience and/or completion of prerequisite courses. Evening activities include lectures, slide shows, field trips, and a graduation banquet.

Typical course titles include Sack-Back Windsor, dedicated to mastering chairmaking by constructing a sack-back Windsor arm chair utilizing such uncommon techniques as riving, working green wood, and steam bending, and such infrequently used tools as scorps, shaves, travishers, and spoon bits; Woodturning — Artistic and Functional, which emphasizes the fluid application of conventional turning tools to produce work that requires only minimal sanding; Shaker Box Making, which begins with the making of necessary jigs and forms followed by the construction of nested boxes and carriers; Basic Hand Tool Joinery, which applies the use, adjustment, and care of handtools and the skill of "tuning" to the construction of a small table; Continuous-Arm/Oval Back Windsor and Sack-Back Windsor Settee, which teach advanced techniques to those who've completed the sack-back Windsor course; Turning for Windsor Chair Makers, a hands-on course in production spindle turning for furniture makers; and Three Shaker Baskets, in which students weave Cathead, round bottom, and Trinket baskets.

Specialties: Woodturning, Windsor chair building, basket weaving.

Faculty: Director Susan Conover and Founder Ernie Conover; Windsor instructors Boyd Hutchison and Kevin Malone; turning instructors Rude Osolnik, Palmer Sharpless, Dave Hout, Leo Doyle, Ray Key, Clead Christiansen, and Pete Hutchinson; John Wilson (Shaker box making), John Dodd (joinery), and Gerrie Kennedy (Shaker baskets).

Costs, Accommodations: Resident student rates, which include lodging, meals, and materials, range from $225 to $699; day student rates, which include materials, noon meal, and final banquet, range from $150 to $599. A $200 deposit must accompany application for each course with balance due two weeks prior. A 50% deposit refund is granted cancellations prior to May 15. Two credit hours per course are available through Hiram College at a cost of $242. Accommodations are single occupancy dormitory rooms. Breakfast and dinner are served cafeteria-style and lunches are catered at the workshop.

Location: The courses are held on the campus of Hiram College, which is handicapped accessible. Round trip shuttle service is available from Cleveland's Hopkins Airport.

Contact: Conover Workshops, Conover Woodcraft Specialties, Inc., 18125 Madison Rd., Parkman, OH 44080; (216) 548-3481.

COOPER-HEWITT MUSEUM
New York, New York
One-day workshops year-round

The Cooper-Hewitt Museum, the Smithsonian Institution's National Museum of Design, offers lectures, seminars, tours, special events, and four to six day-long hands-on workshops each season. Workshop topics have included Jewelry as an Art Form, which covered the techniques of forging, riveting, wire coiling, and creating three-dimensional forms; Purses, Pockets, and Pouches, three workshops in which students learned to make a Victorian evening bag, bead knitted purse, or canvas embroidery pouch; Weaving Techniques From the Orient, in which students wove a Japanese-style flower basket or Oriental rug sampler; Decorated Eggs in the Ukranian Tradition, a family workshop devoted to decorating eggs using an elaborate wax-resist technique. Most workshops are scheduled from 10 am to 4:30 pm.

Specialties: Crafts relating to concurrent exhibitions.

Faculty: Workshops are conducted by distinguished scholars, artists, craftsmen, and designers.

Costs: Tuition averages $65 for nonmembers, $45 for members. Full payment secures reservation and telephone credit card (VISA, MasterCard, American Express) registrations are accepted. A fee is charged cancellations more than two weeks prior; no refunds thereafter. Tuition-free monitorships are available. Annual Cooper-Hewitt membership dues begin at $20 student, $35 individual, and $50 family. Members are entitled to free admission to the

Museum, invitations to viewings and holiday parties, reduced rate tuition on workshops, classes, and tours, a subscription to the Cooper-Hewitt *News*, and discounts at all 13 Smithsonian museum shops.

Location: The Cooper-Hewitt Museum, which is accessible to disabled persons, borders on Central Park on New York's "Museum Mile" on the Upper East Side.

Contact: Programs Department, Cooper-Hewitt Museum, 2 E. 91st St., New York, NY 10128-9990; (212) 860-6868.

CORHAMPTON HOUSE NEEDLEWORK COURSES
Corhampton, Hants, England

One-day and one-week courses in spring and fall

This Georgian Country House school, established in 1987, offers a variety of day courses as well as occasional one-week residential courses for needleworkers of all levels. About a half dozen courses are offered during each season, on such topics as tapestry, Italian quilting, silk shading, and embroidery. Each session is limited to 12 participants and scheduled from 10:30 am until 4:30 pm in the House drawing room. The one-week course includes visits to Hampton Court and the Royal School of Needlework, the city of Winchester, and Harrods in London.

Specialties: Needlework.

Faculty: Instructors from the Royal School of Needlework.

Costs, Accommodations: Tuition, which includes basic materials, VAT, and three-course lunch, is £38.50 per day; lodging, which includes VAT and full breakfast, is £30 single, £39 double. Payment is by check, VISA, MasterCard, and Eurocard. Accommodations in Corhampton House, a no-smoking establishment, have private bathrooms.

Location: Corhampton House is situated on England's South Coast in the countryside of the Meon Valley, 9 miles from the city of Winchester and 60 miles from London. Riding, golf, and sailing are available at nearby Hamble.

Contact: Corhampton House, Corhampton, Hants, SO3 1NB, England; (44) 0489-877845.

COUNTRY WORKSHOPS
Marshall, North Carolina

Five and six-day workshops year-round

Since 1978 Country Workshops, a nonprofit educational organization, has offered a series of workshops in traditional methods of woodworking utilizing hand tools. The programs are designed for beginners to professionals with summer sessions limited to 12 students and winter chairmaking tutorials limited to two. Students arrive on Sunday afternoon and attend classes from 9 am to 6 pm daily, Monday through Friday or Saturday. Four or five workshops are offered each summer, always including one in ladderback and one in Windsor chairmaking and sometimes including Japanese Woodworking, Green Woodworking, Swiss Cooperage, Toolmaking for Woodworkers, Timber Framing, and Scandinavian Woodcarving. Instruction combines traditional methods with contemporary knowledge, designed to teach practical and versatile skills that can lead to a high level of craftsmanship. Theory and hands-on experience are combined in projects that emphasize efficient, safe use of such specialized hand tools as drawknives, spokeshaves, carving knives, and living tools. A special course for children and parents is planned.

An Internship Program from July through August, open to one student a year, provides an opportunity to take classes in return for assistance between and during workshops, tool maintenance, and some farm work. The intern receives room and board and can attend any workshops during the summer.

Specialties: Traditional woodworking.

Faculty: Includes Country Workshops director Drew Langsner (Green Woodworking, Cooperage), apprentice to the last cooper in Switzerland and author of *Country Woodcraft, Green Woodworking,* and other books and magazine articles, full-time chairmakers Dan Mayner (Ladderback Chairmaking) and Curtis Buchanan (Windsor Chairmaking), full-time timber framer and contractor John Koenig (Timber Framing), and retired hand crafts instructor Wille Sundqvist (Scandinavian Woodcarving), author of crafts books in Swedish.

Costs, Accommodations: Tuition, which includes home-cooked meals and materials, is $300 for a five-day workshop, $360 for six days. Those who enroll in two or more workshops receive a 10% discount. Students in Japanese Woodworking must supply their own tool kit, which costs about $100. Lodging in the dorm is $10 per night (bedding not supplied), camp space is free. A $75 nonrefundable deposit must accompany application with balance due four weeks prior. Cancellations postmarked at least two weeks prior receive full refund of balance.

Location: The school is held at the Langsner Farmstead, a 100-acre mountain cove located just beneath the Appalachian Trail, approximately halfway between Asheville, North Carolina, and Johnson City, Tennessee. Nearby attractions include hiking and white water rafting.

Contact: Country Workshops, 90 Mill Creek Rd., Marshall, NC 28753; (704) 656-2280.

COUPEVILLE ARTS CENTER
Coupeville, Washington
Two to five-day workshops in March, June, July, and September

Founded in 1987, this nonprofit organization dedicated to promoting the arts and crafts offers intensive workshops in needleworking, fiber arts, painting, and photography. The daily schedule usually runs from 8:30 am to

4:30 pm and includes lectures, demonstrations, and individual and group critiques. Workshop enrollment averages 15 to 20 participants, primarily advanced amateurs.

Needleworks, a one-week program in mid-March, consists of two and three-day workshops in quilting, knitting, and needlepoint. Fiber Forum, a one-week program in mid-September, offers two and three-day workshops in weaving, color, design, spinning, and dyeing. Palettes Plus, a six-week program in June-July, offers about 14 two to five-day workshops including watercolor, oil, mixed media, calligraphy, papermaking, and marketing.

Specialties: Fiber arts, painting, needlework, photography.

Faculty: Instructors, who are prominent in their fields, include such artists as Sharon Alderman, Peter Collingwood, Ken Hosmer, Betty Chen Louis, Christopher Schink, Meg Swansen, Ann Templeton, and Frederick Wong.

Costs: Tuition ranges from $75 for two days to $230 for a five-day workshop. A $75 deposit must accompany registration, with balance due four weeks prior. Cancellations more than four weeks prior receive a full refund less $25; deposit is forfeited thereafter. Credit cards (VISA, MasterCard) accepted.

Location: Coupeville, the second oldest town in the state, is situated on Whidbey Island, two hours from Seattle. It's accessible by ferry from the south and west, by bridge from the north. Nearby attractions include the catacombs of Fort Casey Park, the forest of Deception Pass, historic Victorian homes and blockhouses, and the Ebey's Landing National Reserve.

Contact: Judy Lynn-Suval, Coupeville Arts Center, P.O. Box 171K, Coupeville, WA 98239; (206) 678-3396.

COWBOY ARTISTS OF AMERICA (CAA) MUSEUM
Kerrville, Texas
Five-day spring and fall workshops

Opened in 1983, the Cowboy Artists of America Museum offers four workshops that are held periodically in the spring and fall and designed for professional level and advanced amateur painters and sculptors. Application for admission is required and students must submit slides of their work for selection by the instructors.

Western Sculpture With the Cowboy Artists of America, a professional level workshop, focuses on sculpting the human head and a continuing study of horse anatomy. The class is limited to 45 students, who are taught by three instructors, and includes lectures, demonstrations, and individual critiques. Another professional level workshop, Expressing Feelings and Emotions in Paint and Bronze, limited to 20 students, is designed to improve expressive skills with emphasis on composition, value, gesture, and movement. Demonstrations, critiques, compositional exercises, and marketing discussions are also a part of the program.

The museum also sponsors beginning, intermediate, and young artists workshops such as Exploring the Third Dimension in Western Art, a two-day discussion and demonstration that covers sculpture from armature construction to the application of clay with special attention to composition, design, and structural anatomy; and Sketching Western Subjects Outdoors, two days of on-location painting at Hill Country sites and area ranches with instruction in color, composition, value, and line.

Dedicated to educating the public to a better understanding and appreciation of America's Western heritage, the CAA Museum displays works of cowboy artists and that of historic Western artists, seves as a repository of information about each artist's life work, and houses a library of Western Americana with special emphasis on the history of the range cattle industry. There are currently 28 active and 6 emeritus CAA members.

Specialties: Art of the American West.

Faculty: Includes William Moyers, author and illustrator of *Famous Indian Tribes* and *Famous Heroes of the West*, Grant Speed, Pat Haptonstall, Jason Scull, and B.R. Greene.

Costs, Accommodations: Professional level five-day workshop fee is $195 ($165, members); two-day workshops cost $55 ($45). An 80% refund is granted cancellations more than one month prior (members receive full refund less $5 cancellation fee); thereafter only if space can be filled, however credit may be applied to a future class. Accommodations are available at area motels, RV parks, and camping facilities.

Location: Located in the Texas Hill Country, Kerrville is 65 miles northwest of San Antonio and 100 miles west of Austin and has bus service and a municipal airport. Facilities are handicapped accessible.

Contact: Cowboy Artists of America Museum, P.O. Box 1716, Kerrville, TX 78029-1716; (512) 896-2553.

THE CRAFTS CENTER
Ripley, West Virginia

Weekend and one-week workshops from March through November

The Crafts Center workshops are sponsored by the West Virginia Department of Education. A variety of workshops are offered from early March through late November for the beginning to advanced craftsperson. Sessions are scheduled daily from 8:30 am until 4:30 pm with classrooms open until late evenings. Weekend workshops, which begin on Friday at 7 pm, have included such subjects as blacksmithing, pieced clothing, natural basketry, watercolor painting, basic wood joinery, glass jewelry, paper marbling, and natural decorations. One-week workshops, which meet from Monday through Friday, have included such subjects as weaving, woodturning, quilting, folk art painting, stained glass, and white oak basketmaking. Credit ia available through the West Virginia College of Graduate Studies.

Specialties: A variety of programs, including blacksmithing, quilting, weaving, woodturning, basketry, stained glass, and calligraphy.

Faculty: Instructors, all of whom have had their work exhibited at crafts fairs or galleries, have included quilters Roberta Farmer and Nancy Pearson, painter Ellen Elmes, production weavers Janet Hamstead and Randall Darwall, blacksmiths Jeff Fetty and Peter Ross, woodworkers David Finck and Palmer Sharpless, and basketmaker Aaron Yakim.

Costs, Accommodations: Tuition, which must accompany application, is $55 for weekend workshops, $100 for week-long workshops, and materials fee ranges from $10 to $45, depending upon class selected. A full refund is granted cancellations at least three weeks prior. One hour of graduate credit is available for a weekend class, two hours of credit for a one-week class at a cost of $170 per hour. Meals and lodging are $18.50 per day for a dormitory room, $24 per day for a semi-private room.

Contact: Crafts Center, Cedar Lakes Conference Center, Ripley, WV 25271; (304) 372-7005.

CREALDE SCHOOL OF ART
Winter Park, Florida
One to three-day weekend workshops

Founded by William S. Jenkins in 1975 as a division of the nonprofit community arts organization, Crealde Arts, Inc., this alternative art educational system offers courses and workshops in sculpture, ceramics, painting and drawing, printmaking, fiber art, stained glass, and photography. Typical weekend workshop titles include Introduction to Bronze Art, two days of lecture, video, and hands-on experience at creating wax sculptures for bronze casting, ending with a bronze pour at Crealde Foundry; Sculptured Jewelry Workshop, a one-day program limited to ten students who design mini-sculptures and jewelry from their own drawings and transform them into silver; and Watercolor Workshop. Credit courses are offered through the University of Central Florida and the school also provides lectures, an art outreach program, fine art gallery exhibits, and open studio time.

Specialties: Painting and drawing, sculpture, ceramics, printmaking, fiber arts, stained glass.

Faculty: Includes David Cumbie, Helen Hickey, Deborah Hildinger-Allen, Susan Hudson, Jackie Otto-Miller, David Reese, Sue Roberts, John Spring.

Costs, Accommodations: Workshop tuition, which must be paid in full three days prior to starting date, ranges from $45 to $90 ($42 to $85 for members); an additional materials fee is charged for some workshops. Cancellations at least three days prior receive full refund less $10. Membership in Crealde Arts begins at $25 for an individual, $50 for a family.

Location, Facilities: The School surrounds a pond in a garden setting in Winter Park, just north of Orlando. Its facilities include a bronze foundry and separate throwing, handbuilding, glazing, and firing areas for ceramics.

Contact: Crealde Arts, 600 St. Andrews Blvd., Winter Park, FL 32792; (407) 671-1886.

THE DAY STUDIO WORKSHOP, INC.
San Francisco, California and New York, New York
One, two, and three-week workshops from March-October

The Day Studio, founded in 1975 as a company specializing in the fine art of surface finishing, is a professional school teaching surface finishing techniques to individuals of all levels who want to expand their practical skills or conceptual abilities in surface finishing (also called faux finishing), an artful treatment applied to any object or interior to create a visual effect. Combinations of paint and other media, applied with special techniques and tools, imitate the texture and depth of marble, stone, lacquer, woodgrain, metallics, fabric, and other materials. Colors vary from pale washes to transparent glazes and bright lacquers and surface textures range from textured to satin smooth. The surface can also incorporate a pictorial or abstract design as an integral part of the finish.

The Studio holds 15 to 20 workshops a year, 10 to 12 in San Francisco and 5 or 6 in New York City, with sessions scheduled from 9 am to 5 pm, Monday through Friday, and a student to teacher ratio of 18 to 1. One-week workshops are Wall Glazing, Color, Woodgraining, and Historical & Complex Stenciling; two-week workshops are Stone & Marble, Glazing & Gilding, and Trompe L'Oeil/Casein; and the three-week Project workshop is for students who have completed Glazing & Gilding and Stone & Marble. Students are taught color balancing techniques, applications, basic preparation, and usable formulas, and are provided with supply sources for tools and materials and guidelines for bidding, contracting, presentation, and selling. They create each finish through hands-on execution of sample boards, which they can utilize in sales presentations. Workshops can be taken in any order, although the Stone and Marble workshop is a foundation for understanding balance and the Glazing and Gilding workshop rounds out the finisher's skills. The other workshops are designed for specific needs with the exception of Color, which applies to all aspects of finishing. During the Project workshop, students design and execute an original three-panel screen, combining the finishing and design skills from the other workshops as well as Oriental and European design techniques.

Specialties: Surface finishing.

Faculty: JoAnne Day studied and earned her journeyman status at the Isabel O'Neil Studio in New York City. Her work has appeared in *Architectural Digest* and been featured in *The Wall Street Journal*. The author of books on decorative stenciling, she is writing and producing a library of surface finishing videotapes. Members of the Day Studio teaching staff are trained by JoAnne Day and are accomplished professional decorative artists with contracting experience and communication skills.

Costs, Accommodations: Tuition, which includes paint brushes, tools, and sample boards, ranges from $750 to $1,000 for the one-week workshops and from $1,750 to $2,000 for the two-week workshops. A $300 deposit is required for one-week workshops, $600 for two-week workshops, with balance due on arrival, payable by check, cash, MasterCard, or VISA.

Cancellations at least 14 days prior receive full refund less $25; no refunds thereafter. A list of recommended accommodations is provided.

Location: The courses are held at The Day Studio in San Francisco and at 225 West 28th Street in New York City. Both facilities are handicapped accessible.

Contact: The Day Studio, Inc., 1504 Bryant St., San Francisco, CA 94103; (415) 626-9300.

DILLMAN'S SAND LAKE LODGE
Lac Du Flambeau, Wisconsin
One to six-day workshops from May-October

Dillman's Lodge, a family resort complex opened in 1935, has offered a wide variety of creative art and photography workshops and travel study programs since 1977. The approximately 70 to 80 visual arts workshops conducted each year by prominent faculty emphasize an informal studio and on-location environment with individual and group instruction and daily critique. Most workshops run for six days and are open to all levels, with a few geared to intermediate and advanced artists. A majority of the programs focus on painting and drawing, primarily watercolor.

Typical titles, which reflect the instructor's specialty, include Watercolor the Creative Experience (Barbara Nechis), Portrait and Figure Painting in Pastel & Oil (Bob Gerbracht), Oil Maritime Seascapes and Portrait (Charles Vickery), Capturing Motion and Light in Watercolor (Doug Lew), For the Love of Portrait Painting (John Naylor), and Wildflowers in Watercolor (Maggie Linn). Other workshops include Intaglio Carving on Gems and Glass (Ute Klein Bernhardt), Stained Glass (Lee Scriver), Rosemaling (Judith Nelson), Quilting: Traditions and Beyond (Frances Ginocchio), Calligraphy (Mary Jane Gormley), Marketing Your Artwork (a one-day workshop by Richard Jamiolkowski), and Wings in Wood (Robert Guge), in which each student carves and paints a bird. Painting trips to Italy and Africa are planned.

Specialties: Drawing and painting, calligraphy, quilting, woodcarving, rosemaling, and other topics.

Faculty: In addition to the above, includes Bridget Austin, Phil Austin, Judi Betts, Larry Blovits, Rose Edin, Nita Engle, Robert Hoffman, Karlyn Holman, Margaret Kessler, Greg Kreutz, Susan Kuznitsky, Maggie Linn, Betty Lynch, Tom Lynch, Maxine Masterfield, Charles Movalli, Carol Orr, Irving Shapiro, Catherine Wilson Smith, Ted Smuskiewicz, Charles Sovek, Tony van Hasselt, Judi Wagner, Frank Webb, Doris White, and Mary Whyte.

Costs, Accommodations: The fee for most workshops ranges from $375 (weekend) to $795 (one week), which includes double occupancy lodging and breakfasts and dinners. Nonparticipant rates are $417 for six days, which includes room and meals; reduced rates for children are also available. A $200 deposit must accompany application and full refund, less $20 service charge, is granted cancellations received six weeks prior to class. Accommodations, which are assigned on the basis of size of party, consist of lakeside vacation homes, inn rooms, or dorm units. CEUs are available through Nicolet College for an additional fee ranging from $15 to $35.

Location: The 250-acre lodge property, which is handicapped accessible, is situated on White Sand Lake in northern Wisconsin, a three-hour drive from Green Bay. Arrangements can be made for meeting guests who fly in to Rhinelander via Northwest Air Link or United Express. On-site facilities include a covered marina with equipment for fishing and water skiing, hiking trails, and tennis. Golf, horseback riding, bowling, shopping, summer theater, and museums are nearby.

Contact: Dillman's Sand Lake Lodge, P.O. Box 98, Lac du Flambeau, WI 54538; (800) 433-2238, (800) 433-6772 in Wisconsin, *or* (715) 588-3143.

DORIS ANNE HOLMAN WATERCOLOR WORKSHOPS
Maine and other locations in the U.S. and Canada
One to four-day workshops

Since 1984, artist Doris Anne Holman has offered one to four-day water-color workshops for 10 to 20 students of all levels. Selected workshop topics include experimental techniques, moods, flowers, and compositional form. Saturday workshops are held once a month at the artists studio in Wayne from November to May and approximately eight summer weekend workshops are given throughout Maine and in New Hampshire and Newburyport, Mass. Workshops outside the U.S. include four days in Bermuda and three days in Grand Manan Island, Canada.

Specialties: Watercolor with gesso and india ink.

Faculty: Doris Anne Holman studied at the Maryland School of Art and Design, the Portland School of Art, and with Edgar A. Whitney, Robert E. Wood, and Milford Zornes. She teaches watercolor at the University of Maine-Augusta, her article on "Value Sketching" was published by *Draw Magazine*, and her work is exhibited in Maine galleries.

Costs, Accommodations: Workshops cost $15 to $20 per day. A $25 deposit must accompany reservation form. Accommodations are at local motels and bed & breakfasts.

Contact: Doris Anne Holman, Box 222, Wayne, ME 04284; (207) 685-4177.

DORIS OLSEN'S PAINTING WORKSHOPS
Sonora, California and Cornwall, England
Six-day Sonora workshops in June; Cornwall workshops in summer/fall

Since 1984, watercolorist Doris Olsen has taught outdoor painting work-shops in all media for students with some drawing and painting experience. Her Gold Country Painting Workshops, offered three times each June, are limited to six students, who live at her home in Sonora. The workshop begins with Sunday night dinner, concludes after breakfast the following Saturday and includes individualized instruction in the studio and a Friday evening group critique. During the first three daily sessions, students begin by painting skies and clouds, then distant and near scenery, and finally buildings, light, and shadow. On the last two days they incorporate the techniques they've learned into paintings.

Workshops in Cornwall, scheduled in July/August and September/October are limited to ten students, who are given painting instruction by the sea.

Specialties: Painting.

Faculty: Doris Olsen attended New York's Art Students League and the Academy of Art in San Francisco. She received first prize (still life) in the Washington, D.C. Miniature Painters & Sculptors Society and has published a series of limited edition prints, *Country Houses and Historic Houses.*

Costs, Accommodations: Cost of the Sonora workshop is $385 per week, which includes double room in the artist's home and studio and home-cooked meals. A $100 deposit is required with application with balance due 30 days prior. Deposit is refundable for cancellations more than 30 days prior and thereafter if space can be filled. The Cornwall workshop fee of $2,500 includes airfare, bed and breakfast lodging, and picnic lunches. A $250 deposit is required with balance due 30 days prior. The deposit is refundable if space can be filled.

Location: The artist's Sonora home is located on 10 acres of oaks with walking path and solar-heated swimming pool. Cornwall is situated on England's southwest coast.

Contact: Doris Olsen, 17364 Overland Trail, Sonora, CA 95370; (209) 586-2472.

D'PHARR PAINTING ADVENTURES
California, Nevada, New Mexico, Wyoming, Europe
Three to seven-day classes from March-November

Established in 1972, D'Pharr Painting Adventures offers approximately ten outdoor painting classes a year at scenic and historic locales. The classes are limited to 12 to 20 students of all levels per instructor and consist of five teaching hours daily with individual assistance and critique. Two units of credit with lifelong learning are available from the University of Pacific.

Specialties: Outdoor painting in oil, watercolor, acrylic, and gouache.

Faculty: Includes prominent artists Dr. Charles Movalli, a contributing editor of *American Artist* magazine and editor of ten books with contemporary artists; Jake Lee, N.W.S., whose watercolors have appeared in one-man shows and won honors and awards in national exhibitions; Edward Norton Ward, a member of the Society of American Impressionists whose work is in public and private collections, including Allen Hancock College and the Bank of California; Ned Mueller, who has studied with Sergei Bongart, David

Leffel, and Richard Schmid, and exhibited at the Frye Art Museum; Zygmund Jankowski, an associate member of the American Watercolor Society who has had more than 40 one-man shows; Carl Miller, member of Watercolor West and Signature member of Midwest Watercolor Society; and artist and teacher D'Pharr, whose works are in collections in the U.S., Mexico, England, Canada, Chile, Australia, and Sweden.

Costs, Accommodations: Tuition, which includes accommodations, ranges from $165 to $200 for five days, $240 for six days. The fee for tuition and housing in the Art Center of Virginia City, Nevada, starts at $215. A $50 deposit is required with balance due six weeks prior. Cancellations at least six weeks prior receive refund less $30 fee; no refunds thereafter unless space can be filled.

Location: Locales in California include Los Gatos, Saratoga; Locke, Historic Chinese Settlement and Stockton, Delta Areas; Mendocino Coast and Ft. Bragg area; and the Monterey Coast. Other locales include Virginia City, Taos, Santa Fe, Jackson Hole, and Europe.

Contact: D'Pharr Painting Adventures, 8527 MacDuff Ct., Stockton, CA 95209; (209) 477-1562.

DUNCONOR WORKSHOPS
Taos, New Mexico
Five-day to three-week workshops in January, May, the summer months, and October

Founded in 1976 by goldsmith Harold O'Connor, Dunconor Workshops offers a series of "learn by doing" intensives in jewelry techniques that emphasize surface embellishment of metals, fabrication and forging methods, gold overlays and granulation, reticulation, and the refinement of design ideas. Participants, limited to six to nine per instructor, are expected to have a basic knowledge of working with metals. Each session focuses on a few techniques and processes with demonstrations by the instructor followed by supervised hands-on practice time.

Typical workshop titles include Innovative Models For Casting, which stresses direct methods for creating wax models that don't appear waxen, the use of materials to facilitate rapid transfer of textured surfaces to rubber molds, and creating gold and silver granulated surfaces through the casting process; Designing With The Computer, which covers the use of computers for developing design series programs, artwork revision, generation of templates and precise angles and curves, and "painting" and "drawing"; The Container As Object, utilizing such basic techniques as raising, forging, and sinking to create small-scale container forms and covering line/shape overlay and heat coloration surface embellishments; Gold Granulation, an intensive introduction that covers the making of special alloys to form sheet and wire, perfect spheres and other forms, techniques and jigs for cutting pallions, applying and fusing beads to the metal surface, and finishing and repairing granulated work; Jewelry Fabrication, an introduction to time saving hints from design concept through layout as well as soldering, forming and finishing, the making of templates, geometric shapes, tubes and wire, necklace segments and catch, and use of the flexibleshaft machine; and Surface Embellishments, an exploration of such methods as alloying, fusing and reticulation of gold and silver alloys, texture transfers to metal surfaces, and the construction of structurally sound objects using a minimum of hand tools and no solder.

Specialties: Jewelry techniques, emphasizing metals.

Faculty: Workshop director Harold O'Connor, a distinguished goldsmith with more than 25 years experience, is a recipient of design awards from the International Jewelry Arts Exhibitions in Tokyo and Jablonec and has authored five books, including the *Jewelers Bench Reference*. Other instructors, usually practicing artists/metalsmiths who are brought in to teach special seminars, have included Jack de Silva, Marilyn Griewank de Silva, Robin McGee, Brian Clarke, Bill Dawe, and Randall Gunther.

Costs, Accommodations: Workshop costs, excluding materials, range from $225 to $600 and one-half payment must accompany application. Refunds are granted if space can be filled. Budget lodging is available at the nearby Adobe Motel and reservations must be made directly. Participants should bring hand tools and the metals they plan to work with.

Location, Facilities: Each student has an individual work station with soldering stand, torch, and lamp. General shop equipment includes rolling mill, forming tools, and casting machine. Motels and restaurants are within walking distance. Taos is about a 90-minute drive from Santa Fe, which is an hour's drive from Albuquerque Airport.

Contact: Harold O'Connor, Director, Dunconor Workshop, Box 149, Taos, NM 87571; (505) 758-9660.

THE EARNLEY CONCOURSE
Chichester, Sussex, England
Two and four-day workshops year-round

This year-round residential center for courses and conferences, established in 1975 by the Earnley Trust, Ltd., an educational charity founded in 1951, offers workshops for craftspersons of all levels of ability. Two-day weekend programs include Stained Glass: Copper Foil Technique, an introduction to the basic techniques for making either a hanging panel or a decorative foiled glass box or terrarium; Yarn Design for Handspinning, for experienced students, which stresses the preparation and techniques of spinning such fibers as dyed tops, silk, mohair, camel, and cashmere; Embroiderers' Weekend, which consists of separate workshops in textile design, decorative wearables, papermaking, and machine embroidery. Other two-day workshops may include Mounting and Framing Pictures, Care and Restoration of Antique Furniture, and Enamelling — Jewelry and Small

Objects. Four-day workshops cover such topics as woodcarving, sculpture, and china restoration.

Specialties: A variety of crafts topics, including china restoration, enameling, stained glass, fiber arts.

Costs, Accommodations: Resident tuition, which includes lodging, all meals, use of facilities, and 15% VAT, ranges from £76 to £145; nonresident tuition ranges from £45 to £83, which includes lunch and beverage breaks and VAT. Breakfast and dinner are available for an additional charge. In addition to the basic charge, a £5 supplement is levied on some courses that incur additional costs. A £27 to £51 deposit (£19 to £29 for nonresidents) must accompany application with balance due 28 days prior. Cancellations more than 28 days prior receive 50% deposit refund; thereafter full deposit is forfeited. Accommodations consist of single and twin-bedded rooms, most with private bath; nonresidents can make arrangements with a local bed and breakfast. Nonparticipants receive a 20% discount if they share a room with a registrant.

Location, Facilities: The center is situated in a rural setting in West Sussex, six miles south of Chichester. Facilities include lecture rooms, arts & crafts studios, conference hall, computer room, heated indoor pool, squash court, and snooker table. Earnley, West Sussex, is located six miles south of Chichester. Ground transportation is available from the Chichester Railway Station and the Concourse mini van meets certain London trains. A route map is sent to those traveling by car.

Contact: The Earnley Concourse, Earnley, Chichester, Sussex, PO20 7JL, England; Bracklesham Bay (44) (0243) 670392.

EDEN VALLEY WOOLLEN MILL
Armathwaite, Cumbria, England

Weekend and five-day courses from April-December

Since 1988, the Eden Valley Woollen Mill has offered spinning, weaving, and dyeing courses for all levels and day workshops for children during school holidays. Enrollment is limited to three to six students, who receive instruction from 9:30 am to 4:30 pm and may continue to work outside these hours. Typical courses, which are mainly practical and supplemented by occasional lectures, include such titles as Spinning, which covers the skills of fleece sorting, cording, spinning, and plying; Dyeing, which focuses on the basic techniques; Weaving, which stresses design and structures, rug and fabric weaving, inkle and tablet weaving, and tapestry; and Finishing, using dry and wet techniques. The weaving school is part of a small working woolen mill that produces a variety of woven textiles and has available a wide selection of yarns for students' use.

Specialties: Weaving, spinning, dyeing.

Faculty: A professional, experienced instructor.

Costs, Accommodations: Tuition of £20 per day includes all materials. A 25% deposit must accompany application with balance due four weeks prior. Refunds for cancellations are granted only if space can be filled. Accommodations are available at nearby hotels and bed & breakfast farmhouses.

Location: The mill and studio are housed in a converted sandstone coachhouse in Armathwaite, a picturesque village in the far northwest of England near the Lake District and just below the Scottish border.

Contact: Eden Valley Woollen Mill, Armathwaite, Carlisle, Cumbria, CA4 9PB, England; (44) 06992 457.

THE ENAMELIST SOCIETY CONVENTION
Location changes each year

Three-day August workshops

Six three-day workshops are scheduled during the annual Enamelist Society Convention, which is usually held in mid-August. Each workshop, limited to 14 experienced students, is taught twice and can be taken either before or after the convention. Typical titles include Sculptural and Architectural Enamels — Designing, Making, and Installation Considerations, which emphasizes working with steel repoussé and such techniques as granular/color spray, TIG welding of copper, and styrofoam modeling for foundry casting of three dimensional shapes; Mixed Media Enameling, which explores the high fired limoges technique, opaques with over and under glazes, forming and texturing the metal surface, and the joining of enameled surfaces with various media; Photo Silkscreening Using Liquid Enamels, which covers design considerations for workable patterns, the making of special screens using RISO paper from Japan, and the use of special water base liquid enamels; Champleve, which focuses on design, transfer procedures, applying resist, etching and enameling procedures, and finishing pieces prior to plating; and Repoussé on Silver.

The Enamelist Society, a nonprofit corporation dedicated to the promotion of the ancient European and Asian art of enameling, sponsors juried exhibitions and publishes a bi-monthly newsletter, *Glass on Metal*.

Specialties: Enameling.

Faculty: Has included art professors John Killmaster, Harlan Butt, and JoAnn Tanzer; artists Harold Balazs, Carol Adams, Peggy Hitchcock, and Trisha Noe; and art research assistant Barbara Minor.

Costs: Workshop cost is $95 for Society members and $135 for nonmembers. Annual Society membership fee ranges from $30 to $50.

Location: Varies with each annual meeting.

Contact: The Enamelist Society, P.O.Box 310, Newport, KY 41072.

ERICA WILSON'S NEEDLEWORK SEMINARS
Nantucket, Massachusetts and New York, New York

Five-day seminars from June-September (Nantucket) and October-May (New York)

Established in 1955, Erica Wilson Needle Works offers embroidery and needlework seminars, each limited to 15 to 40 participants of all levels. The seminar program consists of five slide lectures and workshops, each devoted to a single subject with its own sampler. Each sampler, when completed, serves as a decorative and useful reference. The daily schedule includes a morning lecture and demonstration by Erica Wilson and afternoon small group sessions where students receive individual assistance. Students are encouraged to bring samples of their work and problem pieces. Additional activities in Nantucket include a welcoming cocktail party at Ms. Wilson's home, country house tours, visits to the Nantucket Yacht Club and museums, a New England Clam Bake, and a special evening event.

Specialties: Needlework.

Faculty: Prominent needlework artist Erica Wilson and her teaching staff.

Costs, Accommodations: The $1,500 fee includes all materials, double occupancy lodging, continental breakfast, and planned activities. Full payment secures reservation. Cancellations at least eight weeks prior receive a 50% refund unless space can be filled, in which case $50 is charged. Participants are lodged in the Barnacle Inn, the Ship's Inn, India House, 10 Hussey Street, or the Jared Coffin House.

Location: Nantucket Island, a resort situated 30 miles off the coast of Cape Cod, is served by Continental and Bar Harbour Airlines and ferries from Woods Hole and Hyannis. Seminars are held in Erica Wilson's house or locations on the island. Recreational and cultural activities include swimming, boating, fishing, cycling, golf, tennis, riding, concerts, and theaters. The area is handicapped accessible.

Contact: Mrs. Hampton Lynch, Erica Wilson Needleworks, 717 Madison Ave., New York, NY 10021; (212) 832-7290.

ERNIE MUEHLMATT WILDFOWL CARVING SEMINARS
Springfield, Pennsylvania

One-week seminars from May to August

Ernie Muehlmatt offers approximately seven Sunday to Saturday wildfowl carving and painting seminars during the summer, each limited to ten participants of all levels of experience and covering such topics as research and reference material, pattern development, rough shaping, feather groups and fine carving, texturing and stoning, positioning eyes and bill, burning for tones, preparing birds for painting, color theory and use of washes, designing bases and positioning birds, and habitat. Each seminar is devoted to a different specie of wildfowl, including Bob White Quail, Robin, Woodcock,

Baltimore Oriole, Semi-Palmated Plover, and Carolina Wren. Participants work alongside the instructor in developing and producing a decorative piece.

Specialties: Wildfowl carving and painting.

Faculty: Ernie Muehlmatt, a graduate of the Advertising Art Students League of Philadelphia and wildfowl carver since 1968, received first prize in the 1979 and 1981 Ward Foundation Championship Wildfowl Carving Competition and the 1984 Best in World, Decorative Life-Size Division.

Costs, Accommodations: Tuition for each week-long session is $500, which includes lunch. A nonrefundable $50 deposit must accompany application and balance is billed January 1st. Full refund, less deposit, is granted cancellations more than 30 days prior to class and a 50% refund thereafter, unless space can be filled. A list of materials and tools and details of local motel accommodations and airport pickup is sent to all registrants.

Location: The spacious air-conditioned studio is located in a quiet, wooded Pennsylvania setting, just off Route 1 between Media and Philadelphia. Nearby attractions include Winterthur Museum, the Franklin Mint Museum, the Barnes Foundation, and the Tyler Arboretum.

Contact: Ernie Muehlmatt, 700 Old Marple Rd., Springfield, Pa 19064; (215) 328-2946.

EVANSTON ART CENTER
Center for the Visual Arts
Evanston, Illinois
One-day workshops throughout the year

The Evanston Art Center, a nonprofit visual arts education organization formed in 1929, offers half and all-day art workshops presented by each department and hosted by artists outside the faculty. Designed to explore the various facets of specific media, these workshops provide students of all levels an opportunity to develop skills in one intensive session and focus on aspects not covered in the regular on-going class schedule. Typical workshops include Collotype, a demonstration of the continuous-tone image photo-printmaking process with "recipes" for sensitizing plates and printing techniques; Woodcut, which begins with a brief study of the influence of early Japanese and German Expressionist prints and covers methods of carving and printing, types of paper, and the care of prints and tools; and Ceramics, a slide presentation and discussion of the artist's aesthetic followed by a demonstration of his working methods. The Center also showcases contemporary art and artists from the Midwest, presents 15 to 20 exhibitions and related programs annually, and offers more than 50 classes a semester for more than 1,200 students each year.

Specialties: Ceramics, sculpture, printmaking, fiber, painting, photography.

Faculty: Thirty instructors regularly conduct classes at the Art Center. Guest faculty includes Erin Middleton (collotype), a local printmaker/book artist, who is curator of the Art Institute of Chicago's Artists' Books Collection and assistant director of Artists' Bookworks; Jeanine Coupe Ryding (woodcut), who has taught at Barat College and the Field Museum of Natural History and has had work exhibited at Perimeter Gallery and the SAGA National Print Exhibition; John Leach (ceramics), whose "Black Pots" have been featured in various galleries and museums; and Karen Karnes.

Costs: Students, who must be members of the Evanston Art Center, pay annual dues of $25, which includes invitations to exhibition openings and a 10% discount on purchases. Workshop fees range from $25 to.$45.

Location: The Center, housed in an historic lakefront mansion since 1966, is located in the North Shore Chicago suburb of Evanston.

Contact: Adult Workshop Program, Evanston Art Center, 2603 Sheridan Rd., Evanston, IL 60201; (708) 475-5300.

EXPLORING COLOR WORKSHOPS
Dayton, Ohio and other locations
Five-day workshops

Nita Leland began her Exploring Color workshops in 1980 at the Riverbend Art Center and now teaches them for arts organizations in other locales. The three workshops, each five-days in length and consisting of 25 to 30 hours of class time, emphasize the effective use of color through an understanding of pigments and basic color principles. Enrollment is limited to 25 intermediate to advanced artists.

Part One (Exploring Pigments and Palettes) is an in-depth study of color theory and pigment characteristics with the objective of finding each student's personal basic palette. Projects are based on exercises from the first part of Nita Leland's book, *Exploring Color*. The course includes slide presentations on the history of color in art with painting examples of the principles studied, along with a color critique of finished work. Part Two (Color Contrasts and Color Schemes) deals with expanded palettes and advanced color theory as well as the elements and principles of color design. Projects, based on exercises from *Exploring Color*, are designed to teach students to use color inventively and expressively in their own paintings. Students who enroll in Part Two should have completed Part One or the equivalent in home study of *Exploring Color*. Part Three builds on the principles learned in the first two parts. Participants plan and paint their own works, based on projects suggested by the instructor, to further their understanding and practical experience. Daily color critiques are featured.

Specialties: Painting, with emphasis on understanding and using color.

Faculty: Nita Leland has studied with Homer O. Hacker, Edgar Whitney, Edward Betts, Glenn Bradshaw, and Mario Cooper. Her interest in using color as the primary means of expression evolved out of a workshop with Jeanne Dobie and Chris Schink. Author of *Exploring Color* and *The Creative*

Artist, she serves as a judge for exhibitions, has exhibited in Dayton area galleries, and is an instructor for the North Light Art School.

Costs, Accommodations: Tuition at Riverbend is $10 annual membership plus $80 to $100 for each part. Full nonrefundable payment, payable by VISA or MasterCard, must accompany registration. Motels are located nearby.

Location: Riverbend Art Center is located six minutes from the center of Dayton with easy access to I-75. Other workshop locations include the Southwestern Michigan Watercolor Society in Kalamazoo, Michigan; the Grand Valley Artists in Jenison, Michigan; the Ft. Myers Beach Art Association in Ft. Myers, Florida; and the Haystack Mountain Workshops in Cumberland, Maryland.

Contact: Nita Leland, 1210 Brittany Hills Dr., Dayton, OH 45459; (513) 434-9977.

THE FABRIC CARR COUTURE SEWING CAMP
Carmel, California
Three one-week sessions in July

Begun in 1981 by Roberta Carr, this camp specializing in couture sewing techniques offers three consecutive week-long sessions, each limited to 12 students, such as home sewers, teachers, and dressmakers, who are actively sewing and have at least a basic knowledge of sewing techniques. The course content is different in each session and students may enroll in one, two, or all three. Part of each week is devoted to the instruction and use of Burda patterns, which are inspired by the European couture collections and can be cut exactly to fit. Personalized measurement charts are developed.

Sessions begin with a reception and dinner and each morning is devoted to a three-hour lecture/demonstration on a specific topic, such as couture techniques, tailoring, the psychology of color, elements of design, techniques for mixing grains, methods for choosing and using interfacings, buttonholes, seam construction, decorative finishes, sleeves, pockets, collage, and how to measure, cut, and sew pants. One class may feature the career and philosophy of a specific designer, with techniques used by that designer demonstrated and adapted to commercial patterns or drafted. After lunch, students spend the afternoon on individual projects, drafting their own patterns, testing them in muslin, and practicing newly learned techniques under the instructor's guidance. Following dinner, students have the evenings free or may continue to work on their projects.

Specialties: Couture sewing.

Faculty: Roberta Carr, a graduate of the Tobe-Coburn School for Fashion Careers, has written articles for such publications as *Sew News*, *Threads*, *Vogue Pattern Magazine*, and *The Singer Sewing Reference Library*. She owns the Fabric Carr Sewing Tools Catalog and has produced videotapes on couture techniques.

Costs, Accommodations: The per-session cost of approximately $1,400 includes room, meals, and supplies. A nonrefundable $100 deposit must accompany application, with 50% payable 60 days prior and the balance 30 days prior. Full refund, less $100, is granted cancellations more than 30 days prior. Lodging is in two-bedroom cabins with shared bath. Single supplement is available.

Location, Facilities: The camp is held at Clint Eastwood's Mission Ranch in Carmel, near Monterey and Big Sur. The classroom is an old barn/dance hall and each participant is assigned a permanent work area. Handicapped persons can be accommodated.

Contact: Roberta C. Carr, The Fabric Carr, P.O. Box 32120, San Jose, CA 95152-2120; (408) 929-1651.

FAMOUS ARTISTS WORKSHOP PROGRAM
The Fort Myers Beach Art Association
Fort Myers Beach, Florida
Five-day workshops

Since 1981, The Fort Myers Beach Art Association has sponsored an annual program of three or four workshops taught by prominent artists. Each workshop is limited to 20 to 25 students of all levels, who receive instruction from 9 am to 4 pm, Monday through Friday, and attend a Thursday evening demonstration.

Specialties: Painting.

Faculty: Typical artist/instructors include Nita Leland, a faculty member of the North Light Art School, associate of the Ohio and American Watercolor Societies, and author of *Exploring Color*; Skip Lawrence, a member of local and regional watercolor societies, who has been featured in *American Artist* and *Watercolor '86*; Christopher Schink, a Stamford University graduate and author of *Mastering Color and Design in Watercolor*, whose paintings have appeared in such publications as *Watercolor U.S.A.* and *Watercolor West*; and Joyce Gow.

Costs: Range from $100 to $145 for nonmembers and $75 to $130 for members. A $20 registration deposit is required, which is nonrefundable unless space can be filled.

Location: Workshops are held in the association's art building, which is handicapped accessible, or on location within the immediate area. Fort Myers Beach is on Florida's Gulf Coast.

Contact: Barbara Miller, Workshop Director, 6250 Timber Wood Circle, Ft. Myers, FL 33908; (813) 489-2845 *or* The Fort Myers Beach Art Association, P.O. Box 2359, Donora St., Ft. Myers Beach, FL 33931; (813) 463-3909.

FAMOUS SCULPTORS SEMINARS
Montoya Art Studios, Inc.
West Palm Beach, Florida
Three and four-day seminars from November-May

Established in 1974 as a full service center dedicated to sculpture professionals, the Montoya Art Studios has sponsored sculpture seminars since 1987. Approximately a half-dozen hands-on seminars are offered annually, each taught by a prominent professional and limited to 15 artists of all levels. Typical course titles include Direct Cement Sculpture (Lynn Olson), in which students complete several small sculptures using this medium without molds; Stonecarving — Beginning to Advanced (Bob Lockhart), which focuses on hand tools, stone selection, filing, sanding, finishing, and mounting the sculpture; Stone Carving — Demonstrations & Hard Facts (Luis Montoya), which deals with tools, stone finishing and repairing, creative uses of adhesives for inlays, multi-stone sculptures, and the pointing machine; Wildlife Sculpture in Plasteline Clay (D.H.S. Wehle), covering armature construction, applying plasteline, modeling the finished surface, and modeling from live animals; Modeling A Portrait Head in Clay (Marc Mellon), in which each student develops a clay portrait head from the raw armature through the casting into plaster; Patina Application For Bronze (Andrew Baxter), which emphasizes hot patinas applied with a blow torch and explores such techniques as resin smoked patinas, wet cloth and dry burnishing, Tiffany style and ancient patinas, and the use of pigmented waxes; and Artists' Rights & Marketing (Martin Bressler, Esq.), which addresses such legal issues as artists' rights and their relationships with galleries, museums, and collectors. The Studio also offers two to six-month day and evening sculpture classes.

Specialties: Sculpture.

Faculty: Co-director Luis Montoya, a graduate of the School of Fine Arts of San Fernando, initiated and taught the stone carving sculpture program at the Norton Museum School. His works are in both public and private collections. Guest teachers include Lynn Olson, a professional sculptor and author of *Sculpting With Cement*; Bob Lockhart, a graduate of Chicago's Art Institute and a tenured professor at Bellermine College; D.H.S. Wehle, a Ph.D. in zoology, electee to the Society of Animal Artists, and gold medal-winner for sculpture at the Allied Artists of America Show; Marc Richard Mellon, a realist sculptor and recipient of awards from the National Sculpture Society, The Salmagundi Club, and The National Artists Club; Andrew Baxter, an experienced worker in art foundries who has conducted workshops in patina for the National Trust for Historic Preservation: and Martin Bressler, a Harvard Law School graduate and a practicing attorney specializing in the visual arts.

Costs, Accommodations: Fees, which vary with the length of the seminar, range from $235 to $295. A $125 to $150 deposit must accompany application with balance due 30 days prior. Full deposit refund, less $50, is granted cancellations more than 30 days prior or if space can be filled.

Students are responsible for their own lodging and meals and are asked to supply their own tools.

Location, Facilities: The studio, centrally located in West Palm Beach, is near hotels, motels, restaurants, snack shops, and public transportation and a five-minute drive from both the airport and the beaches. The 15,000-square-foot center, which has an entrance ramp and easy classroom access for handicapped persons, stocks all necessary tools and supplies and provides complete foundry facilities, firing kilns, air compressor stations, hydraulic lifts and hand carts, a stone carving and clay modeling studio, outdoor studio, studio storage, and workshop and studio rental space.

Contact: Montoya Art Studios, Inc., 435 Southern Blvd., West Palm Beach, FL 33405; (407) 832-4401.

FARMINGTON VALLEY ARTS CENTER (FVAC)
Avon, Connecticut

One to four-day workshops year-round

Established in 1972 as a focal point for public awareness of and participation in the visual arts, the nonprofit Farmington Valley Arts Center offers year-round art and craft classes and workshops for all ages and levels, provides studio space to working artists and craftspeople, operates a gift shop and art gallery, and sponsors such special events as an annual Holiday Exhibit and Sale. The mostly one and two-day weekend workshops cover such topics as basketry, design and printing, quilling, drawing and painting, decorative finishes, machine knitting, papermaking, quilt restoration, etching, silkscreening, chair caning, floral design, bookbinding, cartooning and caricature, and weaving. Workshops for young people of all ages are also offered, including a series of four-day summer programs that meet two hours daily and offer children the opportunity to work on a variety of creative projects.

Specialties: Painting, printing, basketry, papermaking, quilting, chair caning, book arts, weaving, and other crafts.

Faculty: The staff consists of more than 20 local artists and craftsman.

Costs: Tuition ranges from $30 to $75 for a one or two-day workshop. Children's workshops range from $15 for one session to $50 for five sessions. Students must be members of FVAC; individual dues are $15, family dues are $20. Payment in full must accompany registration and is refundable if cancellation is more than two weeks in advance.

Location: FVAC is in the Avon Park North commercial park, a park-like setting ten miles west of Hartford. Housed in mid-19th brownstone factory buildings, the Center has 20 studios that are occupied by professional artists and artists' cooperatives.

Contact: Farmington Valley Arts Center, Box 220, Avon Park North, Avon, CT 06001; (203) 678-1867.

THE FECHIN INSTITUTE ART WORKSHOPS
Taos, New Mexico
Five-day workshops from May to October

Since 1986, the Fechin Institute has offered approximately six summer and fall art workshops, each led by a different instructor and limited to 20 students of all levels. Typical courses include Drawing The Female Figure, which covers posing, lighting, and drawing the female subject from life; Figure Drawing And Painting, which focuses on the human figure and the concepts of drawing with solidity and weight and understanding the problems of value, color, edges, and paint quality; Watercolor Painting, in which students paint the regional landscape as well as a local model; and a series of oil painting workshops that emphasize shapes, colors, composition, and light, and such subjects as still life, figure, portrait, and painting models who are dressed in colorful area costumes. The Fechin Institute, a nonprofit educational and cultural institute founded in 1981 in the home designed in the 1920s by Russian/American artist Nicolai Fechin, also offers special exhibitions and concerts during the season.

Specialties: Oil painting, watercolor, drawing.

Faculty: Has included Ned Jacob (female figure), whose work has been exhibited in galleries and museums in the U.S. and abroad; David Leffel (oil painting), an instructor at the Art Students League of New York since 1971 and recipient of awards from the National Academy of Design and the National Academy of Art; Sherrie McGraw (drawing), winner of awards from the National Arts Club and Salmagundi Club and an exhibitor in the "Artists of America" Rotary Show in Denver; Timothy J. Clark (watercolor), who has exhibited at the American Watercolor Society and New York's National Academy of Design and is author of *Focus on Watercolor*, a companion to the PBS series; Mark Daily (oil painting), who studied at the Art Institute of Chicago and the American Academy of Art; Roy Vinella (oil painting), award recipient as one of the top one hundred artists in the U.S. Park Service's Arts-in-the-Parks contest; and Gregg Kreutz, Art Usner, and Mie Shu Ou.

Costs, Accommodations: Tuition ranges from $200 to $275. Room and board (three meals a day) is $275. A $100 tuition deposit and $100 room and board deposit must accompany application with balance due 30 days prior. All deposits are refundable for cancellations more than 30 days prior. Lodging is in rustic, dormitory style housing at the adobe-style Branham Ranch.

Location, Facilities: The Branham Ranch, 18 miles north of Taos on the slopes of the Sangre de Cristo Mountains, is surrounded by 300 acres of woods, meadows, and wildflowers. Classes and meetings are held in a two-story geodesic dome studio building, where a row of east windows receives the morning sun. Taos is a 2 1/2-hour drive from the nearest commercial airport, in Albuquerque.

Contact: The Fechin Institute, P.O. Box 832, Taos, NM 87571; (505) 758-1710.

FENTON AND GAINES GLASS STUDIO
Oakland, California and other locations
One to four-day courses year-round

The Fenton and Gaines Glass Studio offers a variety of glassworking courses, each limited to ten to twelve students of all levels and scheduled daily from 10 am to 6 pm with a one hour lunch break. The studio remains open after hours for those students desiring additional time to work on their projects. Typical course titles include Fusing and Slumping, Flint Knapping: Aboriginal Glasschipping, Enamels on Fired Surface Decoration, Flameworking Glass, Pate De Verre Glass Casting, Moldmaking for Slumping, Moldmaking for Casting, Glass Blowing From a Furnace, Sandblast Shading and Carving, Murrini Making: Advanced Fusing, Painting on Glass, Architectural Model Making, Fine Gold and Metals on Glass, and Sandblasting on Glass. Evening activities are also scheduled.

Specialties: Glassworking.

Faculty: Includes Wayne Archer, Kathy Bradford, Albinas Elskus, Dan Fenton, Larry Fielder, Elizabeth Gaines, Rick Glawson, George Jercich, Dorothy Lenehan, Margaret Mathewson, and Gil Reynolds.

Costs: Tuition, which includes all materials and use of tools, ranges from $70 to $330. A 50% deposit is required, which is refundable for cancellations received more than fifteen days prior to first class or if space can be filled.

Contact: Fenton and Gaines Glass Studio, 4001 San Leandro St., #8, Oakland, CA 94601; (415) 533-5515.

FLETCHER FARM SCHOOL FOR THE ARTS AND CRAFTS
Society of Vermont Craftsmen, Inc.
Ludlow, Vermont
One to five-day workshops from July-August

This 600-acre farm, settled by Revolutionary War soldier Jesse Fletcher in 1783, passed through various generations of the Fletcher family until it was organized as Fletcher Farm, Inc., a nonprofit educational center, in 1933. The Board of Trustees invited the Society of Vermont Craftsmen, Inc., to use the buildings and establish an arts and crafts school, which began in 1947. The school offers a wide variety of workshops for adults and children of all ages with most programs for all levels and others suited to beginning, intermediate, or advanced students. More than 50 workshops are held during the summer with class size ranging from three to twelve students per instructor. Five-day workshops begin with a Sunday evening buffet and orientation and conclude the following Saturday after breakfast. Sessions are scheduled from 9 am to 5 pm, Monday through Thursday, and from 9 am to 3:30 pm on Friday. Weekend workshops begin with a Friday evening buffet and orientation and meet from 9 am to 5 pm Saturday and from 9 am to 3:30 pm on Sunday. A few workshops are specifically designed for children while the rest are open only to those who are 18 or older. The Society provides an outlet — the Fletcher Farm Craft Shop — for the sale of members' handcrafts and holds an annual craft fair with participation by both member and nonmember craftsmen.

The scope of topics includes art (calligraphy, watercolor, drawing), basketry, decorative arts (early American decoration, theorem painting, stenciling, primitive portraiture, gold leaf, woodgraining and marbleizing) Norwegian rosemaling (decorative painting), fiber arts (rag weaving, spinning, four-harness loom weaving, natural rush seating, chair caning), needlework (embroidery, quilt making), woodcarving, and such miscellaneous crafts as stained glass, rug hooking, bandboxes, lampshade construction, paper marbling, and bookcraft. Children's workshop topics include painting and drawing and arts and crafts.

Specialties: A wide variety of subjects, including watercolor, calligraphy, rosemaling, quilting, basketry, tinsmithing, weaving, jewelry, china painting, rug braiding, doll making, woodcarving, pottery, stained glass, needlework, lampshades, stenciling, furniture restoration, floral and herbal arts, spinning, wood graining and marbleizing, chair caning.

Faculty: The more than 30-member faculty of accomplished artists and teachers includes rosemaler Eldrid Skjold Arntzen, textile weaver and designer Betty Atwood, stained glass artists Judith Beals and Kay Frizzle, woodcarver Art Bergstrand, publisher and printer Elena Colin, quilters Nola Forbes and Cyrena Persons, early American decorative artists Dolores Furnari and Alice D. Smith, spinner and dyer Debbie Gile, wood grainer Dorothy Wood Hamblett, weaver Edith F. House, watercolorist George Lawrence, basket maker Jacquelyn Logan, embroiderer Beverly Merritt, theorem painter Maxine O'Brien, fiber artist Marcia Rhodes, calligrapher Beth Elaine Smallheer, rug hooker Amy Soutter, and hand caner Earl A. Thomsen.

Costs, Accommodations: Tuition is $35 for one day, $70 for two days, $95 for three days, and $150 for five days. Some workshops require a materials fee, which ranges from $1.50 to $75. An additional nonrefundable registration fee of $10 ($20 after April 30) and 50% tuition deposit secures a reservation with balance due June 15. Cancellations at least three weeks prior receive a 50% refund less registration fee. Meals and lodging (double occupancy motel-like accommodations with shared baths) range from $70 per person for two nights to $210 per person for six nights. Single accommodations are $10 to $30 additional. College credit may be available.

Location, Facilities: The school is on Route 103, midway between Ludlow and Proctorsville in Vermont's Green Mountains. Bus service is available at the door and the nearest air service is in Rutland. A 200-year-old barn is the center of classroom activity. Weaving and spinning classes are in the old sugarhouse beside the pond. The property has hiking trails and natural woodlands and the village of Ludlow has a landmark historical museum.

Contact: Fletcher Farm School for the Arts and Crafts, RR 1, Box 1041, Ludlow, VT 05149; (802) 228-8770.

FOLK ART INSTITUTE
Museum of American Folk Art
New York, New York

One-day workshops from September-May

A division of the Museum of American Folk Art, which was founded in 1961 and is the leading urban center of folk art scholarship in the nation, the Folk Art Institute offers lectures, courses and hands-on craft workshops that are open to all levels of experience. Workshops are usually scheduled three to four Fridays a month, from 10 am to 4 pm, and offer participants the opportunity to complete a project in a single session. Typical projects include a floral pattern hooked rug, Shaker pin-cushion basket, painted canvas floor rug, folk art portrait (such as the famous "Little Girl in Red"), and contemporary sampler. Some sessions cover specific techniques, such as marbleizing or stenciling.

Specialties: Traditional folk arts and crafts.

Faculty: Includes experienced craft artists Ann Eastwood, Sarah Hilton, Gerrie Kennedy, Sudee Sanders, Rubens Teles, Hildegard Vetter, and Marie Wilson.

Costs: Tuition is $65, materials fee ranges from $5 to $25. Full payment must accompany registration. Museum membership offers such benefits as free admission to exhibitions, a subscription to *The Clarion* folk art magazine, and reduced course fees. Annual dues begin at $35 individual, $50 family.

Location: The Institute is situated across from Lincoln Center on New York City's West Side.

Contact: Folk Art Institute, 61 W. 62nd St., New York, NY 10023-7015; (212) 977-7170.

THE FOOTHILLS ART CENTER, INC.
Golden, Colorado

One-day to one-week workshops year-round

Established as a nonprofit organization in 1968, The Foothills Art Center promotes the understanding and appreciation of the visual arts, poetry, and music by providing a variety of classes, workshops, lectures, demonstrations, poetry readings, concerts and major art exhibitions. Workshops offered as part of the Center's regular schedule are open to all levels and include such titles as Principles of Painting, Sumi-e Floral Painting, Figure Drawing, Airbrush, and Experimental Watermedia. Two to five week-long workshops are scheduled in conjunction with two national shows sponsored by the Center — the North American Sculpture Exhibition (May and June) and the Rocky Mountain National Watermedia Exhibition (August and September). Sessions meet from 10 am to 3 pm daily, are limited to 20 participants, and include demonstrations, lectures, and individual and group critiques.

Specialties: Painting, drawing, sculpture.

Faculty: Regularly scheduled workshops are taught by area professionals. Workshops held during the national exhibitions are taught by the invited judges, who are nationally known artists.

Costs, Accommodations: Tuition ranges from $60 for a two-day workshop to $160 for five days. A 50% tuition deposit must accompany registration with balance due prior to first day of workshop. Full refund less $10 fee is granted cancellations at least two weeks prior; no refunds thereafter unless space can be filled.

Location, Facilities: Situated in a Gothic style building complex that began in 1872 as the First Presbyterian Church of Golden, the Center contains an Art and Poetry Library, art galleries, and a gift shop. It is accessible from Denver via Highway U.S. 6 or Interstate 70.

Contact: The Foothills Art Center, Inc., 809 Fifteenth St., Golden, CO 80401; (303) 279-3922.

FUJISTUDIO SCHOOL OF JEWELRY MAKING, TEXTILE DESIGN, AND FASHION
Florence, Italy

One-month workshops year-round

Established in 1969, Fujistudio is a professional school and art workshop offering monthly and semester courses in jewelry making and textile design. Some courses are open to all levels while others are specifically for beginning, intermediate, or advanced artists. Class enrollment is limited to 10 to 13 students per instructor and all sessions are taught in both English and Italian. The one-month workshops, which begin the first working day of each month, may be taken under the normal option — three hours daily for three days per week — or the intensive option — 14 hours per week. At the end of the fall and spring academic semesters (December and May), the school conducts a juried Student Exhibit and Fashion Show of the work of all students.

Jewelry making courses include Beginning Jewelry Making Levels I and II, which introduce students to materials, tools, and techniques with projects in inlay, married metals, stone setting, scagliola, three-dimensional construction, Mokume, and lamination; Intermediate Jewelry Making, which includes such projects as Repoussé, twist lamination, and faceted stone setting; Advanced Jewelry Making, in which students research and develop their own projects; Casting, including lost wax casting, which includes work in hard and soft wax for modeling, carving, and fabrication and an introduction to mold making and wax burnout; Three-Dimensional Pantography and Tooling I and II, specialized courses in the direct carving of metal, wood, ivory, plastics, and other materials in two and three-dimensional pieces; Gemology, a study of precious and semi-precious stones; and Stone Setting I and II.

Textile design courses include Serigraphy/Silk Screen I and II, in which students can emphasize the techniques for either fine art paper editions or textile surface design; Weaving, which includes both tapestry weaving on frame looms and weaving with four and eight harness looms and experimentation with yarns, weights, settings, colors, textures, and patterns; Batik and Dyeing, which covers wax resist Batik, Shibori, and various systems of pattern design and fiber techniques; Soft Sculpture, emphasizing sculptural, bas relief, and environmental approaches to the fiber arts media; and Fashion As Art I and II, which explore areas of textile art and apply them to fashion and costume design in the construction of finished garments and accessories.

Specialties: Jewelry making and textile design.

Faculty: Fujistudio director and co-founder Tamio Fujimura received an MFA from Rosary College in Illinois and was awarded the De Belli grant, the Montecatini Edison research award, and a grant from Dow Chemical for pioneering the shell ceramic molding process. His work has been exhibited in the U.S. and Europe and is in private collections. Co-founder Kathleen Ann Knippel, a former professor at Rio Hondo College in Whittier, California, has had her textile work published in five books and her soft sculpture of a Volkswagen is in the Volkswagen collection. Professional artists available for consultation during the school year include Susan Wilson Arcamone, Pat Kinsella, Elena Laime, Paul Rooms, and Paolo Pratesi.

Costs, Accommodations: Tuition is 450,000 Lira for the one-month normal course, 690,000 Lira for the one-month intensive. A 40% deposit must accompany application with balance due during the first week of class. Cancellations at least 30 days prior receive a 60% deposit refund. Pension or hotel reservations for the first week are made by the school and, upon arrival, students are assisted in locating appropriate lodging.

Location: The school, which is on the ground floor and handicapped accessible, is situated in Florence's historic district.

Contact: Fujistudio, Via Guelfa 79/A, 50129 Florence, Italy; (39) 55 216877, Fax (39) 55 214500.

GAWTHORPE HALL
Nelson and Colne College
Padiham, Burnley, Lancashire, England
One to four-day courses from March-November

Gawthorpe Hall offers approximately 25 to 30 courses in the needle and fiber arts for all levels of experience. Sessions are scheduled for one day, weekends (Friday evening through Sunday lunch), and four days (Thursday afternoon through Sunday lunch). Course topics include embroidery, hand stitches, bobbin lace, needlepoint, quilting, hand and machine knitting, rug hooking, and screen printing.

Specialties: Embroidery, knitting, screenprinting, other needle and fiber arts.

Faculty: Jan Beaney, Gene Bowen, Hilary Bower, Richard Box, Clare Bryan, Pauline Burbidge, Anne-Marie Cadman, Lauretta Clark, Belinda

Downes, Constance Howard, Ruth Hydes, Jean Littlejohn, Sheena Pawson, Elizabeth Prickett, Lynne Rogers, Sally Taylor, Amanda Townend, Barbara Underwood, Cheryl Welsh, Margaret Williams, Carol Williamson.

Costs, Accommodations: Fees are £18 for a one-day course, £35 to £40 for a weekend, and £80 for a four-day course. A £15 deposit (full fee for day course) must accompany booking at least three weeks prior with balance due two weeks prior. Cancellations at least two weeks prior (and within two weeks if space can be filled) receive full refund less £5 charge. Accommodations can be arranged at a nearby bed and breakfast for approximately £8 per night.

Location: The 17th century Gawthorpe Hall, refurbished by the National Trust in 1987 and managed by Nelson & Colne College, is set on wooded grounds on the northern side of the A671, a half-mile from Padiham centre.

Contact: Theresa Savage, Gawthorpe Hall, Padiham, NR. Burnley, Lancs., BB12 8UA, England; (44) 0282 78511.

GEMOLOGICAL INSTITUTE OF AMERICA (GIA)
Santa Monica, California and major U.S. cities
One to seven-week courses

Founded in 1931 as a nonprofit educational organization, the GIA offers a wide variety of residence, extension, and home study courses in gemology, jewelry manufacturing arts, and business. Jewelry manufacturing courses focus on jewelry making, design, and skills and range from the six-month Jewelry Manufacturing Arts Residence program, geared primarily to those pursuing a career in jewelry repair, stone setting, or manufacturing, to individual one-day to seven-week courses devoted to specific aspects of jewelry manufacture. Classes are held seven hours daily, from Monday through Friday.

Residence courses of interest to individuals with no previous experience include Jewelry Design (seven weeks), in which students learn to create, illustrate, and present designs; and Hand Engraving (seven weeks), which covers lettering, monograms, and ornamental designs. Extension courses include Jewelry Design (one week), which covers basic techniques; Hand Fabrication (one week), which teaches the skills needed to create unique pieces of jewelry directly in metal; Basic and Advanced Stone Setting (each one week), covering a variety of traditional and contemporary settings; Wax Modeling and Casting (two weeks), for translating designs into finished silver and gold jewelry, using the lost wax process.

Specialties: Jewelry manufacturing arts.

Faculty: The more than 40-member faculty includes experienced teachers and professionals from a variety of backgrounds.

Costs, Accommodations: Tuition for each of the seven-week residence programs — Jewelry Design and Hand Engraving — is $1,995. A $100 fee must accompany application with $200 deposit due 60 days prior and balance due on arrival. Cancellations within seven days of signing application receive a full refund, $100 fee is forfeited thereafter. Tuition for the extension courses is $495 or $595 for one-week courses and $895 for the two-week course. A $75 fee must accompany application with balance due 30 days prior. Cancellations within seven days of signing application or more than 30 days prior receive full refund, $75 fee is forfeited thereafter. Prorated refunds are granted after start of course. VISA and MasterCard are accepted and housing information is provided. All course materials are included in the tuition.

Location: GIA's main campus is in Santa Monica, near beaches, UCLA, and the Los Angeles Jewelry District. The two-story building has elevators and parking for handicapped access. Extension courses are offered in major cities, including New York, Orlando, Miami, Tampa, Jacksonville, Atlanta, Boston, Chicago, Dallas, San Francisco, New Orleans, Las Vegas, Philadelphia, Pittsburgh, Nashville, Newark, Cincinnati, Cleveland, Albuquerque, Charlotte, Minneapolis, Hartford, Denver, and Washington.

Contact: Gemological Institute of America, 1660 Stewart St., P.O. Box 2110, Santa Monica, CA 90406; (800) 421-7250, ext. 227 *or* (213) 829-2991, ext. 227.

GEORGE B. SUTHERLAND PAINTING WORKSHOPS
New England, West Indies, Caribbean
Three to seven-day workshops from April-October

Since 1976, painter George B. Sutherland has offered on-location painting workshops, each limited to 6 to 15 students of all levels. Daily demonstrations cover basic techniques, color mixtures, composition, and simple drawing. Students receive individual instruction and critique. Approximately six workshops are held each year.

Specialties: Painting in a variety of media.

Faculty: George B. Sutherland is primarily a painter of the outdoors. He studied at the Art Students League of New York and Parsons School of Design and has created design and illustration work for national magazines. His oil and watercolor paintings are in private and corporate collections.

Costs, Accommodations: Costs for New England area workshops range from $120 for three days to $200 for seven days, not including transportation, meals or lodging. Materials cost about $60. A $50 deposit reserves a space with balance due one month in advance. The seven-day West Indies workshop fee, which includes airfare to and from New York, double occupancy lodging at the Zetland Plantation Inn or Manapany cottages in Nevis or St. Barts, and two meals daily, is approximately $1,360 (based on five students) and requires a $200 deposit. Cost of meals in St. Barts is $130 to $250 per week.

Location: New England workshops are held in such scenic locales as Rockport and Cape Cod, Massachusetts; Mystic Seaport, Connecticut;

Portsmouth, New Hampshire; and Portland, Maine. Nevis, West Indies, is 40 miles from Antigua and two miles from St. Kitts in the eastern Caribbean. It covers an area of 30 square miles with Mount Nevis volcano rising from the center. The Zetland Plantation Inn occupies 750 acres and has tennis courts and a large swimming pool. St. Barts is about 40 miles northwest of Antigua. **Contact:** George B. Sutherland, 65 Hidden Brook Dr., Stamford, CT 06907; (203) 329-0488.

THE GLACIER INSTITUTE
Glacier National Park, Montana
One and two-day summer classes

This nonprofit corporation, established in 1983, sponsors art, photography, and natural science field courses that are taught on-site within the Glacier National Park ecosystem. Typical two-day classes include Watercolor in Glacier, which explores a variety of watercolor techniques with the Park as the inspiration and consists of morning lecture/demonstrations followed by student painting sessions and critiques; and People of the Mountain World, which focuses on the history, crafts, and skills of the Blackfeet Indians and the arts of beading, brain-tanning, and quilling. A series of one-day explorations are also scheduled on such topics as Outdoor Sketching and Introduction to the Creative Journal, which emphasizes both drawing and writing. Most classes include credit from Flathead Valley Community College.

Specialties: Art and crafts indigenous to the Glacier National Park.

Faculty: Includes Karen Noice, a full time painter and veteran instructor at Flathead Community College; Dr. O. Fred Donaldson, who has taught at the University of Washington and the Yellowstone Institute; and Lynne Tuft, who has taught art at Flathead Community College.

Costs, Accommodations: Course fees, which include instruction, transportation, and college credit, are payable with application and range from $85 to $120; one day explorations cost $20 for individuals, $30 for two family members, and $8 for each additional member. An 80% refund is granted cancellations at least two weeks prior to workshop, 50% refund two weeks to two days prior, no refunds thereafter. Lodging options include cabins at the Institute facility, nearby campgrounds, and motels in the West Glacier area. Participants may cook in the basic kitchen at the Institute or purchase meals at nearby cafes and restaurants.

Location, Facilities: Glacier National Park, located on the Canadian border in northwestern Montana, offers a rich variety of wildlife and diverse glaciated landscapes ranging from alpine cirques to broad forested valleys. The Institute's summer office, a rustic facility near West Glacier, consists of an office, meeting hall, spartan wooden cabins, kitchen, and washrooms.

Contact: The Glacier Institute, P.O. Box 1457A, Kalispell, MT 59903; (406) 752-5222 *or* (406) 888-5215 (June 15-Aug. 15).

GRAND MARAIS ART COLONY
Grand Marais, Minnesota
Five-day workshops from June-August

Founded by the late Birney Quick in 1947 as a summer branch of what is now the Minneapolis College of Art and Design, the Art Colony is a nine-week series of visual arts workshops for adults and young people. Most workshops for adults are scheduled from 9 am to 4 pm daily and are limited to 12 to 18 participants. Aside from a beginning watercolor course, the program is designed primarily for serious artists who consider themselves professional and sessions are built around the concept of exploring and unlocking the inner artist rather than his or her technique. Evening activities include a series of Monday night lectures by guest artists.

Typical workshop titles include Making Personal Art, in which students utilize various exercises in order to discover their personal imagery; Asian Painting, which centers on technique and philosophy; Expressive Calligraphy, designed to make words look like what they mean; and Sculpting the Human Figure, with emphasis on gesture, proportion, and spatial relationships. The Watercolor Basics workshop, for beginning to intermediate students, features daily demonstrations in the studio and field and regular critiques. A young people's workshop, Summer Youth Arts Collage, allows students to sample several media within the categories of drawing, painting, and sculpture.

The Arts Colony also offers Saturday classes for children and a six-week residency program, for which slides and a resume are required.

Specialties: Painting, drawing, sculpture, pastels, and other visual arts.

Faculty: Instructors, who change each year, have included freelance graphic designer Maria Mazzara; Elizabeth Erickson, an associate professor in fine art at the Minneapolis College of Art and Design; fiber artist Jean Matzke, who has taught textiles at the College of St. Benedict; Laura Stone, an instructor at the Minneapolis College of Art and Design; Howard Sivertson, whose paintings of the Boundary Waters Canoe Area are in private and public collections; and Paul Granlund, a prominent sculptor.

Costs, Accommodations: Tuition is $180 for a five-day workshop (VISA, MasterCard accepted). A 50% deposit must accompany registration with balance due prior to workshop. Withdrawals at least 30 days prior receive a refund less $20; no refunds thereafter. Students receive aid in finding lodging.

Location, Facilities: The Art Colony is centered in the scenic village of Grand Marais on Lake Superior's North Shore. The old church that serves as the Colony's main studio is within walking distance of the lake. Grand Marais is at the entrance to the Boundary Waters Canoe Area, 40 miles from the Canadian border. Nearby attractions include a marina, golf course, swimming pool, community theater, canoe outfitters, and hiking trails. An art supply store is located adjacent to the main studio and studio space is available for individual artists on a weekly basis.

Contact: Grand Marais Art Colony, Box 626, Grand Marais, MN 55604; (218) 387-2737.

GRIGORY GUREVICH DRAWING AND PASTEL CLASSES
Volosko, Croatia, Yugoslavia
Two-week June workshop

Grigory Gurevich conducts a two-week workshop that includes drawing and pastel lessons in the scenic environs of Volosko, located in Croatia by the Adriatic Sea. The workshop is open to artists of all levels, who receive instruction from 9 am to noon and 1 to 3 pm, Monday through Friday. Mr. Gurevich also teaches a drawing class every Saturday from September 20th to May 1st.

Specialties: Drawing and pastel.

Faculty: Grigory Gurevich is a faculty member of the School of Fine and Industrial Arts in Newark, New Jersey, and the Fine Arts Counsel of the International Center for Educational Advancement. Recipient of a master's degree in art from the Graduate School of Fine Arts in Leningrad, he emigrated to the U.S. in 1976 and became a citizen in 1984. He has been awarded two grants from the New Jersey State Council on the Arts and his sculpture tableau, "Commuters", is installed in Penn Station in Newark. His work is in public and private collections in the U.S.S.R. and the U.S.

Cost, Accommodations: The cost, which includes double occupancy room, breakfast, and round trip transportation from the U.S., is $1,600.

Location: Volosko, a small Mediterranean town strongly influenced by the Italian culture, is 90 minutes from Trieste and about 4 1/2 hours from Vienna.

Contact: Grigory Gurevich, 282 Barrow St., Jersey City, NJ 07302; (201) 451-4862.

GRIMMSTONE POTTERY
Missoula, Montana
One to four weeks in July

Since 1971, ceramist Douglas Grimm has offered intensive, individualized workshop-residencies for anyone interested in the ceramic arts, including beginning to advanced ceramists, sculptural artists, and functional potters. Enrollment is limited to four or five students, who are encouraged to stay for the full four weeks but may sign up for one, two, or three-week periods. Organized instruction is scheduled from noon to 5 pm daily and from 7 to 10 in the evenings and the studio is available for use at all times of the day and night. The teaching format includes demonstrations, slide shows, critiques, lectures, visiting artist presentations, and individual assistance. Students are taught to be self-sufficient and learn how to look for and mix suitable clay, load kilns, mix and correct glazes, build simple outdoor kilns, work on a potters wheel, hand build, and construct a mural for installation in a building. Each student is asked to submit a list of specific interests in advance of arrival so that the workshop can be tailored to the needs of the group. Additional activities may include visits to nearby potters' studios and sightseeing excursions to ghost towns and Glacier National Park.

Specialties: Ceramics.

Faculty: Resident director Douglas Grimm earned an MFA in ceramics from the University of Montana and studied with Rudy Autio, Peter Voulkos, Don Reitz, Bob Sperry, Daniel Rhodes, Ted Randall, Patti Warashina, and Jim Leedy.

Costs, Accommodations: Tuition, which includes lodging in a 13-room log house, is $600 for four weeks or $150 per week. A $25 deposit must accompany application with balance due one month prior. All tools, brushes, and equipment are provided but students should bring $50 for clay and miscellaneous materials. Dormitory-style lodging is provided on "Castle Grimm's" top floor, which has a kitchen, bath and shower, and private entrance. Students can buy and prepare their own meals.

Location: Grimmstone Pottery is a five-minute drive north of central Missoula in the Rocky Mountains of western Montana, a region known for its outdoor activities, which include hiking, camping, skiing, hang gliding, hunting, fishing, horseback riding, river rafting, canoeing, and golf. Missoula, the home of the University of Montana, is situated halfway between Yellowstone and Glacier National Parks. Pickup is available for students arriving at Missoula Airport, which is serviced by Continental, Delta, Horizon, Skywest, and other airlines.

Contact: Douglas Grimm, Grimmstone Pottery, 2524 Sycamore, Missoula, MT 59802; (406) 543-7970.

HF HOLIDAYS LIMITED
Great Britain

Weekend and one-week holidays year-round

Established more than 75 years ago, the nonprofit HF offers a wide variety of special interest holidays, such as birdwatching, garden visits, murder and mystery weekends, literature and music weeks, dancing, sports, and bridge, as well as painting and sketching, cartooning, and crafts for adults of all levels. Art holidays include one-week sessions in landscape and seascape painting at several scenic locales, a cartooning workshop, and programs specifically for beginning artists. Crafts holidays are planned so that instruction is given in the morning and late afternoon or evening, with mid-day free. Featured topics are embroidery, egg decorating, spinning, corn craft, calligraphy, and making greeting cards. Evenings are reserved for such activities as slide shows, lectures, and excursions.

Specialties: Painting and a variety of crafts.

Faculty: Instructors and professionals in their fields.

Costs, Accommodations: Cost, which includes double occupancy lodging and full board, ranges from £99 for a weekend holiday to £245 for a week (seven nights). Single supplement is available. A £5 reduction is granted paid-in-full reservations prior to the end of February. Participants usually stay in HF-owned country houses with lounges, game rooms and, in some cases, tennis courts, libraries, and heated swimming pools.

Location: More than 20 resort locales in Great Britain, including Loch Leven and Loch Awe in the Scottish Highlands, Conwy in North Wales, Derwentwater and Conistonwater in the Lake District, Bourton-on-the-Water in the Cotswolds, and Lyme Regis and Swanage in Dorset.

Contact: HF Holidays Limited, 142-144 Great North Way, London NW4 1EG; Administration (44) 1 203 3381, Reservations (44) 1 203 0433, Fax (44) 1 203 1114.

HALIBURTON SCHOOL OF FINE ARTS (H.S.F.A.)
Haliburton, Ontario, Canada
Weekend and five-day workshops in July and August

The Haliburton School of Fine Arts, founded in 1968 as a branch of Sir Sandford Fleming College, offers more than 150 workshops for adults and children of all levels in a broad spectrum of art and craft topics. The workshops are held during five weekly sessions from early July to early August, with approximately 25 concurrent workshops during each session. Most adult workshops meet daily, Monday through Friday, from 9 am to noon and 1 to 4:30 pm, and a couple of programs are scheduled over the weekend. Subjects include basketry, bird and decoy carving, bookbinding, calligraphy, clay sculpture, drawing and painting, duffle parka making, fabric collage, folk art painting, furniture making, glass blowing and fusing, hand and machine knitting and embroidery, Japanese brush painting, jewelry, knife making, leather, marquetry, miniature cabinet making, papermaking, photography, pottery, printmaking, quilting, rug hooking, silversmithing, stained glass, stenciling, weaving, and woodcarving. Several of the subjects are taught on the beginning, intermediate, and advanced levels. Adult courses are eligible for Post Secondary Credit from Sir Sandford Fleming College. Additional day and evening activities are scheduled throughout the month.

A children's day camp, which operates in conjunction with the children's workshops offered during the five-week summer school, is divided into a morning section for 5 to 8 year olds and an afternoon section for 9 to 12 year olds. Children choose one of two weekly workshops that include such topics as drawing, soapstone carving, papier mâché, weaving, and photo arts.

Specialties: A variety of arts and crafts subjects, including basketry, bird carving, book arts, drawing and painting, fiber arts, glass, knitting, jewelry, photography, pottery, printmaking, quilting, and woodcarving.

Faculty: Includes decoy carver Al Brady, glass workers Clark Guettel and Lou Lynn, Japanese brush painter Cassandra Wyszkowski, jewelrymaker Michael Letki, spinner Ted Carson, machine knitter Marilyn Leonard, ceramist Hanni Rothschild, basketmaker Ankaret Dean, miniaturist June Simpson, papermaker Tootsie Pollard, potters Jeanne McRight and Barbara Joy Peel, woodcarvers Joe Dampf and Christopher Rees, painters Brian

Atyeo and John Leonard, book artist Don Taylor, metalsmith Lois Ethering-
ton Betteridge, screenprinter Sally Glanville, and quilter Laurie Swim.

Costs, Accommodations: Five-day adult course tuition is C$76 (plus a
material fee payable at the first class), weekend tuition is C$35, children's
courses are C$50. Full fee must accompany registration and telephone credit
card (VISA, MasterCard) registrations are accepted. Full refund is granted
written cancellation at least two weeks prior. Accommodations are available
at area bed and breakfasts, motels, cottages and resorts. Breakfasts and
lunches are served at the Haliburton Highlands Secondary School cafeteria.

Location: Courses are held at the Haliburton Highlands Secondary School
and Sir Sandford Fleming College in the south/central region of southern
Ontario.

Contact: Haliburton School of Fine Arts, P.O. Box 339, Haliburton, ON
K0M 1S0, Canada; (705) 457-1680.

HAYSTACK MOUNTAIN SCHOOL OF CRAFTS
Deer Isle, Maine
Two and three-week sessions from June-September

This nonprofit research and studio program in the arts, chartered in 1950,
sponsors five 2 and 3-week summer sessions, with each session consisting of
six studios that are open to adults of varying levels of experience. Studios
include ceramics, drawing, fiber art, glass and glassblowing, metalworking,
woodworking, graphic art, papermaking, basketry, quilting, blacksmithing,
and other crafts. Although most studios are offered for more than one session,
each session has a different faculty and each studio has a unique focus.
Classes are scheduled from Monday through Friday in a flexible manner by
the instructors and studios are open 24 hours a day, seven days a week. Each
session is limited to 80 participants (including staff and faculty), who may
enroll in only one studio per session. Selection is based on the need for
balance and for a range of ages and experience levels. Special session
workshops, offered two or three times during the summer, are open only to
those with an advanced level of experience in the medium.

Specialties: Ceramics, drawing, fiber art, glass and glassblowing, metalworking, woodworking, graphic art, papermaking, baskets, quilting, blacksmithing, and other crafts.

Faculty: Instructors, who are established professionals, are different each
summer. Representative faculty includes Clay: Christine Federighi, Mary Jo
Bole, Chris Staley, Wayne Higby, Warren MacKenzie,and Walter Ostrom.
Drawing: Constance Costigan. Graphics: Susan Groce, Marjorie Moore.
Paper: John Babcock, Betty Oliver. Baskets: Michael Davis, Ferne Jacobs.
Foundry: Tom McGovern. Blacksmithing: Peter Ross. Fibers: Arturo
Sandoval, Nance O'Banion, Cynthia Schira, Mary Anne Jordan, Randall Dar-
wall. Glass: Richard Marquis, Josh Simpson, Stephen Dee Edwards, Lino

Tagliapietra, Michael Scheiner. Metals: Arline Fisch, Peter Jagoda, Susan Kingsley, Eleanor Moty, Charles Crowley, Komelia Okim. Wood: Seth Stem, Bob Trotman, Alphonse Mattia, Michael Pierschalla. Quilts: Pam Studstill.

Costs, Accommodations: Two-week (three-week) session tuition is $340 ($450) and double occupancy twin-bedded room with bath is $480 ($700). Other accommodations range from an open bunkhouse for $230 ($335) to a single room and bath for $725 ($1,070). Shop fees are between $10 and $30 per week, $75 per week for glassblowing and hot glass. Clay and other supplies not provided for in shop fee can be purchased at the school store. Application, accompanied by a nonrefundable $20 fee, should be made by April 15. Upon acceptance, a $200 deposit is required, which is refundable for cancellations received at least three weeks prior. Up to 100 scholarships are awarded annually for periods of up to 13 weeks. Applications for technical assistant/monitor and work/study scholarships must be received by April 1.

Location: The oceanfront school, designed by architect Edward Larrabee Barnes and built in 1962, is located on a remote island off the Maine coast.

Contact: Haystack Mountain School of Crafts, Deer Isle, ME 04627-0087; (207) 348-2306.

HEARTWOOD OWNER-BUILDER SCHOOL
Washington, Massachusetts

Five-day workshops and three-week courses from April-October

Established in 1978 to teach the skills and knowledge it takes to build an energy-efficient house, Heartwood offers three-week house-building courses and a variety of specialized five-day workshops for skilled builders who wish to learn energy efficient house design as well as individuals with no previous construction experience. Enrollment averages 15, with a student to teacher ratio of 5:1.

The three-week house-building course, offered four times each summer, is designed for those who plan to build their home or wish to pursue a home-building career, as well as those who want to design their home and subcontract out all or part of the work. The daily schedule includes morning classroom sessions with demonstrations, slide programs, discussions, mock-ups and models, and student participation. Following lunch, students go to the building site and join in the construction of a custom house, putting into action the skills demonstrated and taught that morning. The specialized five-day workshops, most offered twice each summer, are Contracting, Timber Framing, Cabinetmaking (the only workshop that requires some experience), Finish Carpentry, Renovation, Carpentry for Women, and Masonry. Each workshop consists of classroom sessions and hands-on practice. The Heartwood staff provides free design and construction consulting to graduates.

Specialties: Home-building and renovation, timber framing.

Faculty: The four-member resident faculty, all licensed building contractors, are Will Beemer, who served as construction foreman at Arizona's Arcosanti project and design instructor at Cornell and has 15 years of building and teaching experience; on-site instructor Michele Beemer; Herb Lorentzen, who specializes in older houses and has been a building and remodeling contractor on Cape Cod for ten years; and Robert Jarvie, a toolmaker, cabinetmaker, and finish carpenter for more than years. Guest faculty has included Karla Kavanaugh, a contributor to *Fine Homebuilding* magazine; Ed Bond, president of a design and construction firm; mason and fireplace specialist Joe Sonsini; mason and stone carver Peter Champoux; and architect Jack Sobon, author of *Timber Frame Construction.*

Costs, Accommodations: Tuition for the three-week house-building course, which includes weekday lunches and a copy of Sam Clark's *Designing and Building Your Own House Your Own Way,* is $800 per person, $1,400 per couple, with a $50 discount for registrations before April 1. Tuition for the five-day workshops, including lunches, is $375 per person, $650 per couple taking the same workshop, less $25 prior to April 1. A $200 per person deposit is required for the three-week course, $100 for a five-day workshop, with balance due two weeks prior. Deposit is refundable, less $50, if cancellation is made at least four weeks prior. Local accommodations, breakfasts, and dinners are arranged by students individually. Following receipt of registration, students are send a list of nearby accommodations and required tools, which can be brought or purchased at the Heartwood Tool Store.

Location: The school is approximately two miles from Becket, which is 15 miles southeast of Pittsfield in western Massachusetts.

Contact: Heartwood School, Johnson Hill Rd., Washington, MA 01235; (413) 623-6677.

HERITAGE HANDWEAVING SCHOOL
Orland, California
Five-day classes throughout the year

Established in 1980, this school offers individualized weaving instruction from Monday through Friday with emphasis on cost-cutting measures and time-saving production methods. Participants study the weaving technique of their choice while working at their own pace and are encouraged to bring any materials they wish to use for special projects. Beginners learn such techniques as calculating warp and weft, warping and setting up a loom, reading drafts, and four-harness patterns.

Specialties: Handweaving.

Costs, Accomodations: The $500 tuition includes room with bath, all meals, and airport shuttle service. A nonrefundable $250 deposit is required to reserve the five days of choice, with balance due upon arrival. An antique-filled country home, located on ten secluded acres, houses the studio and facilities, which include a spa.

Location: The nearest airport is at Chico.

Contact: Heritage Handweaving, Rte. 3, Box 3086, Orland, CA 95963; (916) 865-5745.

HERMAN MARGULIES WORKSHOPS IN PASTEL
Washington, Connecticut
One to five-day workshops year-round

Since 1986, Herman Margulies has offered weekly one to five-day pastel workshops, each limited to four artists of all levels. Emphasis is on basic foundations and the preparation of a unique board surface to facilitate the transposing of literal scenes into the artist's personal statement and make the painting sparkle. Using a pure palette, students work with bold strokes, rich color, and strong shapes to interpret the form, texture, and light of the landscape. The instructor conducts several demonstration sessions and personal attention is given to each student throughout the day. Participants learn to paint landscapes from high quality color slides, a method which allows them to continue to work and practice on their own.

Specialties: Pastel.

Faculty: Herman Margulies, a Master Pastelist and former director of the Pastel Society of America, is a distinguished American impressionist who has won 100 awards for his pastel landscapes. His work is exhibited in such museums as the Hermitage Museum in Virginia and Yad Vashem in Jerusalem as well as galleries and corporate collections.

Costs, Accommodations: The $750 five-day workshop fee includes materials, three meals daily, in-studio sleeping loft, Sunday dinner and Saturday breakfast, and airport transportation. A $150 deposit must be submitted one month in advance with balance due upon arrival. Daily fees are $75, tuition only; or $100, which includes lunch and use of homemade board and pastels. A $75 deposit must be submitted two weeks in advance, with balance due each day. Requests for cancellations should be submitted more than two weeks prior to allow place to be filled by another artist.

Location, Facilities: The studio is located in the northwest hills of Connecticut's Litchfield County, in a wooded, countryside setting. Facilities include 800-square-feet of floor space, skylights to allow north light, and large screens to project landscape slides. The nearest airport is Hartford's Bradley International and the limousine depot in Southbury services the New York airports.

Contact: Herman Margulies Workshops in Pastel, 32 Revere Rd., Washington, CT 06793; (203) 868-0496.

HEWITT PAINTING WORKSHOPS
Various locations, mostly abroad

Seven to sixteen-day workshops

Begun in 1955, the Hewitt Painting Workshops conducts seven to ten traveling art workshops each year to various locations throughout the world. One member of a faculty of nine teachers, all experienced artists, conducts each tour for 10 to 30 students of all levels. Most classes are scheduled for the mornings, leaving the remainder of the day free for individual pursuits. Emphasis is on watercolor but students may work in any medium.

Specialties: Painting, with emphasis on watercolor.

Faculty: Includes Robert E. Wood, a member of the National Watercolor Society, former vice-president of the American Watercolor Society, and author of *Watercolor Workshop*, whose work has been shown in one-man and competitive exhibitions and received a variety of awards; Dong Kingman, recipient of such awards as Guggenheim Fellowships, the Philadelphia Watercolor Prize, and the Pennell Medal, and whose work is represented in the permanent collections of more than 30 museums; Robert Wade, author of *Painting More Than the Eye Can See*, recipient of the 1983 Cornelissen Award, an elected member of the Australian Watercolor Institute, the Salmagundi Club, and a Fellow of the Royal Society of Arts, whose work has been exhibited with many watercolor societies; and Joan and Rex Brandt, George Post, Charles Reid, Frank Webb, Christopher Schink, Gerald Brommer, and Tony Sheets.

Costs, Accommodations: Cost ranges from $895 to $4,500, which usually includes airfare, lodging, meals, and local transportation. A deposit is required to confirm reservation with balance payable eight weeks prior to departure. Accommodations are in hotels.

Location: Typical trip itineraries include Bali, Japan, and Hong Kong; Sydney, Leura, Melbourne, and Fiji; and Samoa, Pago Pago, and Apia.

Contact: Hewitt Painting Workshops, P.O. Box 6980, San Diego, CA 92106-0980; (619) 222-4405.

HILL COUNTRY ARTS FOUNDATION (HCAF)
Ingram, Texas

Weekend to five-day workshops from May-August

Established in 1959, The Hill Country Arts Foundation offers more than 30 summer workshops for artists of all ages and levels. Classes are held from 9 am to 3 pm, Monday through Friday, with studios open until 5 pm. Typical workshop titles are Acrylic Painting (Marilynn Branham), Multi-Media Painting (Fred Samuelson), Pastels and Oils (Ben Konis), Sculpting With Clay (Ann Armstrong), Ceramics (Don Herron), Etching (Marie Leterme), Creative Oil Painting (Ann Templeton), Large Format Painting (Julie Locke Eskoff), and Beginning Spinning (Faye Drozd).

Specialties: A variety of art and craft topics.

Faculty: Changes each year. Instructors are prominent artists and teachers.

Costs, Accommodations: Tuition ranges from $50 for a weekend workshop to $175 for five days and some classes require a materials or model fee. HCAF members (annual dues begin at $25) receive a $10 discount. A $50 nonrefundable deposit must accompany registration at least four weeks prior with balance due at start of workshop. Partial scholarships are available. A list of nearby private homes and commercial lodging establishments is provided.

Location, Facilities: HCAF is situated on the banks of the Johnson Creek at its confluence with the Guadalupe River. Facilities include an art gallery, three art studios, photographic and fiber laboratories, and a pottery studio.

Contact: Hill Country Arts Foundation, P.O. Box 176, Ingram, TX 78025; (512) 367-5121.

HILLTOP WOOLS
Prescott, Ontario, Canada
Three-day summer courses

Established in 1976, Hilltop Wools offers three-day summer courses in spinning, weaving, and natural dying for 8 to 20 beginning to experienced craftspersons.

Specialties: Spinning, weaving, dyeing.

Faculty: Proprietor Trudy Van Stralen, an experienced teacher who has published articles with Interweave Press, teaches dyeing. The spinning and weaving courses are taught by guest instructors.

Costs, Accommodations: The three-day course fee is C$125 plus a C$10 to C$25 materials fee. A 50% deposit must accompany application with balance due 30 days prior. MasterCard and VISA accepted. Refund of deposit is granted cancellations more than 30 days prior; thereafter, a 90% refund is given only if space can be filled. Accommodations are available in local motels at rates ranging from C$40 to C$75 per day. Lunch at the studio is C$5 and remaining meals are taken in area restaurants.

Location: The facility, 50 miles from Ottawa, is located on a sheep farm near the major Montreal-Toronto highway. Regional attractions include the Thousand Islands tourist area, Upper Canada Village, and Ottawa, the nation's capitol city.

Contact: Jan Van Stralen, Hilltop Wools, R.R.4, Prescott, ON, Canada K0E 1T0; (613) 925-4502.

HIMALAYAN WEAVING WORKSHOP
Craft World Tours (CWT)
Northern India

Three-week workshop in spring and fall

Established in 1981, Craft World Tours are international travel programs designed for persons with an interest in the crafts and folk arts of the world. Twice a year CWT sponsors the Himalayan Weaving Workshop, limited to 20 participants of all levels, which combines sightseeing and visits to craftspeople in the foothills of the Himalayas of northern India with hands-on instruction at a family farm in the Himalayas. Participants travel through the Kulu and Kangra Valleys, visiting handcraft centers and artisans' workshops, and spend five days weaving at Dharamkot, a protected nature reserve located on top of a mountain. The workshop format is flexible, to meet the needs of the participants, who have opportunities to card and spin mountain wool on a traditional Gandhi spinning wheel and dye fibers utilizing plants and roots indigenous to India. The emphasis is on learning the traditional "bar" method of Tibetan carpet weaving, including making a design, setting up a loom, and weaving a small sample under the tutelage of local women carpet weavers. Evenings are reserved for informal discussions on Tibetan and Himalayan design and carpet weaving in general.

Specialties: Weaving.

Faculty: Lesley Butterworth lives at Dharamkot, where she is involved with the operation of small-scale cottage industry projects with local village people in northern India, creating products based on traditional designs.

Costs, Accommodations; The cost, which includes round trip airfare from New York City, double occupancy lodging, and some meals, is $3,215; single supplement is $258 and travel from Seattle is $150 additional. A $250 deposit must accompany reservation with balance due 60 days prior.

Location: The tour arrives at and departs from Delhi and includes stops at Bhuntar, Manali, Vashist, Naggar Castle, Mandi, Tashi Zong, McLeod Ganj, Naddi Village, Chandni Chowk, and Agra, site of the Taj Mahal.

Contact: Craft World Tours, 6776 Warboys Rd., Byron, NY 14422; (716) 548-2667.

HORIZONS: THE NEW ENGLAND CRAFT PROGRAM
Williamsburg, Massachusetts

Year-round weekend and five-day intensives for adults; two three-week sessions in July and August for high school students

Established in 1983 as a year-round craft school, Horizons offers arts programs encompassing eight studios: Drawing and Color, Ceramics, Weaving, Surface Design, Wood Sculpture and Furniture Design, Metalsmithing and Jewelry Construction, Glass Blowing, and Photography. Weekend and five-day adult workshops, limited to three students per instructor (12 per studio), are offered throughout the year as well as six one-week intensives under the auspices of Elderhostel. The summer intensive art program for high school students allows participants to enroll in either of two three-week sessions or the full six-weeks. Each studio is limited to eight students, who enroll in two studios and spend mornings (three hours) in one and afternoons (three hours) in the other. Weekends feature four guest artists, who discuss their work at a Friday evening slide presentation and conduct hands-on workshops on Saturday. High school credit is available.

The adult intensives, which include formal instruction and independent practice, offer artists of all levels the opportunity to explore new techniques. Typical titles include Japanese & African Dye Techniques, in which students create a wide range of designs and produce fabric suitable for wall hangings, quilts, and clothing; Weaving, including various methods and patterns as well as drafting, project planning, and finishing techniques; Painting and Illustrating on Fabric, an exploration of batik and dyepainting on fabric; Color and Collage, in which students complete several experimental pieces in traditional and modern mediums; and Images on Clay, which addresses ceramic tile-forming with emphasis on the decoration and design of ceramic tiles that are suitable for wall pieces and small murals.

Specialties: Drawing and painting, ceramics, weaving, surface design, woodworking, metalsmithing, jewelry, glassblowing, and photography.

Faculty: Founder and Director Jane Sinauer, a graduate of Smith College and a studio potter for 12 years, has had her large porcelain forms exhibited in museums and galleries in the U.S. and abroad, including the Corning Glass Museum, World Trade Center, DeCordova Museum, and Delaware Art Museum. Workshops are conducted by prominent artists and craftsmen, assisted by graduate students or those embarking on a career.

Costs, Accommodations: Cost of the summer program for high school students is $1,325 per three-week session or $2,475 for both, which includes room and board. Applicants must submit a personal statement, two reference letters, and a $280 deposit, which includes a $40 nonrefundable registration fee. Cancellations at least eight weeks prior receive a full refund less fee. Adult workshop fees range from $125 for a weekend to $225 for a five-day workshop. Studio, field trip, and supplies fees are additional. Horizons' four living modules are designed as a series of double rooms, each of which opens out onto a large outdoor deck.

Location, Facilities: Horizons is located in the five-college community of Amherst/Northampton close to Old Deerfield Village, in the foothills of the Berkshires. near the 5-college community of Amherst/Northampton. Facilities blend 1700's farm and contemporary stuctures and include professionally equipped studios.

Contact: Horizons, 374 Old Montague Rd., Amherst, MA 01002; (413) 549-4841.

HUDSON RIVER VALLEY PAINTING WORKSHOPS
Greenville, New York
Six-day workshops from May-October

The Greenville Arms, a Victorian country home built in the Queen Anne style of the late 1800's by William Vanderbilt, is host to more than a dozen painting workshops from late spring to early fall. Each six-day session begins with a Sunday evening dinner and orientation, followed by studio and on-location classes that are scheduled from 9 am to 4 pm, Monday through Friday. Participants receive daily group and individual instruction and one evening is reserved for a critique, demonstration, or slide presentation. Most of the workshops are open to all levels with a few limited to intermediate to advanced artists.

Specialties: Painting in watercolor, water media, oil, pastel, pencil.

Faculty: Includes such prominent artists as Don Andrews, Americo DiFranza, Zygmund Jankowski, Skip Lawrence, Paul Leveille, Stanley Maltzman, Maxine Masterfield, Charles Movalli, Barbara Nechis, Tom Nicholas, Alex Powers, Christopher Schink, Betty Lou Schlemm, and Don Stone.

Costs, Accommodations: Tuition, which includes double occupancy lodging and country-style breakfasts and dinners at the Greenville Arms, ranges from $435 to $520. Single supplement is $95 and nonparticipant fee is $325. A $100 deposit secures booking with balance due on arrival. Refund, less $25 charge, is granted cancellations at least three weeks prior; thereafter if space can be filled.

Location, Facilities: The Greenville Arms is situated in the small village of Greenville in Greene County, near the Hudson River and the northern Catskill Mountains, approximately 130 miles from New York City and 185 miles from Boston. A swimming pool is on the grounds and golf, horseback riding, and tennis are nearby. The town is also convenient to country auctions, antique shops, and historic sites.

Contact: Hudson River Valley Painting Workshops, Greenville Arms, South St., Greenville, NY 12083; (518) 966-5219.

IDYLLWILD SCHOOL OF MUSIC AND THE ARTS (ISOMATA)
Idyllwild, California
Weekend and week long workshops from June-September

Established in 1950 as the nonprofit educational Idyllwild Arts Foundation (IAF), ISOMATA offers a ten-week annual Summer Program of workshops for young people and adults of all levels in dance, music, native arts, theatre, writing, and the visual arts. The program begins with Sunday evening orientation and classes meet six hours daily, five or six days a week, with evenings reserved for concerts, artist lectures, gallery openings, potluck dinners, and recreational activities. Most workshops are open to all levels and enrollment in adult workshops is limited to 10 to 15 participants. A variety of subjects are taught, including painting and drawing, printmaking, paper-making, sculpture, ceramics, jewelry, and such native arts and crafts as Papago basketmaking, Navajo weaving, Hopi sculpture carving, and Acoma pottery. ISOMATA also sponsors travel workshops, such as a 15-day Maori Arts and Cultures program in the Bay of Islands, New Zealand. Students study in one of three classes — carving, painting, and weaving — taught by native experts. Other activities include lectures, presentations, and field trips.

Typical summer workshop titles include Painting and Drawing, which emphasizes the science and art of drawing and includes exposure to mono-type; Techniques and Concepts in Papermaking, which explores ways to create pieces quickly, enabling the development of more ideas rather than just techniques, and Specialized Ceramics — Musical Instruments, in which students make and fire sculptured musical instruments and are taught a variety of sound-producing and tuning techniques. Workshops for young people include Visual Arts, which concentrates on a wide variety of media and techniques with emphasis on applying art principles to transforming ideas into group and individual projects.

Specialties: A variety of visual and folk arts and crafts.

Faculty: Includes Sandy Adsett, David Brunn, Blue Corn, Delores Garcia, Joe Gray, Donna Guadagni, Delbridge Honanie, Greg Kennedy, Clinton D. MacKenzie, Frances Manuel, Emma Mitchell, Joseph Mugnaini, Walter Nottingham, Brian Ransom, Bertha Stevens, and Beverly Worlock.

Costs, Accommodations: Tuition is $525 for the young people's workshops (includes dormitory housing and board) and $375 for the one-week adult workshops (not including room and board). Scholarships and financial aid are available. Applications must be accompanied by a $25 application fee and a nonrefundable $125 deposit for each course, with balance due 30 days prior. Full refund less $25 fee is granted cancellations before March 15; cancella-tions afterwards but more than 30 days prior to workshop also forfeit the $125 deposit; no refunds within 30 days. Most adult workshops offer one unit of college credit per week ($100) through the University of Redlands. Adult housing consists of motels, homes, campgrounds, and on-campus residence halls, which range from $275 to $375 per week, including meals.

Location: The 205-acre school site is located at a 5,500-foot elevation in the San Jacinto Mountains, approximately a 2 1/2 hour drive from both Los Angeles and San Diego.

Contact: Steven Fraider, Director of Summer Programs, Idyllwild School of Music and the Arts, Box 38, 52500 Temecula Rd., Idyllwild, CA 92349; (714) 659-2171, Fax (714) 659-5463. Winter address: 849 South Broadway, #816, Los Angeles, CA 90014; (213) 622-0355.

INNIEMORE SCHOOL OF PAINTING
Isle of Mull, Scotland and Mallorca, Spain

Two twelve-day workshops in March (Mallorca) and one-week workshops most weeks from May-September (Isle of Mull)

Established in 1967, this school offers residential painting courses for artists of all ages and abilities. Twelve-day workshops run from Friday to Wednesday, one-week workshops from Saturday to Saturday, and both are limited to 16 students per two faculty members. Instruction includes demonstrations in oil, watercolors, and other media, and discussions of drawing composition and color theory. The emphasis is on landscape painting, with portrait and still life reserved for inclement weather. The week includes an illustrated talk on painting or theatre performance, expeditions to other parts of the island, including Iona, and an exhibition and review at week's end. A two-week stay is recommended, though students may stay any number of weeks.

Specialties: Landscape painting.

Faculty: School principal Julia Wroughton studied at the Colchester School of Art under John O'Connor and Hugh Cronyn and at the Royal College of Art under Carel Weight, Roger de Grey, and Colin Hayes. She has lectured at Gloucester College of Art and her art is in the collections of the Royal West of England Academy and the Nuffield Foundation.

Costs, Accommodations: The weekly fee, which includes VAT, room, and full board, ranges from £210 to £260. Single room supplement is £20 and nonpainters who share a room receive a 5% fee reduction. A 20% deposit secures booking with balance due on completion of course. Cancellations more than six weeks prior receive a 50% deposit refund, no refunds thereafter. Students are lodged in double and single rooms with hot and cold water (no private baths) in Inniemore Lodge. One ground floor room is suitable for handicapped persons. A nearby two-bedroom cottage with wood-burning stove is also available.

Location, Facilities: The Isle of Mull, off Scotland's West Coast, is reached by boat from Oban to Criagnure, which is 25 miles from Inniemore Lodge, a Victorian hunting lodge situated on 25 acres of wooded ground overlooking the Firth of Lorne to Jura, Colonsay, and other islands. The Lodge has two studios and a shop with supplies. Nearby attractions include fishing and boating, golf, pony trekking, and visits to Torosay and Duart Castles.

Contact: Julia Wroughton, Inniemore School of Painting, Inniemore Lodge, Carsaig, Isle of Mull, PA70 6HD, Scotland; (44) 06814 201.

INSTITUTE OF PENNSYLVANIA RURAL LIFE AND CULTURE
The Landis Valley Museum
Lancaster, Pennsylvania
Four days of workshops and seminars in late June

Since 1957, the Landis Valley Museum has offered an annual program of seminars and workshops that teaches a broad array of traditional 18th and 19th century Pennsylvania crafts and skills. Classes, limited to 8 to 15 students, are held from 9:30 am to noon and from 1:30 to 4 pm. Seminars cover such topics as log construction, which focuses on squaring logs and corner construction and the building of a small smoke house; and Southeastern Pennsylvania quilts, a lecture that uses actual examples and slides. Typical workshop titles include Basketry, where students weave a medium-sized market basket with a wrapped rattan handle; Blacksmithing, which encourages students to make an item that suits their ability and interest; Bobbin Lace, focusing on basic techniques and the making of a lace bookmark and a decorative strip; Cabinet Making, which teaches pattern layout, cutting dovetails and other joint types, and construction methods; Leather Working, in which beginners learn hand sewing and dyeing and make an oval box, intermediates learn blind stitching and make a dice cup and ball pouch, and advanced students make a travelling case; Pottery, which emphasizes wheel and hand-building techniques with earthenware and stoneware; Show Towels, in which students use counted cross stitching to make a decorated hand towel; Tin Punching, where students make decorative punched tin panels that are placed in wood frames to construct a cupboard; Tinsmithing, which deals with the principles of pattern layout and cutting, forming, and soldering antique articles; Wood Graining, where students decorate a picture frame and cheese box; and Writing With A Quill Pen, where students learn how to cut and use a quill pen. Evening activities include opening reception and lecture, and dinner with entertainment. Craft classes are also offered the first two Saturday mornings in November and April and afford the opportunity to construct at least one object using traditional techniques.

Landis Valley, opened in 1925, is the largest museum of Pennsylvania German rural life in operation. In conjunction with Landis Valley Associates, the 1,300-member support group that sponsors the annual Institute, the museum also offers special events, lectures, and school programs.

Specialties: Early American crafts, including basketry, leather working, tinsmithing, pottery, wood graining, cabinet making, and blacksmithing.

Faculty: The 13-member faculty has included Dale Lehmer (log building), president of Recycle the Barn People; Patricia Herr (quilting), an authority on Pennsylvania quilts and former guest curator at the Philadelphia Museum of Art; Vivian Aron (basketry), a basketry teacher at Albright College; Jim Kieffer (blacksmithing), an experienced professional blacksmith; Terry Glick (leather working), a full-time craftsman since 1980; and Clair Garman (cabinetmaking), a third generation Lancaster cabinet maker.

Costs, Accommodations: Registration fee, which includes lunches, light breakfasts, reception, and dinner is $170. Materials fee is additional and ranges from $5 to $30. Full refund is granted cancellations more than two weeks prior. Accommodations, which cost approximately $50 per night, are available at a nearby motel.

Location: The Museum, which consists of two farmsteads, exhibit buildings, a cross roads settlement, tavern, country store, and hotel, is located two miles north of Lancaster along the Oregon Pike, easily accessible from the Pennsylvania Turnpike. Lancaster, in the heart of the Pennsylvania Dutch Country, offers a variety of restaurants, a farmer's market, museums, and walking tours of its historic areas.

Contact: Registrar, Institute of Pennsylvania Rural Life and Culture, The Landis Valley Museum, 2451 Kissel Hill Rd., Lancaster, PA 17601; (717) 569-0401.

INSTITUTO DE ARTES
Puerto Juarez, Cancun, Mexico

One to four-week seminars year-round

Established in 1988, the Instituto de Artes offers one to four-week art seminars that are instructed by prominent American and Mexican artists. Approximately 30 seminars are scheduled annually, each limited to 15 to 20 participants (an average of 8 per teacher) who range from the vacationer desiring a new skill to the serious student who wants to study in depth. Seminar topics include pastel, oil, watercolor, acrylic, sculpture, ceramics, monoprint, figure drawing, and art to wear.

Specialties: Drawing, painting, sculpture, ceramics, art to wear.

Faculty: Has included Dorothy Barta, Bennett Bradbury, Goldie Sandman Conway, Lawrence Goldsmith, Albert Handell, Clay Kent, Ben Konis, Susan Kuznitsky, Al Lachman, Nancy McDonald, McKenzie Smith, Justine Parish, Rowena Smith, Ann Templeton, Lillian Trotta, Freda Tschumy, Millard Wells, Larry Weston, and Mary Whyte.

Costs, Accommodations: Weekly course fee, which includes orientation/reception, double occupancy hotel lodging, and two meals daily, ranges from $350 to $667, with a discount for nonparticipant guests. A nonrefundable $100 deposit must accompany application with balance due 30 days prior to departure. Cancellations within two weeks are charged an additional fee.

Location: The Casa Caribela, home of the Instituto de Arts, is a Yucatecan inn located on a cove beach near the old fishing village of Puerto Juarez, 10 minutes from downtown Cancun and 30 minutes from the airport.

Contact: Instituto de Artes, 12101 S. Dixie Hwy., Miami FL 33156; (800) 327-3012, (800) 432-0011 (in Fla.), *or* (305) 232-2111.

INTERNATIONAL ART PROGRAMS, LTD.
Lake Como, Italy
Three-week summer sessions

Established in 1984, International Art Programs, Ltd., sponsors four intensive three-week sessions — each offering workshops in pastel, oil, watercolor, and sculpture — between June 30 and September 2. Each workshop is limited to ten students of all levels, who receive individualized instruction and work at their chosen medium on-location and in the studio for five hours daily, five days a week. One to three-hour demonstrations, scheduled at least twice a week, highlight new approaches and specific techniques. Students may work in one medium for the entire three weeks or select two, working in one in the morning and one in the afternoon or one for one week and the other for two. Pastel, oil, and watercolor workshop time is divided between morning and afternoon classes, from 9:30 am to noon and 2 to 4:30 pm; sculpture workshops run from 9:30 to 3 pm with an on-location picnic lunch break. Group excursions and evening activities are also planned.

Pastels: Portraiture, Still Life and Figure Painting covers basic techniques, color interlocking (to achieve luminosity), blending, and composition, as well as the appropriate use of papers and grounds. Oil: Portraiture and Landscapes emphasizes composition, masses, color values, and glazing. Both Old Masters and Impressionist color palettes are taught, with landscape painting on location and portraiture in the studio. Watercolor: Landscapes, Village Scenes and Florals features on location and studio work, stressing color and composition. Sculpture: Modeling the Head and Figure, Carving in Stone pursues two techniques. Students may choose the art of modeling three-dimensional portraiture and figure work (adding clay or plasteline in a continuing process until the desired form is developed) or the art of hand carving (subtracting from the sculptural material to create the form).

Specialties: Portrait, landscape, and still life painting; modeling and stone carving.

Faculty: Director Diana Willis, P.S.A., a portrait and still life artist, has had one-person shows at Hofstra University and Kew Gallery in New York. Her awards include the Best Pastel in Show Award at the Knickerbocker Artists show and the Ada Cerere Memorial Award at the National Association of Women Artists annual and her work is in private and corporate collections in the U.S. and Italy. Al Krnc, a full-time artist since 1979, has received awards at the Euclid Fine Arts Show and the Hi-Country Invitational in Fort Collins. His work is in corporate collections. Grigory Gurevich, a faculty member of the School of Fine and Industrial Arts in Newark and the Fine Arts Counsel of the International Center for Educational Advancement, was awarded two grants from the New Jersey State Council on the Arts and his sculpture tableau, "Commuters", is installed in Penn Station in Newark.

Costs, Accommodations: The workshop cost of $2,850 includes double occupancy lodging (single supplement ranges from $600 to $900), welcoming reception, breakfasts and dinners for 23 days, and round-trip airfare between Milan and the workshop location. Round-trip air transportation from

New York City must be arranged through International Art Programs, Ltd. Students may enroll in two workshops at no additional charge. A $600 deposit must accompany reservation. Cancellations more than 45 days prior receive a full refund of land costs less $175 fee. Lodging and studio sessions are in the first-class Hotel Bellevue in the village of Cadenabbia.

Location: Cadenabbia is centrally located in northern Italy's Lake Como region, one hour from Switzerland and close to Milan, Lugano, and Venice. On-location oil painting and sculpture sessions are conducted in the gardens of the Villa Carlotta, a national museum adjacent to the hotel. Watercolorists visit neighboring villages and towns.

Contact: International Art Programs, Ltd., 41 Union Square, #314, New York, NY 10003; (212) 980-7053.

INTERNATIONAL WORKSHOPS
Various cities worldwide

Thirteen-day workshop in July-August

Begun in 1971, International Workshops offers an annual 13-day summer workshop in Strings, Piano, Choral Conducting, and Watercolor Art. Student to faculty ratio ranges from 9 to 12 to one and there are no student qualifications for the art program, which consists of on-location sketching and painting, lecture-demonstrations, and individual and small group critiques. A series of discussions and demonstrations on topics of general interest is also scheduled for the entire group.

Specialties: Watercolor.

Faculty: Has included Lou Rizzolo, Professor of Art at Western Michigan University, whose work is represented in such corporate collections as Westinghouse Co. and Upjohn Co.; and Howard Watson, who has had works commissioned by Wyeth Laboratories and *Gourmet* magazine and has taught at the Philadelphia College of Art, the Abdington, Oreland, and Wayne Art Centers, and the Hussian School of Art.

Costs, Accommodations: Basic tuition of $995 includes room, breakfasts, and all dinners. Reduced rates are available for participating and nonparticipating family members. A $150 deposit must accompany application with balance due by June 15. Lodging is in apartments on campus; single supplement and housing upgrade options are available. Three hours of undergraduate or graduate credit are offered through Western Michigan University for a fee of $150 or $195.

Location: The workshops are held in a different city each year. The 1990 location is Calgary.

Contact: International Workshops, 187 Aqua View Rd., Cedarburg, WI 53012; (414) 377-7451.

IRVING SHAPIRO, A.W.S., WATERCOLOR WORKSHOPS
Various locations in U.S., Canada, and Mexico
Three to five-day workshops

A watercolorist and teacher since 1945, Irving Shapiro has presented watercolor workshops since 1967 under the sponsorship of art groups, organizations, and educational institutions. Workshops are from three to five days long, conducted indoors, and open to 15 to 25 artists of all levels. Included in the daily sessions, which begin at 9 am and end in late afternoon, are demonstrations, critiques, student painting time, and slide presentations.
Specialties: Watercolor.

Faculty: Irving Shapiro is past president and director of the American Academy of Art, an electee to the American Watercolor Society, and author of *How To Make a Painting: Planning, Procedures, and Techniques for the Watercolorist.* He is recipient of many awards, including the National Academy of Design's Henry Ward Ranger Award, the Grumbacher Silver Medal, and the Mary Litt Medal and Award, and his work has been exhibited at the Art Institute of Chicago, the Norfolk Museum of Art, the Tweed Museum and other museums and galleries.

Costs: Costs and other arrangements are determined by the sponsoring group or institution.

Contact: Irving Shapiro, A.W.S., 1335 N. Astor St., Chicago, IL 60610; (312) 943-0213.

ISABEL O'NEIL STUDIO WORKSHOP
New York, New York
Two-week courses in June and July

The Studio Workshop of the Isabel O'Neil Foundation for the Art of the Painted Finish offers two concentrated two-week summer courses in the techniques used to produce fine quality painted furniture. Each course is scheduled from 9 am to 6 pm, Monday through Friday, and encompasses the material covered in two courses that meet for three hours once weekly over a span of 7 or 14 weeks during spring and fall. No previous experience is required.

Accelerated I, which is a combination of the Basic Course and the Leafing and Gilding Course, covers surface presentation, color matching and comprehension, striping, antiquing, leafing common and precious metals in the tradition of the Renaissance Master Gilders, patinas, and an introduction to decorative design. Accelerated II, a combination of the Glazing and Distressing Course and the Casein Course, covers physical and surface distressing, glazing, application of decoration, antiquing patinas, gesso-like base, gouache medium, antiquing methods, design in casein and gouache, and fantasy marble. On completion of these two courses, which must be taken in order, students may enroll in Varnishing (two half-days), which covers the

application of shellac and varnish, and Color (four full days), which covers
neutralizing agents, interrelation of color, and analysis of paintings. Students
who wish to continue their studies can enroll in the more advanced courses,
come of which must be taken in sequence and all of which meet once weekly
for 14 weeks.

Specialties: Painted finish for furniture and decoration.

Faculty: Students work under direct supervision of instructors who have
completed the Studio Workshop course of studies.

Costs, Accommodations: Tuition is $1,400 for Accelerated I, $1,500 for
Accelerated II, and students provide their own furniture. Full payment must
accompany registration, which opens in January. A full refund is granted
cancellations at least 30 days prior.

Location: The Studio is situated on New York City's Upper East Side.

Contact: Studio Workshop for the Art of the Painted Finish, 177 E. 87th St.,
New York, NY 10128; (212) 348-4464.

JACQUELINE PENNEY ART GALLERY AND STUDIO
Cutchogue, New York
One to four-day workshops year-round

Established at its present location in 1976, the Penney Studio offers on-
going classes and six to eight workshops a year, with some specifically for
beginners and others for advanced students. Topics include water media,
acrylics, watercolor, collage, and monotype. Beginner workshop titles
include From Drawing to Painting and Exploring Your Own Creativity.

Specialties: Painting and drawing.

Faculty: Jacqueline Penney has studied at the Art Students League and
Phoenix School of Design in New York, Black Mountain College in North
Carolina, the Institute of Design in Chicago, and with Charles Reid, Robert
E. Wood, Tom Hill, Miles Batt, Henry Fukuhara, Frank Webb, Paul Wood,
Daniel Green, Mario Cooper, and Barbara Nechis. She has had solo and group
exhibitions in galleries in New York and New Jersey and is represented in
private, public, and corporate collections. Guest faculty includes master
printmaker Dan Welden, watercolorist Frank Webb, A.W.S., and Carl
Molno, who teaches water media.

Costs: Tuition ranges from $40 for a one-day workshop to $165 for four days.
Students can enroll in some workshops by the day. A nonrefundable $40 to
$60 deposit must accompany registration with balance due at start of work-
shop.

Location: The studio is situated in a redesigned 1840's livestock barn in
Cutchogue on the eastern tip of Long Island, a tourist area known for its
vineyards and wineries.

Contact: Penney Studio, P.O. Box 959, 270 North St., Cutchogue, NY
11935; (516) 734-5426.

JAMES GODWIN SCOTT WATERCOLOR WORKSHOPS
Patagonia, Arizona; Somerset Island, Bermuda; and other scenic locales
One to two-week workshops

Since 1974, James Godwin Scott has taught watercolor painting to artists of all levels and currently offers about a dozen workshops annually. Held in diverse scenic locales, his programs consist of both location and studio work, with emphasis on strengthening individual style. The daily schedule includes lecture-demonstrations, individual assistance, and group critiques.

Specialties: Watercolor.

Faculty: James Godwin Scott studied with Robert Brackman, Frank B. Nuderscher, and Jack Merriott. His paintings are in corporate and private collections, including that of H.R.H. Prince Charles of England, and have been accepted by such juried exhibitions as the American Watercolor Society, The Royal Institute Summer Salon, and the Annuelles des Beaux Arts. He also has produced a set of on-location lecture-demonstration videotapes.

Costs, Accommodations: Costs and accommodations vary widely, depending upon location, facilities, and length of program. Nonparticipant spouses and guests are welcome.

Location: Annual locales are Patagonia, Arizona and Somerset Island, Bermuda. Other locations may include California, Vermont, Hawaii, Illinois, Maine, Missouri, Nova Scotia, Switzerland, and Tortola in the British Virgin Islands.

Contact: James Godwin Scott Watercolor Workshops, 1221 Locust St., #1401, St. Louis, MO 63103; (314) 421-1459.

JANE E. JONES ART STUDIO
Dallas, Texas
Two to four-day workshops

Since 1974, Jane E. Jones has taught painting and drawing to artists of all levels. She offers two to four-day summer and winter art workshops as well as on-going daytime and evening classes. The workshops, which run from 9:30 am to 3:30 pm and are usually limited to 12 to 16 students, include such titles as Collage I and II, Color I and II, Wet Into Wet, Christmas Cards, and Design, which emphasizes an understanding of design elements and principles and their application to painting.

Specialties: Painting, collage, design.

Faculty: Jane E. Jones is recipent of such awards as 1989 Artists & Craftsmen Association Honorable Mention, the 1988 National Watercolor Oklahoma Best of Show, and the 1988 House of Heydenryk Award. She has studied with more than 40 prominent artists and teachers and is the designer and manufacturer of the Jones Watercolor Palette and Plastiform, Inc. Her work is in the collections of Mary Kay Cosmetics, Republic National Bank in Dallas, Sea World in Orlando, and other corporations.

Costs: Workshop tuition ranges from $50 to $125. A $25 deposit must accompany application with balance due the first day of class. Full refund is granted cancellations more than two weeks prior.

Location: The ground floor studio in Dallas is handicapped accessible.

Contact: Jane E. Jones, 13221 Bee St., Dallas, TX 75234; (214) 243-6164.

JAPANESE ARTS SEMINAR
California School of Japanese Arts
Muir Beach, California

Ten-day retreat from late July-early August

First offered in 1987 and modeled after the Oomoto School of Traditional Japanese Arts, Japan, this ten-day intensive retreat emphasizes learning the basic techniques and concepts of the arts through actual practice. Featured arts consist of comic theater (Kyogen), sword movement (Shintaiso Kenjutso), tea ceremony (Chanoyu), and brushwork (Bokugi). The brushwork seminar is devoted to a study of traditional Chinese/Japanese-style calligraphy and contemporary abstract work. In addition to six hours of daily instruction, time is set aside for other activities including discussions, Zen practice, and demonstrations of Japanese flower arrangement. A series of evening lectures covers such topics as woodblock prints, textiles, and pottery, which covers the making of tea bowls to be used in the final tea ceremony. The California School of Japanese Arts, a nonprofit organization dedicated to promoting traditional Japanese arts in the United States, also sponsors various arts and master teachers programs and publishes a newsletter.

Specialties: Japanese arts.

Faculty: Includes Seminar Director Liz Kenner, who studied flower arrangement and tea ceremony in Japan; painter and calligrapher Kazuaki Tanahashi, formerly scholar-in-residence at the San Francisco Zen Center and author of *Penetrating Laughter: Hakuin's Zen* and *Art and Moon in a Dewdrop: Writings of Zen Master Dogen*; and Haruyoshi Ito, Christy Bartlett, and Yuriko Doi.

Costs, Accommodations: Fee of $1,000 includes double occupancy (single supplement available) lodging, vegetarian meals, art supplies, instructional materials, and Japanese-style clothes. A $200 deposit must accompany application; additional $400 is due three months prior with balance payable on arrival. A $200 refund, less $20 processing fee, is granted cancellations more than three months prior; thereafter only if space can be filled. Some scholarships are available. Participants are housed in a new guest facility.

Location: Green Gulch Farm at Muir Beach, one of the San Francisco Zen Center's monastic practicing communities, provides a serene and natural environment and includes a traditional Japanese-style tea house. It is approximately a 25-minute drive from San Francisco.

Contact: The California School of Japanese Arts, 526 Ashbury Ave., Santa Rosa, CA 95404; (707) 578-8014.

THE JOHN C. CAMPBELL FOLK SCHOOL
Brasstown, North Carolina
Weekend and one-week workshops year-round

Founded in 1925, John C. Campbell Folk School is the nation's oldest and largest craft school, offering more than 350 craft workshops and music and dance programs throughout the year. Six to eight craft workshops run concurrently during most weekend and one-week sessions with some workshops arranged back-to-back so that students may spend more than one week either with the same instructor or with two different instructors. Subjects taught include fiber arts, basketry, book arts, jewelry, blacksmithing, woodworking, watercolor, clay, woodcarving, enameling, and photography. Most craft workshop enrollments are limited to 10 to 12 adult students of all levels of ability. Weekend workshops begin with Friday supper, followed by orientation and class. Classes meet from 9 am to noon, 1:30 to 4:30 pm, and after supper on Saturday, and from 9 am to noon on Sunday. One-week workshops begin with Sunday supper and orientation and classes meet from 9 am to noon and 1:30 to 4:30 pm, Monday through Friday, with Friday afternoon reserved for student exhibits. Additional activities include morning campus walks, exercise, and song programs; afternoon and evening slide shows; videos, picnics, campus tours with historical lectures, craft studio demonstrations, music and dance, and such annual special events as sales, auctions, and festivals. The School is host to more than 30 Elderhostel sessions a year and the annual Little/Middle Folk School, a crafts and recreation week for local children ages 6 to 14.

In addition to the above, specific crafts courses include Marbling, Batik, Kaleidoscopes, Calligraphy, Chair Caning, Enameling, Spinning, Wood Bowl Turning, Broom Making, Quilting, Tatting, Bobbin Lace, Knitting, Weaving, Cornshuck Dolls, Dulcimer Building, and Smocking. Some weeks are devoted to such single crafts as basketry, quilting, or woodcarving.

Specialties: Fiber arts, basketry, book arts, jewelry, blacksmithing, woodworking, watercolor, clay, enameling, and photography.

Faculty: Instructors are recognized experts in their fields, some of them second-generation craftsmen whose families have been associated with the School for years. Others have moved permanently to the area and maintain their own private studios nearby.

Costs, Accommodations: Tuition, lab fee, room and full meal plan is approximately $330 per week, $150 per weekend. A deposit of $75 per week or $30 for weekend is required. Camping facilities are also available.

Location, Facilities: The 365-acre campus, a national historic site in the southwest corner of North Carolina, is located in a scenic mountain setting, seven miles east of Murphy, 100 miles southwest of Asheville, and 100 miles north of Atlanta. The School is located within 50 miles of the Cherokee Indian reservation, Joyce Kilmer National Forest, Georgia Mountain Fair, whitewater kayaking, and rafting. Facilities, which are handicapped accessible, include a crafts shop, which displays and sells handcrafted items created by local artisans and instructors, Fiber Arts Studio, Jewelry Studio, Blacksmith Shop, Woodworking Studio, Pottery Studio, Carving Studio, and Enameling Studio, as well as guest houses, open-air pavilions, and a log cabin museum.

Contact: John C. Campbell Folk School, Route 1, Box 14A, Brasstown, NC 28902; (800) 562-2440 *or* (704) 837-2775.

JOHN J. HODGINS WATERCOLOR WORKSHOPS
Connecticut, Florida, Maine, New York

Five-day workshops from April to October

Since 1974, John Hodgins has conducted five-day outdoor painting workshops that emphasize design, composition, and creativity. About six or seven workshops for all levels are scheduled during the months from April to October. The class meets at 9 am each day, Monday through Friday, and then drives to the day's location, where the session begins with a critique of the previous day's work followed by a lecture/demonstration in watercolor. The remainder of the day is devoted to painting, with the instructor available for individual assistance. An afternoon demonstration in oil is given if any students are using this medium.

Specialties: Outdoor painting, with emphasis on watercolor.

Faculty: John J. Hodgins, an experienced full-time painter, runs his own studio/gallery and is author of *An Appalachian Trail Sketchbook.*

Costs, Accommodations: Tuition for the week is $100. A $25 deposit is required with application. Students are responsible for their own food and lodging and non-painting spouses are welcome.

Location: The workshops are held in different locations during the year including Florida (Boynton Beach and Stuart) in the spring, Maine (Kennebunkport) and Connecticut (Farmington) in the summer, and New York (Schenectady, Batavia, and Long Lake) in the fall.

Contact: John J. Hodgins, 117 Ross St., P.O. Box 911, Batavia, NY 14020.

KALI WORKSHOPS AND
HISTORIC MONUMENTS PRESERVATION COURSE
Káli Basin Environment Protection Society
Mérték and Kánon Architectural Studios
Kovágóörs, Hungary

Two-week courses in July and August

Established in 1988, this summer program consists of a variety of crafts workshops for all levels and a two-week course in historic monuments preservation for university students and graduates with an interest in architecture or ethnology. The courses are taught in both English and German and are organized in groups of 10 to 20 students with a student to teacher ratio of 4 to 1. In addition to scheduled activities, participants are invited to wine cellars and artists' studios in the Káli Basin and visit Tihany and Budapest. A public exhibition of students' work concludes each course.

The crafts workshops, offered during three two-week periods in July and August, are sponsored by the Káli Basin Environment Protection Society. The emphasis is on both traditional techniques and new processes in such subjects as drawing, painting, photography, graphics, weaving, leather work, dressmaking, ceramics, and woodcarving. The daily schedule includes four-hour morning workshops and evening lectures that revolve around the theme of contemporary and conventional folk art and music in Hungarian and universal culture. Late night activities include movies, camp-fires, folk dancing, and folk music.

The historic monuments preservation course, offered for two weeks in August and sponsored by the Mérték and Kánon Architectural Studios, provides a detailed introduction to Hungarian theory and methodology, as well as art history, archeology, and restoration. Included in the twelve days of study and two days of excursions are 40 hours of research, surveying, and planning exercises and 20 lectures, with equal emphasis on theory and practical issues. Students receive instruction in preservation of dwellings, press-houses, and common buildings, from historical and sociologic research to technical surveying and planning to the final execution. They also observe such traditional building processes as adobe plastering and roof thatching.

Specialties: Drawing, painting, photography, graphics, weaving, leather work, dressmaking, ceramics, and woodcarving; historic monuments preservation.

Faculty: The crafts workshops are taught by local working artists and craftsmen. The historic monuments preservation course is taught by the architects and art historians of Mérték Architectural Studio and Kánon Architectural Studio with visiting lecturers from the Budapest Technical University and museum and environmental protection experts of Veszprém County.

Costs, Accommodations: The fee, which includes course materials, evening activities, and medical insurance, is $400 for the crafts workshops, $500 for the historic monuments preservation course. Double accommodations with bath in a restored summer cottage are $195 and board (breakfast and dinner) is $85. Discounts are available for tour organizers.

Location, Facilities: The courses are held in the Lake Balaton region of Hungary, an area of rolling hills, vineyards, historic architecture, and fine cuisine. Studios are in a restored building with modern audio-visual equipment. Students can bathe, wind-surf, and sail on Lake Balaton; cycle, hike, ride horseback, and play tennis in the Káli Basin Environment Protection Area; and fish in Kornyi Lake.

Contact for craft workshops: Káli Basin Environment Protection Society, 8254 Kovágóörs, Pf 9 Hungary. **Contact for historic monuments preservation course:** Mérték and Kánon Architectural Studios, 1075 Budapest, Majakovszkij utca 17 Hungary; (36) 1-427-134/425-303.

KEES HOOGENDAM CERAMIC WORKSHOPS
Oosterwolde, Netherlands
Five-day summer workshops

Since 1979, Kees Hoogendam has taught ceramics workshops for beginning and advanced ceramists. Approximately four workshops are offered during July and August, each scheduled from 10 am to 5 pm, Monday through Friday, with a mid-week excursion to a local museum. Each week focuses on a specific theme, such as primitive and traditional pottery, raku, reduction stoneware and porcelain, or salt glazing. Instruction covers clay preparation, glazing, handbuilding, throwing, and kiln building and firing techniques with gas, oil, and wood.

Specialties: Ceramics.

Faculty: Kees Hoogendam has worked as a potter since 1968.

Costs, Accommodations: Course fee, which includes materials, is 200 Dutch Florins. Live-in lodging at the workshop is an additional 200 Florins. Payment is due at the beginning of the workshop and refund is granted for cancellations received more than two weeks prior.

Location: The workshop is located southeast of Friesland, near Groningen and Leeuwarden, and may be reached by train to Assen and by bus to Oosterwolde. Regional attractions include museums, architectural monuments, and lakes.

Contact: Kees Hoogendam, De Knolle 3A, 8431 RJ Oosterwolde (Fochteloo), Netherlands, (31) 05160-88238.

KELLY PLACE
Cortez, Colorado
One and two-week workshops in July and August

Founded by George and Sue Kelly in 1965, Kelly Place, a living history and archaeological education facility in southwestern Colorado, offers summer workshops in Sand Canyon Primitive Pottery and Native Weaving. Each workshop is open to approximately 24 participants of all levels, who can enroll for either one or two weeks.

The pottery workshop, offered twice each summer, is designed to teach the techniques used in gathering clays and creating prehistoric Anasazi pottery in authentic surroundings. The program includes lectures on prehistoric culture, clay getting, and pottery making with pregathered clays and includes tours of trading posts, archeological sites, and Anasazi cliff dwellings. Students are taught a variety of clay processes and firing methods so that they can replicate the pottery and work on individual projects using clays, pigments, tools, and fuels from the workshop area. The weaving workshop, also offered twice each summer, covers loom construction, hand spinning and dyeing using natural materials, and Navajo methods of designing with wool.

Hands-on workshops in landscape gardening and horticulture, portrait photography, draft horse harness and hitching, and Southwest archaeology are also offered as well as opportunities to excavate and restore Indian ruins under the supervision of an archeologist, visit nearby cliff dwellings and national parks and monuments, and practice the farming and ranching principles of early Colorado families.

Specialties: Anasazi pottery and Navajo weaving.

Faculty: Professional craftsmen.

Costs, Accommodations: The $500 weekly workshop fee includes room and board at Kelly Place. A 20% nonrefundable deposit is required 60 days in advance with balance due on arrival.

Location: Kelly Place, a 100-acre re-creation of a 19th century pioneer's farm in the Red Rocks Desert is in the southwestern corner of Colorado, midway between Mesa Verde and Hovenweep. Within the property is McElmo Canyon, the site of at least five Indian communities dating back 1,000 years or more.

Contact: Kelly Place, 14663 County Road G, Cortez, CO 81321; (303) 565-3125.

KONIS ART WORKSHOP
A variety of locations in the Southwest U.S. and Mexico
Two to seven-day workshops year-round

Since 1969, Ben Konis has offered pastel and oil workshops, each limited to 25 artists of all levels. Sponsored by arts organizations, the more than 20 programs scheduled annually cover landscape painting, portraiture, figure, and still life, with emphasis on draughtsmanship, color schemes, and technique combining an impressionistic and realistic approach. Demonstrations and individual assistance are a part of each session.

Specialties: Pastel and oil painting.

Faculty: Ben Konis specializes in the art of the Southwest. His work has appeared in *American Artist*, *Southwest Art*, and *New Mexico Magazine* and has won such honors as the Best Pastel gold medal in the Texas 150th Anniversary exhibition.

Costs, Accommodations: Fees and accommodations vary, depending on sponsor and location. A typical five-day workshop is $225 and deposit is $75. Credit cards (Visa, MasterCard) accepted. Konis workshops for groups and organizations range from $50 per person for a two to three-day workshop to $200 per person for a five-day workshop, plus transportation.

Location: An annual summer workshop is held at Carrizo Lodge in Ruidoso, New Mexico, and other seminars are held throughout the Southwest and in the Mexican villages of San Miguel de Allende and Puerto Vallerta. Facilities are handicapped accessible.

Contact: Ben Konis, 712 W. 17th Ave., Amarillo, TX 79102; (806) 373-8458.

LA ROMITA SCHOOL OF ART, INC.
Terini, Italy
Two to four-week programs

Founded in 1966, La Romita School of Art offers four summer painting and sketching programs, each taught by a prominent artist, that range from two to four weeks and are geared for the serious beginner to the advanced student. Emphasis is on developing visual expression and skills in the student's medium of choice, both on-location and in the school's studio, and evenings are devoted to preparatory critiques, discussion sessions, and slide presentations. Additional activities include bus tours of the region's hill towns and visits to museums and such Renaissance cities as Pisa and Florence or Siena and San Gimignano.

Specialties: Painting, drawing.

Faculty: Has included watercolorists Lisa Guthrie, a past president of the Marin Arts Guild, who studied watercolor with Richard Yip, Rex Brandt, Robert E. Wood, and George Post; and Betty Lynch, winner of a Texas Watercolor Society Show purchase prize and the 1987 American Watercolor Society's Ed Whitney Award; and full-time painter and experienced teacher Tom Mulder.

Costs, Accommodations: Tuition, which includes double occupancy lodging, most meals, and ground transportation, ranges from $1,300 to $2,300. A $250 deposit must accompany application with balance due eight weeks prior. Written cancellations more than 30 days prior receive a full refund less $50; thereafter a 30% penalty is charged. Students are housed in dormitory rooms in La Romita and meals are served on an open porch.

Location: A 16th century monastery that has been converted to modern quarters, La Romita is situated in the Umbrian mountainside above Terni, a few miles from Spoleto, Orvieto, Perugia, Assisi, Viterbo, Todi, and Lake Piediluco.

Contact: La Romita School of Art, Inc., 1712 Old Town NW, Albuquerque, NM 87104; (505) 243-1924.

LEECH STUDIO WORKSHOPS
Friends of the Arts and Sciences
Sarasota, Florida and scenic locales

Three and four-day workshops and one to two-week travel programs year-round

The Friends of the Arts and Sciences, a nonprofit organization chartered in 1963 by a group that grew up around the late watercolorist Hilton Leech, has offered art demonstrations, classes, and workshops since 1976 in the studio that housed his art school. The annual program includes demonstrations, classes, exhibitions, workshops devoted to sketching, painting, and photography, as well as arts travel workshops with a nature focus. Most workshops are scheduled from 9:30 am to 3:30 pm, Monday through Thursday, January through March, and include demonstrations, group critiques and individual instruction.

Arts nature trips, open to anyone interested in nature-oriented travel, visit scenic and photogenic locales. A series of sketching and painting workshop/ trips, "On the Trail of Winslow Homer", visits areas painted by the turn-of-the-century American artist.

Specialties: Watermedia, painting, sketching, photography.

Faculty: Includes such accomplished artists and writers as Frank Webb, A.W.S., author of *Watercolor Energies*; Barbara Nechis, A.W.S., author of *Watercolor, The Creative Experience*; Judi Betts, N.W.S., author of *Watercolor, Let's Think About It*; Valfred Thelin, A.W.S.-N.W.S., author of *Watercolor: Let the Medium Do It*; Maxine Masterfield, A.W.S., author of *Painting the Spirit of Nature*; Fred Messersmith, A.W.S., who has been featured in *American Artist* magazine; and Emily Holmes, who collaborated with Hilton Leech on his book, *The Joys of Watercolor*.

Costs, Accommodations: Tuition ranges from $50 for a three-morning workshop to $150 for four days. A $10 nonrefundable deposit must accompany registration. Trip costs vary, depending on length and locale.

Location: Sarasota, on Florida's Gulf Coast, has many cultural facilities and attractions. Art trips have visited such locations as Tucson, Nova Scotia and Prince Edward Island, and Alaska. "On the Trail of Winslow Homer" locales include Homosassa, Florida; Prouts Neck, Maine; the Bahama Islands; Bermuda; Tynemouth, England; and Quebec, Canada.

Contact: Friends of the Arts and Sciences, P.O. Box 15766, Sarasota, FL 34277-1766; (813) 923-3031/924-5770.

LEELANAU ENRICHMENT PROGRAMS
Glen Arbor, Michigan
One-week workshops in July and August

Established in 1982, The Leelanau Center for Education sponsors summer art workshops, a writers conference, and outdoor natural history classrooms that include nature photography. Approximately a half-dozen Deer-track Art Workshops are offered during July, including such titles as Painting the Landscapes of Leelanau; Collage: An Abstract Approach, which combines collage with paint and other media and focuses on a variety of motifs; and On Location in Leelanau County, an opportunity to sketch and paint at several sites.

Specialties: Painting in a variety of media.

Faculty: Has included Paul St. Denis, former director of the summer art program at Interlochen Center for the Arts and professor of art at The

Cleveland Institute of Art; Pat Norton, a juror and teacher in Michigan and Wisconsin who is affiliated with The Clearing; and Charles Murphy, a Traverse City artist specializing in watercolors..

Costs, Accommodations: The $180 enrollment fee includes lunches and local transportation and room and board ranges from $175 to $290. A $100 deposit must accompany application. Full refund, less $15 fee, is granted cancellations more than 30 days prior; cancellations within 30 days forfeit deposit. Accommodations consist of on-campus single or double dormitories and rustic cabins sleeping six. Meals are served cafeteria style.

Location: The Center is located on 83 acres of forest within Sleeping Bear Dunes National Lakeshore, 30 miles west of Traverse City. Facilities include a library, tennis courts, a private beach on Lake Michigan, and canoes.

Contact: Leelanau Enrichment Programs, One Old Homestead Rd., Glen Arbor, MI 49636; (616) 334-3072.

LIGHTHOUSE ART CENTER (LAC)
Crescent City, California
Two to five-day workshops from February-October

Established in 1986 as a nonprofit local arts corporation, the Lighthouse Art Center hosts more than 60 workshops annually in a variety of arts and crafts topics. Most workshops are open to all levels while some are for intermediate or advanced artists. Topics include color pencil drawing, cartooning, sculpture, woodcarving, basketry, etched glass, printmaking, jewelry making, and fish, songbird, and decoy carving. Several workshops are devoted to the various aspects of painting, such as portrait and figure, landscape, seascapes, florals, wildlife, and Western and Oriental themes. The student to instructor ratio and daily schedule vary with each workshop. Sessions are usually scheduled from 9 am to 4 pm and evening activities may include slide presentations and lectures.

Specialties: A variety of arts and crafts, including painting, woodcarving, basketry, printmaking, jewelry making, and etched glass.

Faculty: Consists of prominent artists and craftspeople from throughout the U.S., who may include fish carver Bob Berry, songbird carver Peter Kaune, cartoonist Jim Snook, realist oil painter Dale Gehrman, printmaker Steven L. Ball, impressionist Gail Robinson, pastel artist Ben Konis, watercolorists Dorothy Barta, Barbara Janusz, Julie Simmons, Judith Campbell-Reed, Kolan Peterson, Stan Miller, Naomi Brotherton, Duane Light, Maxine Masterfield, and Jan Kunz.

Costs, Accommodations: Tuition ranges from $135 to $300 and materials are extra. A 50% tuition deposit, of which $60 is nonrefundable, must accompany registration with balance due 30 days prior. A list of nearby accommodations is provided.

Location: The Lighthouse Art Center consists of a gallery and studio space housed in a restored 1949 dance hall on U.S. Highway 101 — the Redwood Highway — across from the Crescent City Harbor. Facilities are handicapped accessible. The community is located in Del Norte County, the northernmost and one of the smallest California counties.

Contact: Lighthouse Art Center, 575 Redwood Highway 101 South, Crescent City, CA 95531; (707) 464-4137.

THE LITTLE ACORN: A QUILT EMPORIUM
Kensington, Connecticut
One-day workshops year-round

Established in 1986, The Little Acorn offers a variety of one-day quilting workshops and two to five-session classes, each limited to four to six participants of all levels. Workshops are scheduled on Saturdays from 10 am until 1 to 3 pm or weeknights from 7 to 9 pm in a teaching area of the retail establishment. Topics include various patterns and techniques, color and design, aging quilts, and fabric-covered boxes.

Specialties: Quilting.

Faculty: Includes professional quilters and teachers Pat Karambay, proprietor of The Little Acorn and Connecticut winner of the Great American Quilt Contest; Barbara Wysocki, newsletter editor of the New England Quilt Museum; and Greater Hartford Quilt Guild president Judy White, past president Mickey Lawler, and vice president Christine Goldschmidt.

Costs: Tuition ranges from $25 to $40.

Contact: The Little Acorn, 1204 Farmington Ave., Kensington, CT 06037; (203) 828-1193.

THE LOOM SHED SCHOOL OF WEAVING
Oberlin, Ohio
Individualized half-day to five-day courses year-round

Established in 1980 by Charles A. Lermond, The Loom Shed retail establishment and weaving studio offers a variety of weaving courses for all levels. Sessions are scheduled daily from 9 am until 5 pm and each student follows a curriculum tailored to his or her specific needs. Course titles include Basic Weaving (five days or more); Drafting (one to three days), including the use of computers; Rug Weaving (five days or more), in which students complete rugs in twill and summer/winter weaves; Overshot Weaving (five days), covering the variations in treadling techniques; Shaft-Switching (five days or more), which works with a four-harness loom with a working equivalent of 30-70 harnesses; Moorman Technique (three to five days), a double weave/double-warp 4-harness technique; and Summer/Winter (five days), a special case of three/one twill.

Specialties: Weaving.

Faculty: Charles Lermond received an Ohio Arts Council Individual Artists Fellowship for 1988, his weaving represented the State of Ohio at Convergence '86, and he is instructor at Convergence '90. Author of articles in the *Weaver's Journal*, including one on Overshot Weaving, he demonstrates weaving at local schools and has had his work shown at the Gund Gallery and other exhibits.

Costs, Accommodations: Tuition is $125 for Monday morning to Friday afternoon, including some evenings; tuition and room and board in the Lermond home is $200 (no smoking). Shorter sessions are $30 per day or $18 for three hours. Materials are extra and available at The Loom Shed. Workshops for groups are $150 per day plus expenses.

Location: The Loom Shed is situated south and east of Oberlin's business district, one block east of Rte. 58 between Edison and Hamilton Streets.

Contact: The Loom Shed, 278 S. Pleasant St., Oberlin, OH 44074; (216) 774-3500.

MAINE COAST ART WORKSHOPS
Port Clyde, Maine

Four and five-day workshops from June-September

Since 1984, Merle Donovan has sponsored painting workshops taught by prominent artists. More than a dozen workshops are held during the summer months, each limited to 20 artists of all levels. Media include watercolor, oil, watermedia, pastel, and acrylic.

Specialties: Landscape, figure, and portrait painting.

Faculty: Has included Judi Betts, Gerald Brommer, Roberta Carter Clark, Alan Flattman, Serge Hollerbach, Cathy Johnson, Charles Movalli, Barbara Nechis, Tom Nicholas, Ron Ranson, Christopher Schink, Betty Lou Schlemm, Don Stone, Robert A. Wade, Frank Webb, and Frederick Wong.

Costs, Accommodations: Tuition of $295 includes model fee. A $75 deposit must accompany enrollment with balance due four weeks prior. A full refund less $30 fee is granted cancellations more than six week prior, thereafter only if space can be filled. A list of accommodations is provided. Single rooms start at $35 per night.

Location: Port Clyde, located on a 13 mile-long peninsula off the Maine coast, is accessible via Greyhound Bus from Portland Airport to Thomaston. The closest airport is Knox County in Rockland, which is serviced by flights from Portland and Boston.

Contact: Ms. Merle Donovan, Maine Coast Art Workshops, P.O. Box 236, Port Clyde, ME 04855; (207) 372-8200.

MAINE WATERCOLOR WORKSHOPS
WITH CARLTON PLUMMER
Boothbay, Maine

Two to six-day workshops the last three weeks in June

Since 1965, Carlton Plummer, A.W.S., has offered summer workshops that are limited to 20 artists with some knowledge of watercolors. Although the workshop is offered as a six-day program beginning with a Sunday evening reception and concluding the following Saturday morning, registrations are accepted for two days or more. The daily schedule from Monday through Friday includes a one-hour morning on-location demonstration and after lunch critique and discussion of the visual environment. Students paint on their own the rest of the day, receiving assistance and critique as needed, with emphasis on developing each individual's unique abilities.

Faculty: Former illustrator, art coordinator, combat artist, and University of Lowell painting professor Carlton Plummer earned an MFA from Boston University, is the recipient of more than 100 national painting awards, and is listed in *Who's Who in American Art*. A painter for more than 30 years, his work is part of museum, corporate, university, and private collections and is included in such painting books as *Learning From the Pros*, *Exploring Color*, and *Let the Media Do It*. He has written articles for *American Artist* and *Palette Talk*.

Costs, Accommodations: The six-day workshop fee, which includes lodging and five continental breakfasts, is $345. Tuition for nonresident day students is $45 per day, with a two-day minimum. A $100 deposit secures reservation with balance due on arrival. Refund, less $20, is granted cancellation at least 30 days prior. Lodging is provided in twin-bedded chalets with kitchen facilities.

Location: Boothbay is situated on the Maine Coast. The nearest airport is in Portland and the nearest Greyhound bus stop is in Wicasset, where pick-up can be arranged.

Contact: Carlton Plummer, 10 Monument Hill Rd., Chelmsford, MA 01824; (508) 256-7937.

MARBLE & ART INSTITUTE and LA CORTE DELLA MINIERA
Italy

Three and four-week sessions from June-September

Established in 1986, the Marble & Art Institute offers four consecutive four-week summer workshops, each limited to five to twelve beginning to advanced artists (with one or two instructors plus an assistant), that focus on the sculpting of marble and other stones. The course includes twice weekly lessons on marble technique with detailed demonstrations and lectures, art theory and criticism discussions, and visits to marble studios and foundries, a handmade tool factory, and a working marble quarry. Studio work hours are from 8 am to 5 pm, Monday through Friday.

Begun in 1990, La Corte della Miniera workshop in etching, lithography, and ceramics consists of three three-week sessions, each limited to seven to fifteen students of all levels who work with one instructor and one or two technicians.

Specialties: Sculpting, with emphasis on marble; printmaking, ceramics.

Faculty: Marble & Art Institute faculty includes Lynne Streeter, an experienced sculptor who received her MFA from the University of California-Berkeley; Pasquale Martini, who received an MA from Penne Institute and teaches at the State Artistic School in Varese; and Cesare Riva, who attended Milan's Castello Sforzesco Art School. La Corte della Miniera faculty is selected from prominent exhibiting American and European artists.

Costs, Accommodations: The Marble & Art Institute fee of $2,700 per session includes hotel lodging, two meals daily, studio space, and some related trips. Materials and tools are additional. A deposit of $700 must accompany registration, with a $1,000 installment due April 1 and balance prior to May 15. Full refund, less $400, is granted cancellations received in writing prior to April 1; cancellations between April 1 and May 1 are charged an $700 fee; no refunds thereafter unless space can be filled. La Corte della Miniera fee of $2,300 per session includes accommodations in mini-apartment, three meals daily, studio space, and tools and materials. An $800 deposit must accompany registration with balance due by May 1. Full refund, less $300, is granted cancellations received in writing prior to April 1; cancellations between April 1 and May 1 are charged an $800 fee; no refunds thereafter unless space can be filled.

Location: Marble & Art Institute workshops are held in a spacious studio located in Pietrasanta, a small northern Tuscany town that is noted for its local marble. Nearby cities include Florence, Pisa, and Lucca. La Corte della Miniera workshops are held in newly-constructed studios on the site of an old sulphur mine in the central Italian countryside near Urbino, which is conveniently located for trips to Venice, Rome, and Florence.

Contact: Lynne Streeter, 627 Adams St., Albany, CA 94706; (415) 524-7115 *or* c/o Casella Postale 244, 55045 Pietrasanta (LU), Italy; (39) 0584 71436 (from May 25-Oct. 1).

THE MARCHUTZ SCHOOL OF PAINTING AND DRAWING
Institute for American Universities (IAU)
Aix-en-Provence and Avignon, France
Six-week summer program

Established in 1972 as an outgrowth of the teachings of painter, lithographer, and Cézannien Leo Marchutz, who advocated the study of the masters and of nature as the path to self-discovery for the artist, The Marchutz School offers a full academic year program, divided into two semesters (September-December and January-May), and a drawing and painting summer program from mid-June to the end of July. All programs are open to beginning to advanced students, who receive instruction according to their specific needs. The student to instructor ratio is about 7 to 1.

The summer program offers a foundation in drawing and painting, encouraging the student to observe and interpret nature and acquire the skills and self-discipline required for sustained creative work. Most work is done from landscape, the model, still life, architecture, and reproductions of masterpieces. Watercolor, oil, and gouache are suggested for painting and pencil and lithographic crayon for drawing. Formal classes are held Monday through Thursday mornings from 9 am until noon and students are expected to work independently in the afternoons. Fridays are reserved for field trips to Arles, Montpellier, Marseille, and the Luberon. While instruction is in English, daily French conversation classes are available.

Specialties: Painting and drawing in the European tradition.

Faculty: American artists, who have been painting and teaching in France for several years and who have either studied with Leo Marchutz or earned the Certificat d'Etudes from The Marchutz School, include school director Alan Roberts, assistant director John Gasparach, and painting and drawing instructors Samuel Ernest Bjorklund and James Toub.

Costs, Accommodations: Six-week tuition, which includes field trips and health insurance, is $1,300 and a nonrefundable $25 fee must accompany application. For college-age students, room and half board (room only) in French homes is $820 ($540). Older students may stay in a studio apartment, which ranges from 3,000 FF to 6,000 FF, or a one or two-star hotel, which ranges from 8,400 FF to 16,000 FF. Cancellations receive a full refund (except $25 fee) prior to May 1, an 80% refund from May 1 to June 1, no refund thereafter.

Location: Students may take the summer program in either Aix-en-Provence or Avignon, located in the Rhône Valley in the south of France. The school in Aix is located on the Route du Tholonet in the atelier designed for Leo Marchutz by the noted architect Fernand Pouillon. The site is near Mont St. Victoire and Châteaunoir, whose motifs were painted by Cézanne. The workshops in Avignon are held on the third floor of the ancient restored Chapelle Saint Antoine, in the heart of the city, a cultural center and site of the International Summer Festival of Drama, Cinema, and Dance. Six units of academic credit may be granted through the student's home university.

Contact: Art in Provence, Institute for American Universities, 27, Place de l'Université, 13625 Aix-en-Provence, Cédex, France; (33) 42 23 39 35.

MARLBOROUGH COLLEGE SUMMER SCHOOL
Marlborough, Wiltshire, England
One-week courses in July and August

Since 1976, Marlborough College has offered a three-week summer school of Sunday to Saturday residential and day courses that cover a variety of subjects including arts and crafts. Two-hour morning and afternoon sessions are scheduled daily and participants may elect two half-day courses or one full-day course each week. A special children's program for ages 7 to 13 and 13 to 16, which combines special courses and recreation, affords parents the opportunity to pursue their own activities. Evening activities consist of concerts, lectures, films, dances, and end-of-week entertainment.

Typical course titles include Basketry and Chair Seating, which emphasizes basic techniques and the use of such natural materials as rush, willow, and cane; Dolls' Houses and Miniatures (sessions for both adults and ages 13 to 16), which concentrates on electrifying and decorating of a doll house or construction of detailed furniture pieces as well as instruction in the use of hand and power tools; Woodcrafts, which covers woodturning, elementary cabinet making, and simple repairs; Basic Pottery, which explores the expressive qualities of clay rather than producing a finished piece; China Restoration, which consists of a basic course devoted to such skills as cleaning, bonding, making missing pieces, drilling, moulding, painting, and glazing and an intermediate course where students work on their own pieces under guidance in a workshop setting; Basic Bookbinding, an overview of the different methods of binding and repair including pulling, resewing, endpapering, casemaking, and casing-in hardcover books; and Rag Dolls, which demonstrates the use of a variety of materials to produce dolls.

Specialties: A variety of arts and crafts topics.

Faculty: Summer School instructors are experts in their fields and many are drawn from the teaching staff of the College.

Costs, Accommodations: Resident weekly tuition, which includes all meals and lodging inclusive of VAT, ranges from £220 to £265; nonresident weekly course fees range from £68 (single half-day) to £130 (full-day or two half-day); children's program is £62 to £118. Cancellations are subject to a £15 per person administration charge and no refunds are given after June 1. Accommodations are in single rooms and dormitories and some double and family rooms are available; children are housed in single sex dormitories near their parents. Meals are served cafeteria-style in the College dining hall.

Location: The College, a prominent independent boarding school, is located in the small country town of Wiltshire, about a one-hour drive from Bath, Bristol, Oxford, Salisbury, Stratford, Southampton, and Heathrow Airport.

Contact: Summer School, Marlborough College, Marlborough, Wiltshire SN8 1PA, England; (44) 0672 53888.

MARTIN HOMER SCHOOL OF POTTERY AND PAINTING
Tenbury Wells. Worcestershire, England

Weekend workshops in May, June, and October; one-week workshops in July and August

Established in 1981, this school offers small group pottery and painting courses for beginners to experienced amateurs. One-week courses, which begin with Sunday dinner and end after breakfast on Saturday, are offered each week during July and August; weekend courses, which begin with Friday dinner and end Sunday evening, are offered once or twice monthly during May and June and weekly during October. The daily schedule is usually from 10 am to 1 pm and 2 to 5 pm and the size of each class is limited to eight students per instructor.

The painting course features practical demonstrations and talks on the application of various media (oil, watercolor, pastel, pen and wash, and sketching) and techniques (composition, line, texture, tone, and colour mixing). Subjects include the local landscape and studio still life subjects, such as rural artifacts, farm implements, flowers, and natural forms. The course concludes with an appraisal and discussion of each student's work.

The pottery course begins with a lump of clay (usually stoneware) and goes through the various stages of throwing, pulling handles and spouts, turning and modelling, to the final glazed and fired pot. Instructions are given in handbuilding by slab and coil as well as press moulding and decorating. At the end of the week, each student's five best pots are fired and glazed.

Specialties: Painting (landscape and still life) and pottery making.

Faculty: Proprietor Martin Homer, an established potter, teaches the pottery courses. Brian Tandy, N.D.D., and Eve Gregory, N.D.D., teach painting.

Costs, Accommodations: The £198 (£79) cost of the one-week (weekend) courses includes double occupancy room and full board and up to five (two) canvas boards or watercolor papers for painting students or the five (two) best pots glazed and fired for the pottery students. Single supplement is £25 (£8). A £30 nonrefundable deposit secures booking with balance due four weeks prior. Students are lodged and eat breakfast and dinner at three nearby country houses; lunch is served at the school. Nonresident students are welcome.

Location, Facilities: Lower Aston House, a 17th century farmhouse set in a large garden, has newly converted pottery and painting studios situated in the barn and hop kilns attached to the house. Each pottery student has individual equipment and a seated kick wheel. Nearby painting subjects include hop fields, river scenes, water mills, ancient churches, and timber-framed houses. The school is located two miles from the small market town of Tenbury Wells and nine miles from Ludlow.

Contact: Martin Homer, Lower Aston House, Aston Bank, Knighton-on-Teme, Tenbury Wells, Worcestershire, WR15 8LW, England; (44) 058479 404.

MASTER WORKSHOP IN ART
Long Island University
Southampton, New York

Four-week summer workshop

Long Island University offers a four-week practical and in-depth studio workshop limited to 35 artists who have mastered the basic techniques of painting, drawing, and sculpture. Those selected live and work in shared studios on the campus and have the opportunity to interact with a faculty of distinguished visiting artists. The program includes critiques, discussions, and visits to the artists' studios. An instructional printing workshop, which focuses on unique methods of monotype, is conducted once a week by a master printmaker.

The University also offers one and two-week summer fine arts workshops for artists of all levels, with sessions scheduled for four hours each weekday morning. Typical titles include Landscape Painting & Drawing, Weaving, and Primitive Pottery Techniques (Sawdust/Sagger Firing and Raku Firing).

Specialties: Painting and drawing, ceramics, weaving.

Faculty: Visiting artists include Larry Rivers, Eric Fischl, Miriam Schapiro, April Gornik, Bob Dash, Dan Welden, Steve Wood, Berenice D'Vorzon, Leslie Neumann, Alexander Russo, and Katherine Carter.

Costs, Accommodations: The $1,550 tuition includes dormitory housing and cafeteria-style meals; cost for nonresident students is $1,050. Application must include five to ten slides of student's work, a letter describing educational background and reasons for wishing to attend the program, and a $10 fee. Four undergraduate or graduate credits are available.

Location: The 110-acre campus, which is located in the Hamptons of eastern Long Island, overlooks Shinnecock Bay and the Atlantic Ocean and is accessible to major museums, galleries, and noted artists and critics. The campus is regularly served by the Long Island Railroad and jitney service to New York City. Facilities include athletic playing fields, tennis courts, fitness trails, and pool.

Contact: Ann Chwatsky, Master Workshop in Art, Fine Arts Dept., L.I.U. Southampton Campus, Southampton, NY 11968; (516) 283-4000, ext. 427.

METCHOSIN INTERNATIONAL SUMMER SCHOOL OF THE ARTS (M.I.S.S.A.)
Victoria, British Columbia, Canada
Two-week school in late June-early July

Established in 1985, this two-week school offers approximately ten weekend to two-week specialized intensive courses for serious and professional artists and teachers. The teaching approach is of a diagnostic nature with the aim to encourage a greater understanding of the arts in general and personal growth in the areas of study. Most courses are limited to 12 students with at least a basic knowledge and some instructors require applicants to submit a portfolio and curriculum vitae prior to admission. Course topics include basketry, ceramics, papermaking, silk painting, woodcuts, fabric collage, raku pottery, Mandala painting, watercolor painting, and drawing and vision. Evening activities include slide presentations, lectures by visiting artists, films, readings, seminars, and concerts.

Typical workshop titles include Ceramics — Glaze and Colour Development, a combination of daily lectures and practical work including one day of museum study at the Art Gallery of Greater Victoria; The Basket as Sculpture: Concept to Completion, which focuses on developing a basket from a variety of materials; Hand Papermaking, which explores the use of plant fiber as a culture medium through traditional European, Oriental, and contemporary casting techniques; Advanced Japanese Woodcut Printmaking, covering multiple block printing and experimental surfaces and processes; and Introduction to Silk Painting, which covers contemporary dyeing and resist techniques for silk.

Specialties: Ceramics, drawing, painting, textiles, printmaking, and other crafts.

Faculty: The changing faculty of distinguished artists and teachers has included basket maker Len Bentham, whose work has appeared in *American Craft Magazine* and is in private collections; Raku potter Walter Dexter, who won a silver medal at the Prague International Ceramics Exhibition; Saidye Bronfman Award-winning ceramist Robin Hopper; artist Glenn E. Howarth, a Fellow of the Royal Canadian Academy of Art; watercolorist Flemming Jorgensen, who teaches at Pearson College and the University of Victoria; silk painter Bill Morton, who serves on the faculty of the Alberta College of Art; woodcutter Noburo Sawai, who has won eight grants and awards and has had 15 solo exhibitions; fabric artist Marion Spanjerdt, who has exhibited in Holland and Canada; Mandala painter Jack Wise; and papermaker Sharyn Yuen, proprietor of Kakali Handmade Papers.

Costs, Accommodations: Tuition is C$250 for the two-week course (ten days of instruction), C$125 for one week (five days instruction), and C$75 for a weekend workshop, which includes lunches. Materials fee for ceramics course is C$50. Dormitory housing and three meals are C$53 per day double, C$62 per day single occupancy. Day students in the two-week courses pay C$185 for two weeks, which includes use of studios and college facilities, lunches, and refreshments. A C$100 deposit required with application is refundable only if student is not accepted or notice of cancellation is received at least one month prior. Balance, payable in Canadian funds, is due in advance.

Location, Facilities: The summer school is held on the campus of Lester B. Pearson College of the Pacific, set on the wooded hillside of an inlet to Pedder Bay on Vancouver Island, a 45-minute drive west of Victoria. Campus facilities include tennis courts, a heated pool, canoes, boat docks, fishing, and nature trails. Victoria is accessible through Victoria Airport, which has regularly scheduled flights from Vancouver and Seattle.

Contact: Elizabeth Travis, Administrator, Metchosin International Summer School of the Arts, 911a Linden Ave., Victoria, BC, V8V 4G8, Canada; (604) 384-1698.

MINNEAPOLIS COLLEGE OF ART AND DESIGN (MCAD) CONTINUING STUDIES
Summer Arts for Teens
Minneapolis, Minnesota
Two-week courses in June and July

MCAD Continuing Studies sponsors Summer Arts for Teens, a series of summer courses designed for ages 13 to 16. Sessions meet for 2 1/2 to 3 hours in the morning or afternoon, Monday through Friday, and cover such subjects as fine arts, papermaking, and mixed media. Typical courses include Color Theory, in which participants use paints and colored paper to learn the use of color and its application to all the arts; Drawing I, which explores fundamental visual elements using ink, pencil, charcoal, and pastels; Drawing II, which examines traditional and experimental techniques using such media as graphite, gouache, watercolor, and pastels for still lifes and landscapes; Painting, designed to encourage individual creativity and develop skills using oils or acrylics; Mixed Media: Self Portraits Inside Out, in which participants study the self-portraits of many artists and then create their own 3-D self portrait image as well as personal items that have special meaning; Papermaking, which begins with the basic skills and then moves on to pulp painting and assemblage, hand papermaking, and such decorative paper techniques as marbling, suminagashi, and fish prints; Sulpture, in which students work with a variety of materials — from cardboard to welded steel — to explore techniques and how content and subject matter can define their work; and Photography and Video.

MCAD, part of an arts complex that includes the Minneapolis Institute of Arts and the Children's Theatre, also offers a summer schedule of day and evening design and fine arts classes and a one-week Elderhostel program covering such subjects as drawing, painting, and art history.

Specialties: Color theory, drawing, painting, mixed media, papermaking, sculpture, photography.

Faculty: Has included Julie Baugnet (drawing), a 1981 State of Alaska Fellowship Award recipient; Amanda Degener (papermaking), who has taught at Haystack School, Women's Studio Workshop, and Minnesota Center for Book Arts; Gail Jacobson (drawing and color theory), who has taught at the University of Minnesota and Washington University; Leslie Hawk (sculpture), a 1988 Jerome Foundation Fellow and Minnesota State Arts Board grant recipient; Jacqueline Kielkopf (painting), a 1984 McKnight Foundation Fellowship and 1985 Bush Foundation Fellowship recipient; Barbara Kreft (mixed media:self-portraits), a McKnight Foundation Fellowship recipient whose work is included in such collections as Citicorp and First Bank Minneapolis.

Costs: Tuition is $135 and some courses also have a lab fee ranging from $5 to $10. Full refund, less $15 registration fee, is granted cancellations prior to start of class; a 75% and 50% refund is granted prior to the second and third class meeting, respectively; no refunds thereafter. Credit cards (VISA, MasterCard) accepted. Financial assistance is available through the Summer

Scholarship for Academic Enrichment Program. Membership is available in the Minneapolis Institute of Arts (MIA) and members receive a 10% tuition discount.

Location: MCAD is located just south of downtown Minneapolis in the Fine Arts Complex, which includes the College, the Minneapolis Institute of Arts, and the Children's Theatre.

Contact: Continuing Studies, Minneapolis College of Art and Design, 2501 Stevens Ave. South, Minneapolis, MN 55404; (612) 874-3765, (800) 872-6223 (in Minnesota), (800) 874-6223 (out of state).

MOON FISH SUMMER PROGRAM IN THE ARTS
Oregon Coast Community College
Yachats, Oregon
One to two weeks in August

Established in 1989, this annual program for artists and writers of all levels provides a forum for those interested in the creative process. Two to five-day workshops in painting and writing are featured as well as special presentations and art shows. Classes meet from 9 am until 4 pm on weekdays and the workshop culminates in a presentation of the week's accomplishments. Students paint on-location using a variety of media and have opportunities to schedule individual sessions with faculty members. Special workshops have included such topics as Japanese wood block printing.

Specialties: Painting, Japanese woodblock printing, and adjunct activities such as framing.

Faculty: Has included landscape artist Michael Gibbons, a member of Allied Artists of America, whose work has been exhibited in the U.S. and England; marine painter Phillip Schuster, who studied at the Chicago Academy of Arts, Northwestern Illinois University, and with Charles Vickery; and Paul Gunn, a specialist in wood block printing, who has taught at Oregon State University.

Costs, Accommodations: Workshop fee is $150. Cancellations more than a week prior forfeit $15; within the week prior 50% is refunded; no refunds thereafter. A limited number of scholarships are available. Upon registration, participants are provided with a list of nearby accommodations.

Location: An inn in Yachats, which is situated on the scenic Oregon Coast, 80 miles west of Eugene and 135 miles southwest of Portland, both of which are served by bus, rail, and air transportation.

Contact: Director, South County, Oregon Coast Community College, 322 SW Coast Hwy., Newport, OR 97365; (503) 265-2283 *or* 547-3122.

MORAVIAN POTTERY AND TILE WORKS
APPRENTICE/WORKSHOPS
Doylestown, Pennsylvania

Two 12-week apprentice/workshops annually

The Moravian Pottery and Tile Works, a National Historic Landmark, operates as a "living history" museum producing tiles in a manner similar to that employed in the early 1900's by its founder and builder, Henry Chapman Mercer. Devoting his life to preserving the arts and crafts of pre-industrial America, he learned pottery making as practiced by early Pennsylvania German settlers and established a successful tile factory. Following his death in 1930, a succession of owners ran the factory until it was purchased by the County of Bucks in 1967.

Since 1975, the Tile Works has offered apprentice/workshops that teach, through practical experience in a production setting, the tile-making methods of Henry Chapman Mercer and relate them to the needs and interests of ceramists working today. Two 12-week workshops are offered each year with each limited to three apprentices, who are accepted on the basis of previous experience (not necessarily in tile), direction of personal work, and commitment to the three days of tedious labor that follow a production schedule. Apprentices learn various forming and reproduction techniques, including mosaic making, moldwork, glaze application, sagger firing for controlled smoking of the clay body, and concrete installation. Slabs of red clay are rolled out and cut to form quarry tiles or mosaics or pressed into copies of Mercer's original molds to form decorative tiles. Some are then finished by being fired unglazed while others are fired, glazed, and fired again. Field trips of related interest are arranged throughout the program and each workshop concludes with an exhibition of apprentice work.

Specialties: Decorative and quarry tiles handcrafted according to the early methods of Henry Chapman Mercer, a major proponent of the American arts and crafts movement.

Faculty: The six-member full-time production staff is headed by ceramist Adam Zayas.

Costs: Apprentices work 24 hours per week in exchange for an hourly wage, studio space, and the use of materials and limited facilities for their own work. They are expected to use the studio independently, with instruction and critiques provided by the staff. Applicants are required to submit a resume, ten slides of previous work, and a statement of intent, which includes what is expected to be gained from the experience and what is hoped for in return.

Location: Located on Swamp Road (Rte. 313) next to Fonthill, Henry Mercer's 40-room home, which is now a National Historic Landmark and museum, the Tile Works is open to the public and offers self-guided tours throughout the day.

Contact: Moravian Pottery and Tile Works, Swamp Rd., Doylestown, PA 18901; (215) 345-6722.

MOREA WEAVING CENTER
Leonidion, Greece
Two-week courses from June-September

Established in 1984 by Katerina Kalamitsi, Morea Weaving Center offers weavers of all levels of experience the opportunity to spend two weeks with a Greek weaver in a Greek environment, learning about weaving as well as traditional and modern life in Greece. Three courses are offered: Traditional Greek Weaving Techniques (held three times each summer), Oriental Knotted Pile Carpets, and Kilim Weaving (both held once). Each course begins on Monday and is limited to eight participants, who spend a minimum of 60 hours in the studio. The daily schedule includes morning and evening classes and four hours in between for relaxation or swimming. Each course features an excursion to Nafplion with a visit to the Folk Art Museum and study of the costume, textile, and tool collections. One evening is devoted to Greek folk dancing, with a slide lecture and instruction.

In the Traditional Greek Weaving Techniques course, students learn finger manipulated and loom-controlled decorative techniques as well as methods for weaving rugs and clothing. They weave three rugs, a bag, an apron, a towel, and samples of cloth. Participants in the Oriental Knotted Pile Carpets course warp an upright loom and weave a pile rug. Looms, materials, dyes, knots, finishings, and carpet care are also covered. In the Kilim Weaving course, each student warps an upright loom and weaves a kilim, utilizing traditional patterns and techniques.

Specialties: Greek weaving techniques.

Faculty: A weaver since 1973, Katerina Kalamitsi has taught in Athens and in courses organized and financed by the Ministry of Agriculture and the EEC. She has also participated in research projects on old costumes and embroideries.

Costs, Accommodations: The cost of each course is approximately $950, which includes materials, lodging, continental breakfast, dinner, folk dancing, the Nafplion excursion, and transportation to and from Athens. A $230 nonrefundable deposit, payable by certified check, must accompany registration at least six weeks prior with balance due on arrival. Students are lodged in double bedded rooms with private baths at a hotel near the studio. Breakfast is served at the hotel and dinners are taken at local outdoor tavernas.

Location, Facilities: Leonidion, an Arcadian traditional settlement on the eastern coast of the Peloponnese, is a non-tourist town noted for its woven rugs. Inhabitants preserve the old traditions and the elderly people use a dialect derived from the ancient Doric language. The studio occupies a late 19th century house and is equipped with 15 horizontal floor looms and 9 upright looms.

Contact: Katerina Kalamitsi, Morea Weaving Center, 22300 Leonidion, Greece; (30) 0757 23124.

MOUNTS BAY ART CENTRE PAINTING AND DRAWING HOLIDAY COURSES
Newlyn, Penzance, Cornwall, England

One-week courses from May-October

Established in 1977, this art center offers approximately 15 summer landscape painting and drawing courses for beginning to experienced artists. Each course is limited to ten students, who arrive prior to Thursday dinner and depart the following Thursday after breakfast. Students can work outdoors on location or, when weather is inclement, paint or draw still lifes and portraits in the studio. The week's schedule for the painting course, which is offered most weeks, includes slide-illustrated lectures and demonstrations of materials, composition, color, and tone. The program for the drawing course, which is offered three times during June and September, includes illustrated talks on pencil, pen and wash, charcoal and chalk, pastel, and on the use of line, tone, and perspective. Each course features daily excursions with individual instruction as needed. Evening entertainment includes a country dance band organized by the Centre proprietors, Bernard and Audrey Evans.

Specialties: Landscape painting and drawing.

Faculty: Course tutor Bernard Evans is a practicing painter who has taught in England and the U.S. and is a member of the Newlyn Society of Artists. He has had one-man exhibitions in Newlyn, Penzance, London, and Plymouth.

Costs, Accommodations: The £180 fee for the one-week course includes lodging and all meals; tuition only is £50; nonparticipant guest fee is £160. A £30 nonrefundable deposit (£10 for nonresident students) secures booking with balance payable three weeks prior. No refunds within three weeks unless space can be filled. Accommodations are single, twin bedded, and double rooms with wash basins and heaters.

Location, Facilities: The studio, which has been converted from an old granite barn, is fully equipped with easels and drawing desks. Outdoor sketching easels, boards, and stools are available and art materials can be purchased at a discount in the studio shop. Newlyn, now a busy seaport, was noted as an artists colony 100 years ago. Mousehole, with its granite piers and stone cottages, is two miles away and St. Michael's Mount and Marazion are three miles away across the bay. A series of coves and cliffs stretch around to Land's End and beyond to Cape Cornwall.

Contact: Mounts Bay Art Centre, Trevatha, Faugan Lane, Newlyn, Penzance, Cornwall, TR18 5DJ, England; (44) 0736 66284.

NAROPA INSTITUTE
Boulder, Colorado

Four weeks in summer

Since 1974, the Naropa Institute has offered an intensive four-week summer program in visual arts, music, dance, writing, traditional arts, and contemplative disciplines. The Visual Arts Program affords an opportunity to explore the arts from both Eastern and Western traditions, ancient and modern. Typical topics include drawing, watercolor, oil and acrylic painting, Tibetan Thangka painting, and Chinese brush painting. A variety of special summer events are also scheduled, including faculty, guest, and student performances, readings, and talks. Naropa is the only accredited North American college whose educational philosophy is rooted in the Buddhist contemplative tradition at the heart of which is sitting meditation practice.

Specialties: Visual arts, emphasizing both Eastern and Western traditions.

Faculty: Has included Barbara Bash, Sanje Elliott, Sherry Hart, Virginia Maitland, Michael Newhall, Shou Cheng Zhang, and special guests David Hockney and Henry Geldzahler.

Costs: The tuition for each course in the summer program is approximately $250, noncredit. Students from other institutions may elect to attend the month-long intensive with a six to eight-credit option.

Location: The Institute, located in Boulder, is situated against the foothills of the Rocky Mountains. Students share in the cultural and educational environment of the Boulder/Denver area.

Contact: Mary McHenry, Director, Naropa Summer Institute, 2130 Arapahoe Ave., Boulder, CO 80302; (303) 444-0202.

A NATURALIST'S SKETCHBOOK
THE ART OF NATURE DRAWING
Massachusetts Audubon Society — Wellfleet Bay Wildlife Sanctuary
South Wellfleet, Massachusetts
Two days in late August

Since 1984, the Wellfleet Bay Wildlife Sanctuary has sponsored the Cape Cod Natural History Field School's two-day to one-week courses in writing, photography, and art for adults interested in learning more about the Cape Cod coast. The two-day nature drawing course, for the beginner to advanced artist or naturalist, emphasizes a variety of techniques, from detailed studies to rapid field sketches, for illustrating plants, animals, landscapes, and such local habitats as saltmarsh, dunes, pine woodland, and seashore. The course is held outdoors, with workshops on form and line using pen or pencil, shadows and light, and on color theory using colored pencils, which are complemented by drawing sessions in the field.

Massachusetts Audubon Society, one of the oldest conservation groups in the world and the largest in New England, is a voluntary association open to all who value preservation of the environment. Programs sponsored by the Society encompass the areas of conservation, education, and research. Wellfleet Bay Wildlife Sanctuary, one of 17 staffed sanctuaries, also presents a variety of programs dedicated to the interpretation, exploration, and protection of Cape Cod and its environs.

Specialties: Nature drawing.

Faculty: Clare Walker, an artist, naturalist, educator, and illustrator, is author of *Nature Drawing: A Tool for Learning, Notes From a Naturalist's Sketchbook,* and *A Naturalist's Sketchbook: Pages from the Seasons of the Year.*

Costs, Accommodations: Course fee is $175 for Society members and $200 for non-members, which includes one-year membership. A nonrefundable $50 deposit must accompany application with balance due 30 days prior. No refunds less than 30 days prior. Accommodations in shared rooms are $15 for the course and private rooms for couples are available on a first-come, first-served basis. First and last evening dinners are included and participants are responsible for remaining meals.

Location: Wellfleet Bay Wildlife Sanctuary preserves over 700 acres of pine woods, moorland, fresh water ponds, tidal creeks, and saltmarsh. Lodging is in a secluded house with small kitchen overlooking Nauset Marsh in the Cape Cod National Seashore with a view past a barrier beach to the Atlantic Ocean. There are a number of nearby restaurants.

Contact: Massachusetts Audubon Society, Wellfleet Bay Wildlife Sanctuary, P.O. Box 236, South Wellfleet, MA 02663; (508) 349-2615.

NEW BRUNSWICK CRAFT SCHOOL
Fredericton, New Brunswick, Canada
Three to seven-day workshops

Established in 1938 by the New Brunswick Government to provide skills and work for young people in small communities throughout the province, the School now offers a three-year program of study in ceramics, fashion design and construction, fabric printing and painting, textiles, jewelry, woodworking, and photography, as well as approximately eight workshops from September through April. The workshops, limited to ten to fifteen participants, are taught by noted professionals in the various studios and are designed for students with a thorough grounding in the subject.

Typical programs, each three days, include Visual Design on the MacIntosh, an introduction that emphasizes hands-on experience in computer-based design; Multi-Metal Lamination, which concentrates on the marriage of such metals as copper with sterling and nickle silver to create patterns on sheet, around a rod, and from multi-twisted wires; Seeing the Art Process, which focuses on drawing techniques and basic painting; Mechanisms For Jewelry, covering the techniques of hingemaking and latch construction, the making of tubing, findings, catches, and several varieties of chains and clasps. Other programs include a five-day tapestry workshop, a seven-day class on soft sculpture using various fabrics, and a week-long participatory workshop with potter Jeff Oestreich.

Specialties: Painting, drawing, ceramics, sculpture, tapestry, jewelry.

Faculty: Includes fiber artist Barbara Falkowska, artists Graham Metson and Joyce Weiland, jewelry artist Tim McCreight, fabric sculptor Lisa Lichtenfels, and potter Jeff Oestreich.

Costs: Workshop tuition is approximately C$50 to C$70. Full payment must accompany application at least two weeks prior to workshop.

Location: The heart of Fredericton, on the banks of the Saint John River.

Contact: New Brunswick Craft School, Box 6000, Fredericton, NB, E3B 5H1, Canada; (506) 453-2305.

NEW ENGLAND ART THERAPY INSTITUTE
Sunderland, Massachusetts
Week-end courses

This nonprofit educational organization, founded in 1981, offers two or three new weekend courses each semester that focus on the use of art as therapy in the reconciling of emotional conflicts and the fostering of self-awareness and personal growth. Designed for people interested in integrating art into therapeutic or educational settings and artists who want to deepen their creative process, typical courses include Drawing From Within, which stresses the importance of inner motivation in creativity and techniques to facilitate the creative process in others, and The Therapeutic Use of Art Materials, which focuses on the qualities of art materials and their appropriate therapeutic applications. The Institute also sponsors a week-long summer residential intensive and a certificate program and provides in-service training to organizations and art therapy to individuals of all ages.

Specialties: Art therapy.

Faculty: Includes Executive Director Robin Dale Schwarz, M.Ed., a registered art therapist and fabric artist, and Associate Director Guillermo Cuellar, Ed.D., an artist trained in gestalt and family therapy, creativity, and organizational development. Both maintain a private practice in the Amherst area.

Costs: Weekend course tuition is $130. Upon receipt of registration form, which must include $10 fee, applicants are contacted for a telephone interview. Once accepted, 50% of the total fee is required within ten days with balance due ten days prior to course. A 75% tuition refund is granted cancellations more than seven days prior and withdrawals within three days receive a 50% refund.

Location: Courses are held in the Amherst/Northampton area.

Contact: The New England Art Therapy Institute, 216 Silver Ln., #20, Sunderland, MA 01375; (413) 665-4880.

NEWPORT WICKFORD WATERCOLOR SEMINAR
Newport and Wickford, Rhode Island
Six-day August seminar

Since 1974, Spencer Crooks has offered an intensive six-day on-location seminar for 12 to 20 artists of all levels. Sessions meet for six hours a day — 9 am to 4 pm — and students can enroll on a daily basis with a minimum of three days desired. The teaching format includes morning lectures and demonstrations with the afternoon reserved for individual instruction and critique. The workshop concludes with a party, presentation of certificates, and drawing for a watercolor by Spencer Crooks.

Wednesday sessions are offered from September until the last week of July. Students meet from 9:30 am to 1 pm and paint on-location.

Specialties: Watercolor.

Faculty: Spencer Crooks received an honorary doctorate of fine arts from Roger Williams College and serves on the board of directors of the Rhode Island Heritage Hall of Fame. He has earned such awards as the Eliza Gardiner Memorial Award, the Eliza Radeke Memorial Award, and the Florence B. Kane Memorial Award and his works are in the collections of such notables as Mrs. Anwar Sadat, Anna Moffo, Michael Dukakis, the late Arthur Fiedler, and Jack Lynch, former Prime Minister of Ireland.

Costs: Tuition for the six-day seminar is $160 or $29 per day. A $29 deposit secures reservation. Wednesday sessions are $17 each.

Location: Outdoor seminar sessions are held at such Wickford and Newport locations as Gold Street, at the Town Dock, Wickford Cove Marina, Ida Lewis Yacht Club, Casey Farm, and the Pleasant Street boat yard. In case of inclement weather, seminar sessions are held in St. Paul's Episcopal Parish Hall in Wickford. Wednesday sessions are held at the Barrington Congregational Church Recreational Building on County Road in Barrington.

Contact: Newport/Wickford Watercolor, 84 Davis Ave., Cranston, RI 02910; (401) 941-2251.

NINA ROSA IRWIN PAINTING WORKSHOPS
Coxsackie, New York

Five to twelve-day workshops from July-October; one-week travel workshop

Since 1974, Nina Rosa Irwin has conducted workshops and classes for artists of all levels. Approximately a half dozen workshops are offered each summer, divided equally between Landscaping on Location (6 or 12 days) and Portrait and Figure Study (5 or 10 days). Both programs cover drawing, color theory, linear and aerial perspective, art history, and study of the masters. Instruction is provided in a variety of media, including pencil, oil, watercolor, acrylics, and pastel. An annual painting holiday visits a scenic locale, such as the island of Maui, Hawaii.

Enrollment in the Landscaping on Location workshop is limited to 20 students, who paint outdoors daily from 10 am until 2 pm, Monday through Friday, at the sites made famous by Thomas Cole, Frederick Church, Asher Durand, and other artists of the Hudson River School. The Portrait and Figure Study workshop, limited to 10 students, is scheduled daily from 9 am to noon and 1 to 4 pm, Monday through Friday, in the Ms. Irwin's studio. The day begins with pencil sketching and figure study and demonstrations by the instructor. During the afternoon, students paint from a live model and receive individual assistance.

Specialties: Landscape, portrait, and figure painting.

Faculty: Nina Rosa Irwin has been a professional artist for more than 30 years and a teacher for more than 15. Her works include landscapes, still life, florals, and portraiture.

Costs, Accommodations: Tuition for the Landscaping on Location workshop is $100 for 6 days, $190 for 12; the Portrait and Figure Study workshop is $200 for 5 days, $380 for 10. A $30 deposit reserves a space and balance is due two weeks prior. A list of nearby accommodations is provided.

Location: Coxsackie is in the Catskill Mountains and Hudson River Valley, across the river from Frederick Church's palatial home, Olana, which is open to the public. The town is 20 miles south of the tri-city area of Albany, Troy, and Schenectady, which offer museums, performing arts centers, and other cultural attractions.

Contact: Nina Rosa Irwin, 19 Elm St., Coxsackie, NY 12051; (518) 731-6403.

NORTHERN MICHIGAN WORKSHOPS
Northwestern Michigan Artists and Craftsmen
Traverse City, Michigan
Five-day workshops from June-November

Established in 1971, the nonprofit Northwestern Michigan Artists and Craftsmen sponsors five-day painting workshops for intermediate to advanced artists. Approximately eight to ten workshops are scheduled during the summer and fall, each limited to about 20 students per instructor. Daily sessions begin at 9 am with a demonstration and conclude at about 3:30 pm. Typical workshop titles include Landscape and Pencil Drawing, an on-location workshop that covers perspective, values, size relationship, and lighting technique; Catching Light in Your Paintings, an indoor and outdoor workshop that focuses on the principles of color mixtures, tonal organization, patterns, and other components; Designing With Watercolor and Acrylic, which emphasizes design-composition, observation, translation, and creation and includes a slide lecture and demonstrations; and Wildlife Workshop, devoted to wildlife illustration with various media, both on-location and using stuffed bird and mammal specimens.

Specialties: Drawing and painting.

Faculty: Includes Ferdinand Petrie, author of *Drawing Landscapes in Pencil*, whose work is represented in the Smithsonian Institution, Kennedy Library, and the Audubon Society; Charles Slovek, contributing editor of *The Artist's Magazine*, who has published *Catching Light in Your Paintings* and *Painting Indoors*; Al Brouillette, recently elected Associate National Academy and author and illustrator of *The Evolving Picture*; Gijsbert van Frankenhuyzen, recipient of awards from Roger Tory Peterson and *Communica-*

tions Arts Magazine; Roland Roycroft, a commercial artist and art director for more than 35 years and featured artist in *The Artist's Magazine*; Paul Leveille, artist for the U.S. Coast Guard and member of the Copley Society, Salmagundi Club, and American Portrait Society; and Judi Betts, Tony Couch, and Irving Shapiro.

Costs, Accommodations: Workshop fees range from $150 to $200. Dormitory housing (five nights) at the local college and meals are available for an additional $112. Payment in full must accompany registration. Full refund, less $20 processing fee, is granted cancellations more than one month prior; thereafter if space can be filled. Participants can also reserve lodging at area hotels and motels.

Location: Traverse is a popular summer tourist area. Nearby attractions include Macinac Island.

Contact: Pat Ford, Northern Michigan Workshops, 11138 W. Bayshore Dr., Traverse City, MI 49684; (616) 947-8714.

NORTHWEST NATIVE AMERICAN ART AND BASKETRY SYMPOSIA
Pacific Cascade Marketing
Union, Washington
Four-day symposia in July and August

Since 1987, Pacific Cascade Marketing has sponsored symposia that include basket weaving instruction by Native American artists. Two programs are offered during the summer, with instructional sessions limited to 15 participants of all levels with two instructors. The July symposia, titled Indian Basketry: Woven Traditions, features three basket weaving sessions including a Skokomish Cedar Bark Spear and Harpoon Basket, Puget Sound Indian Cedar Clam Gathering Basket, and a traditional Lummi Cedar Bark and Sweetgrass Basket. The August symposia, titled From the Hands of our Ancestors, includes the Skokomish Spear and Harpoon Baskets, an authentic Makah decorated deer hide drum, and an Eastern Washington, Colville, red cedar coiled hard basket. A variety of other activities are scheduled, such as an Indian game night, Indian salmon or venison and fry bread dinner at the Skokomish Tribal Center, Indian story-telling, a cultural presentation by Skokomish Tribe members, traditional tribal dances and drumming, and visits with Indian artists and crafts persons. Pacific Cascade Marketing also sponsors basketry classes throughout the year at different locations.

Specialties: Indian basketry and drum making.

Faculty: Includes Native Americans Bruce Miller (Skokomish Tribe), a tribal leader, author, fiber artist, lecturer, woodcarver, and honored by Bowling Green College as one of the top Indian storytellers in the U.S.; Melissa Peterson (Makah), a teacher and basketry specialist at the Neah Bay Museum; drum making artist Linda Colfax (Makah); and basket weavers Anna Jefferson and Marie Morris (Lummi), Ed Carrier (Suquamish), and Elaine Emerson (Colville).

Costs, Accommodations: The cost, which includes meals and accommodations, is $395. A $200 deposit, of which $50 is nonrefundable, must accompany registration with balance due four weeks prior. Cancellations at least five weeks prior receive refund less $50; two to five weeks prior a 50% refund less $50is granted; no refund thereafter. Lodging is provided at St. Andrew's Retreat House, which has nine rooms that are each equipped for two to five guests. Evergreen State College offers four hours of college credit.

Location: The Retreat House is situated on a hillside overlooking Hood Canal and the Olympic Mountains, six miles west of Twanoh State Park and 2 1/2 miles east of Union.

Contact: Patricia M. Martinelli, Pacific Cascade Marketing, P.O. Box 5838, Aloha, OR 97007; (503) 649-7124/9131.

NORTHWEST SCHOOL OF WOODEN BOATBUILDING
Port Townsend, Washington

Weekend workshops, one-week seminars, and six-month program

The Northwest School of Wooden Boatbuilding, a nonprofit corporation established in 1980 to teach and preserve the skills of craftsmanship associated with the art and science of traditional wooden boatbuilding, offers a variety of workshops and seminars that are held from 9 am to 4 pm throughout the year. Typical Saturday workshop titles include Spar Making, a discussion/demonstration of the design, engineering, lay out, and construction techniques for building wooden solid pole and hollow box spars; Galvanized Hardware Fabrication, which covers design considerations and techniques of fabricating traditional galvanized metal fittings; Ship Nameboard Carving, featuring lectures and demonstrations of the basics of nameboard carving, including tools, choice and preparation of woods, layout and designs, and hands-on practice; Oar Making, which covers different styles of oars and their uses plus a demonstration of carving a set of Pete Culler oars; and Planking, Interior Joinery, Painting, and Varnishing and Caulking. Two-day weekend workshops include Deck and Cabin Construction and Flat Bottom Skiff. Five one-week seminars offered each year, usually during the summer months, include Small Boat Construction, in which participants build a small lapstrake boat (moulds, stem, keel, transom, and planking); and Wooden Boat Repair, which deals with structural hull repair techniques. The school also offers a full-time six month program that consists of classroom instruction and hands-on sections designed to provide practical boatbuilding experience.

Specialties: Traditional wooden boatbuilding.

Faculty: Includes experienced boatbuilders Kit Africa, Lee Ehrheart, Carl Brownstein, Richard Golden, Charles Moore, Les Schnick, Ray Speck, Pat Woodland, and head instructor Jeff Hammond.

Costs: Tuition is $25 per day for weekend workshops, $260 (includes $50 registration fee) for five day seminars. These programs are free to students enrolled in the six-month program.

Location, Facilities: Port Townsend, on Washington's Olympic Peninsula, is noted for its concentration of shipbuilding and marine related activities. The school's 10,000-square-foot primary building contains a shop with work benches, industrial machinery, construction space for three 40' vessels and a loft area with space for lofting vessels to 65'. A secondary building provides covered storage for lumber and building space for four mid-size vessels.

Contact: Northwest School of Wooden Boatbuilding, 251 Otto St., Port Townsend, WA 98368; (206) 385-4948.

OLD CHURCH CULTURAL CENTER SCHOOL OF ART
Demarest, New Jersey
One to three-day workshops in January

Established in 1974 as a nonprofit community education facility, the Old Church Cultural Center offers approximately 45 on-going arts and crafts classes a week, year-round, as well as about a dozen one to three-day workshops during the month of January. Typical workshops, which are open to all levels, include Hand Painted Silk, in which students design and paint a unique accessory; Monotype: The Painterly Print, which teaches both subtractive and additive methods of this direct printmaking process; Papermaking, which covers traditional methods along with experimental and interpretive ideas; and Pysanka-Ukranian Egg Decoration, a folk art that uses the batik method. The Center also sponsors a year round program of exhibitions, cultural events, and special seminars. Members receive a discount on classes and workshops, are invited to artists' openings, and receive the Newsletters.

Specialties: A variety of arts and crafts topics.

Faculty: Includes area artists and craftspersons Dorothy Cochran, Denise Collins, Caroline Gangi, Gerry Geltman, Robin Ives, Bruno La Verdiere, Imari Nacht, Janice Mauro, Barbara Neumann, and Karen Vierno.

Costs: Workshop fees range from $25 ($10 for members) to $180 ($165). Annual membership dues are $10 to $25. Senior citizens discount is 10%.

Location: The Center, housed in a 100-year-old, barrier-free former church building, is located in Northern Bergen County, two miles from Exit 2 on the Palisades Interstate Parkway.

Contact: Old Church Cultural Center School of Art, 561 Piermont Rd., Demarest, NJ 07627; (201) 767-7160.

OLYMPIC FIELD SEMINARS
Olympic Park Institute (OPI)
Olympic National Park, Washington
Three to five-day summer workshops

Since 1984, the Olympic Field Seminar series has offered programs on a variety of nature-oriented topics. In 1987, the series came under the umbrella of the Olympic Park Institute, a nonprofit educational organization and one of three campuses operated by the Yosemite National Institutes. Approximately 50 seminars are scheduled during the spring, summer, and fall, including six devoted to arts and crafts, with nature and the environs of Olympic National Park as the focus. Typical workshops include Biological Illustration, which focuses on nature sketching, measurement and scientific lighting of specimens, and the tools for producing pen and ink, watercolor, wash, or carbon dust drawings; Native Basketry, in which participants gather a variety of materials — roots, limbs, bark, grasses and ferns — and weave them into useful containers using both traditional and contemporary methods; Northwest Coast Indian Carving, which emphasizes how to interpret and identify designs on various artifacts and the construction of traditional carving tools for completing a project. Other workshops may include Cedar Bark Basketry of the Northwest Coast, The Olympic Landscape in Watercolor, and Nature Drawing of the Olympic Peninsula.

Specialties: Drawing, painting, illustration, woodcarving, basketry, and other crafts relating to the natural environs of Olympic National Park.

Faculty: Has included Scott Jensen, an experienced Northwest woodcarver who has done commission work for several museums and has exhibited statewide; Phyllis Pearson, a teacher at the Basketry School and the University of Washington Experimental College; Dr. Charles Wood, founder and president of Biomedical Illustrations and instructor of scientific ilustration at the University of Washington; and Chuck Webster and Cliff Wood.

Costs, Accommodations: Costs range from $115 to $220 and payment by check or money order should accompany application. A 5% to 8% discount is available to Friends of the Institute (tax-deductible annual membership dues begin at $25 for an individual and $35 for a family). Full refund, less $15 fee, is granted cancellations at least four weeks prior; no refunds thereafter. Accommodations are available in rustic cabins at Rosemary Inn, an historic landmark built in 1914 and now the home of the Institute. Restroom and shower facilities are located in a separate building. The per person nightly fee of $31, double occupancy, includes three meals. Other housing can be arranged at campgrounds, the Log Cabin Resort, and Lake Crescent Lodge, which offers more formal facilities.

Location: Olympic National Park, a complete ecosystem encompassing 938,000 acres, contains the largest temperate rain forest in the western hemisphere, 60 glaciers, 80 kilometers of roadless ocean coastline, large areas of subalpine meadows, and the largest mixed coniferous forest in the U.S.

Contact: Olympic Park Institute, HC 62 Box 9T, Port Angeles, WA 98362; (206) 928-3720.

OMEGA INSTITUTE FOR HOLISTIC STUDIES
Rhinebeck, New York
Weekend and week long workshops from mid-June to mid-September

The Institute, founded in 1977, is a nonprofit learning center offering more than 200 workshops on topics in the arts, psychology, health, business, spirituality, preventive medicine, and global thinking. At least eight workshops are offered in the fine arts, including such titles as The Alchemy of Medieval Illumination, Traditional Hmong Stitchery, Drawing from Nature, Creativity in Clay and Words, Painting the Creativeness of Dreams, Stone Masonry (building stone walls), and Byzantine Icon Painting: The Light That Comes From Within, which emphasizes traditional painting techniques and an understanding of the spiritual language contained in the symbols, colors, and divine images of the icon. Classes meet daily, with ample time for individual work, and optional classes are also offered each day in yoga, t'ai chi, dance movement, and meditation. Evening activities include community gatherings, films, dances, performances, and networking.

Specialties: Graphic and fine arts.

Faculty: Includes potter M.C. Richards, author of *Centering: In Pottery* and *Pottery and the Person*; icon painter Vladislav Andreyev and calligrapher, illuminator, and book illustrator Karen Gorst, both instructors at Manhattan's School of Sacred Arts; and Jeffrey Brown, Elizabeth Ciz, Rachel Heller, Carol Ann Morley, and Yee Yang.

Costs, Accommodations: Tuition ranges from $225 to $320 with materials fees of $25 to $75. Camping facilities, dorms, and shared or private cottage rooms are available for $60 to $250. All housing fees are per person and include meals, which are primarily vegetarian. A sauna, lake for boating and swimming, massage center, and two flotation tanks are available for participants. Full refund less a $35 fee is granted for cancellations more than 21 days prior to the workshop. Credit voucher good for one year is granted those who cancel less than 21 days prior. A limited number of partial scholarships are available.

Location: Omega Institute is located near the village of Rhinebeck on 80 acres of lakefront woodlands and rolling hills in the Hudson River Valley, two hours north of New York City. Most buildings are accessible for participants in wheelchairs but not all classrooms or housing units are barrier-free.

Contact: Omega Institute, RD 2, Box 377, Rhinebeck, NY, 12572; (914) 338-6030 (Sept.15-May 15) *or* (914) 266-4301 (May 15-Sept.15).

OREGON SCHOOL OF ARTS AND CRAFTS (OSAC)
Portland, Oregon

Three to ten-day summer workshops; weekend workshops during the academic year

Established in 1906 as a resource for crafts education in the Pacific Northwest, the Oregon School of Arts and Crafts is the only accredited post-secondary school in the nation with the sole purpose of addressing traditional and contemporary issues of the crafts as significant forms for artistic expression. Approximately 15 to 20 intensives are offered from mid-June through mid-August as well as year-round weekend workshops in seven disciplines — Book Arts, Ceramics, Drawing, Photography, Fibers, Metal, and Woodworking. Classes, which enroll a maximum of 15 students, meet daily from 9 am to 4 pm and some programs are open to all levels while specialized topics are geared to those with intermediate to advanced skills. The School also offers short-term summer classes; 10-session classes in fall, winter, and spring; year-long residencies for emerging artists; and a three-year Certificate Program built on intensive studio training. Students pursuing a BFA at Pacific University take a portion of their crafts requirements at OSAC.

Typical workshops for all levels include Book Structures, Basketry, Toolmaking, and Papermaking, which covers making suitable pulps, deep casting into various molds, and using found molds. Workshops for those with some experience may include Handbuilding Using Pressmolds (for making large ceramic vessels), Illustration, Woven Tapestry, Imaginative Jewelry Design, and Marquetry, Veneering, and Inlay, in which students develop and complete a marquetry project.

Specialties: Book arts, ceramics, drawing, photography, fibers, metal, and woodworking.

Faculty: Includes such accomplished artists as book artists Lillian Bell, Tim Ely, Hedi Kyle, and Mark Van Stone; ceramists Andrea Gill and Tim Mather; illustrator Marshall Arisman, fiber artists Jim Bassler, Kay Lawrence, Tom Lundberg, Jane Sauer, and Joy Stocksdale; metalsmiths Leslie Leupp and Bruce Metcalf; and woodworkers Silas Kopf and Emmett Turner.

Costs, Accommodations: Tuition ranges from $80 ($76 for members) for a two-day workshop to approximately $270 ($240) for five days, depending upon the course and instructor. Studio fee and college credit is additional. Full payment, payable by VISA and MasterCard, must accompany registration. Cancellations for summer workshops must be received three weeks before the workshop begins to receive a 75% refund. Work study and scholarship opportunities are available based on need and merit. The school housing referral service assists students in finding accommodations.

Location: The seven-acre landscaped campus, built in 1979, comprises nine buildings with studios, cafe dining facility, library, and exhibition and sales galleries. Portland's city center is ten minutes away with direct bus service.

Contact: Oregon School of Arts and Crafts, 8245 S.W. Barnes Rd., Portland, OR 97225; (503) 297-5544.

PAINT AND PHOTOGRAPH ITALY
The Umbria and Tuscany Regions of Italy
Sixteen-days in late summer

Roberta Kritzia conducts a 16-day travel program, limited to 15 artists and photographers, that features concentrated time to paint, photograph, and explore the medieval Italian hill towns and countryside of Umbria and Tuscany.

Specialities: Painting, photography.

Faculty: Roberta Kritzia, a professional etcher and painter and a member of the Los Angeles Printmakers Society, has work in private and corporate collections and has exhibited in Italy; Pamela Lowrie, Professor of Fine Arts at the College of DuPage, has had work exhibited, published articles, and produced a series of art-related films.

Costs, Accommodations: Program cost of $2,200 includes accommodations, most meals, and motorcoach transportation. Airfare is extra. Previous participants and early registrants receive a $100 discount. A $250 deposit is required with registration with balance due 60 days prior.

Location: The trip is headquartered at the Villa S. Regina in Siena and at Hotel Casalago on Lake Piediluco. The trip also includes a three-day excursion to the medieval walled city of Gubbio.

Contact: Roberta Kritzia, 5455 Sylmar Ave., #902, Van Nuys, CA 91401; (818) 994-2402.

PAINT YOSEMITE WORKSHOP
Yosemite National Park, California
Five days in early November

This annual watercolor workshop, held in the scenic environs of Yosemite National Park each November since 1982, is open to artists of all levels, although most participants have had some instruction or experience. The daily schedule includes a morning lecture and demonstration with afternoons free for painting and consultations with instructors. The student to teacher ratio is 25 to 1.

Specialties: Watercolor painting.

Faculty: Features prominent artists and always includes Jane Burnham, a Signature member of the American Watercolor Society, the National Watercolor Society, and Society of Western Artists, and the West Coast Watercolor Society. Her work is in galleries in Scottsdale, Denver, Carmel, Tahoe, Los Angeles, and San Francisco and private collections. Other faculty may include Miles Batt, who has received more than 80 national and regional awards, Millard Sheets, Rex Brandt, Joan Irving, and Jade Fon.

Costs, Accommodations: Tuition is $160. A nonrefundable $50 deposit secures reservation with balance due on arrival. Lodging and meals are available at Yosemite Lodge, a modern, handicapped-accessible facility in Yosemite Valley.

Location: Yosemite Valley can be reached by car on Rte. 41 from Fresno, Rte. 140 from Merced, and Rte. 120 from Sonora.

Contact: Jane Burnham, 51301 Dorstan Dr., Oakhurst, CA 93644.

PAINT WITH PITTARD WORKSHOPS
Various locations in the U.S.

Two to four-day workshops; eight-day Hawaii workshop

Lynne Pittard presents two to four-day "Paint-along" workshops under the sponsorship of various groups and organizations. The sessions are scheduled from 9:30 am to 4:30 pm and limited to 12 to 20 students of all levels. Each student completes an oil painting during the class, choosing from one of a variety of scenes. An eight-day travel workshop to Hawaii is offered each year and trips to other locales are planned.

Specialties: Painting.

Costs: Costs and other arrangements are determined by the sponsoring group or organization. The Hawaii travel workshop fee of $899 includes condominium lodging, rental car, and round-trip airfare (from California to Kona); fee for nonparticipant guests is $699.

Location: In addition to Hawaii, workshop locations may include Florida, New York, North Carolina, South Carolina, Texas, Massachusetts, Virginia, California, and Georgia.

Contact (for schedule): Paint With Pittard Workshops, P.O. Box 3616, Lantana, FL 33465-3616; (407) 586-6702.

PAPER PRESS
Chicago, Illinois

Workshops and tours year-round

This nonprofit studio for experimental hand papermaking offers workshops, courses, lectures, and tours for beginning to advanced artists of all ages. Included in all presentations is a history of paper with emphasis on its decorative and sculptural aspects and use as a painting without paint. The two to three-day workshops usually meet for four hours daily and feature such topics as Oriental paper, two and three dimensional paper, and photographic paper techniques. Typical travel programs are a five-day tour of hand papermakers of the Southwest and a two-week tour of the crafts of Bali. Paper Press also sponsors half and full-day hands-on workshops for groups, 15-day residencies, workshops conducted by guest artists, and exhibitions. Special presentations are provided for teachers and the studio is available to artists for individual projects.

Specialties: Papermaking.

Faculty: Founding member Linda Sorkin-Eisenberg has had her work featured in *Fiber Arts* magazine. She has taught in public schools and her paper garments are in public and private collections. Marilyn Sward teaches papermaking at Columbia College and is co-author of *The New Photography*, which deals with printing photographs on handmade paper.

Costs: Most workshops range from $100 to $125 with an additional $10 to $15 for materials. A nonrefundable $25 to $50 deposit secures reservation.

Location: Paper Press is located at Morgan and Jackson, north of the University of Illinois.

Contact: Paper Press, 1017 W. Jackson, Chicago, IL 60607; (312) 226-6300.

PARSONS SCHOOL OF DESIGN
West Africa and other locations
Three to four-week summer study programs

Since 1984, Parsons School of Design, in collaboration with The Society for International Exchange, has sponsored a three-and-a-half week in-depth study of the Ivory Coast's artistic heritage. The program provides the opportunity to examine the continent's traditions in ceramics, fibers, and metals, and to work directly with African craftsmen in their villages and workshops. Participants, who should have some knowledge of French, register for two courses: Introduction to African Culture and one of the specialized disciplines — ceramics, fibers, metals, or photography. Following the general introduction to African culture and artistic heritage, students travel to small villages in the interior where they study and work. The ceramics group explores the traditions of two very different ethnic groups — the Senufo and the Baule — and take an active part in all aspects of the pottery process. The fibers course surveys the arts of narrow strip loom weaving, ikat and wax resist dyeing, and basketry among the Baule, Senufo, and Dyula, and students have the opportunity to apprentice themselves to village artists. The course in traditional metalwork, which includes lost-wax casting in brass and gold, ironsmithing, and the crafting of gold and silver jewelry, focuses on techniques, cultural uses, and the aesthetic and historic importance of artwork in metal. An additional three-week curriculum in Mali — available as a separate option or a continuation of the Ivory Coast program — is offered as an historical introduction to the region's traditional art and architecture.

Specialties: Ceramics, fibers, and metals of West Africa.

Faculty: Includes Program Director Jerome Vogel, formerly a professor at the University of Abidjan and Executive Director of Operation Crossroads Africa; Victor Diabate, director of Archaeology at the Institute of African History, Art, and Archaeology in Abidjan; Victor Santoni, a painter and professor of mural art at the National Institute of Fine Arts in Abidjan; Alpha Oomar Konare, formerly the Minister of Culture, Art, and Sports in Mali;

Christine M. Kreamer, research assistant at the Smithsonian Institution's National Museum of Natural History; and village craftspeople.

Costs, Accommodations: Cost of the Ivory Coast curriculum, which includes round-trip airfare from New York, continental breakfasts, hotel accommodations, land transfers, and six undergraduate credits, is approximately $4,000. Parsons and New School students must submit a $350 deposit with application; other applicants should submit a nonrefundable $30 application fee and $350 upon acceptance. Half the total cost is due April 15 with the balance due May 15. Written cancellations prior to May 15 receive full refund of deposit; thereafter the $350 is forfeited. On the Ivory Coast, students are housed in modern, European-style hotels in the major towns.

Location: Participants in the Ivory Coast program travel to the northern Senufo region and the central Baule region, using the cities of Korhogo and Bouak as bases for excursions to villages in the bush.

Contact: Office of Special Programs, Parsons School of Design, 66 Fifth Ave., New York, NY 10011; (212) 741-8975.

PASTEL SOCIETY OF AMERICA (PSA)
New York, New York
Six-session workshops year-round

The Pastel Society of America, founded in 1973 as a nonprofit professional association of elected artists who all work in the pastel medium, offers open workshops, where students work under the guidance of accomplished artists, and on-going classes that allow students to follow a specific curriculum and work towards a certificate upon completion. Topics include portraiture, still life, anatomy, composition, figure painting, landscape, perspective, and color. Workshops are scheduled from 9:30 am to 12:30 pm and 1:30 to 4:30 pm and enrollment is limited to 10 students.

Specialties: Pastel.

Faculty: Members of the Pastel Society of America.

Costs: Cost is $100 for six sessions.

Location: The classes and workshops are held in the Society's new facility in the Historic National Arts Club in New York City's Gramercy Park.

Contact: Flora Giffuni, Pastel Society of America, 15 Gramercy Park South, New York, NY 10003; (212) 533-6931.

PAWLEYS ISLAND LANDSCAPE WORKSHOP
BY ALEX POWERS
Sea View Inn, Pawleys Island, South Carolina

One-week spring workshop

Since 1976, Alex Powers has offered a seven-day watercolor landscape workshop for 25 intermediate to advanced artists. Each day begins with an on-location demonstration and class exercises and students then paint with individual help in the late mornings and the afternoons. Three critiques are scheduled during the week at 4 pm. The artist also teaches watercolor workshops under the sponsorship of arts organizations. These workshops, which emphasize design and individual painting style, usually utilize portrait and figure models although students may choose to work abstractly or from their own subject matter.

Specialties: Watercolor.

Faculty: Alex Powers, author of *Painting People in Watercolor* and a winner of Best-Show Awards in three national watercolor competitions, has been published in *American Artist* magazine and *The Artist's Magazine* and was included in Carole Katchen's *Painting Faces and Figures.*

Costs, Accommodations: Workshop fee, which includes room, all meals, and 15% gratuity, is $575 double or $622 single occupancy. A $150 deposit is required prior to April 8. Non-participant fee is $385.

Location: The Sea View Inn, a rustic, oceanfront boarding house, is located in the resort community of Pawleys Island, 24 miles south of Myrtle Beach.

Contact: Alex Powers, 401 72nd Ave. N., Apt. 1, Myrtle Beach, SC 29577; (803) 497-7204.

PEGGY OSTERKAMP WEAVING INSTRUCTION
San Rafael, California and other locations

One and two-day workshops

Artist, textile designer, and weaver Peggy Osterkamp offers one and two-day workshops, semester-length classes, and private instruction for students of all levels. Workshops, which are limited to ten participants, cover theory and basic techniques as well as weave drafting, enabling students to develop original structures, analyze existing textiles, and read drafts in books. Students are taught multi-harness weaving and how to warp and set up the loom themselves, using production techniques. Consultations, career counseling, evaluations, and critiques can be arranged.

Specialties: Weaving.

Faculty: Peggy Osterkamp studied at Pacific Basin School of Textile Arts in Berkeley, California, and apprenticed with Jim Ahrens, designer of AVL production and dobby looms. Her work has been shown at juried exhibitions and is represented in corporate and private collections. She has lectured at the Metropolitan Museum of Art, the Cooper-Hewitt Museum, and Parsons

School of Design in New York City and at the Textile Museum in Washington, D.C. and has written articles for *Threads* and other publications.

Costs: Workshop tuition starts at $65 per day; individual instruction is $50 per hour. Prepayment is required and full refund is granted cancellations more than 30 days prior.

Location: The studio is located in Marin County, across the Golden Gate Bridge and 30 minutes from San Francisco.

Contact: Peggy Osterkamp, 354 Holly Dr., San Rafael, CA 94903; (415) 491-1924.

PENINSULA ART SCHOOL
Fish Creek, Wisconsin
One to five-day summer-fall workshops

Established in 1979, the Peninsula Art School is sponsored by the nonprofit Peninsula Arts Association, which is dedicated to the support and enrichment of the arts in Door County. During the months from June through September the School offers more than 40 workshops in a variety of art media for adults and young people of all levels. Typical adult workshops, each limited to 15 students or less, include Portrait, Drawing and Composition, Life Drawing, Watercolor, Batik, Pastel Portraits, Raku Pottery, Clay Sculpture, Exploring Oil Painting, Jewelry, Monotype, Acrylic Painting, Printmaking, Colored Pencil, Introduction to Color, Open Media Drawing, Painting From Nature, Basic Photography, Papermaking, and Figure and Relief Carving. Young artists (ages 6-12 and 12-16) classes may include Raku, Hand-Built Pottery, Watercolor, Wearable Art, and Contemporary Jewelry.

Specialties: Watercolor, painting and drawing, sculpture, ceramics, papermaking, jewelry, photography.

Faculty: Instructors, who are experienced working artists, include Dan Anderson, Kari Anderson, Wendell Arneson, Jeanne Aurelius, Bridget Austin, Phil Austin, Julia Bresnahan, Kirsten Christianson, Chris Davitt, Deborah Dendler, John Gruenwald, Michele Gutierrez, Emmett Johns, Flora Langlois, Charles Lyons, Bob McCurdy, Evelyn McNamara, Gerhard Miller, Susan Lobe O'Hare, Ruth Philipon, William Pribble, Tom Seagard, Allan Servoss, Mary Ellen Sisulak, Bonnie Oehlert Smith, Rosemary Utzinger, Lionel Wathall, Doris White, and Sylvia Youell.

Costs, Accommodations: The workshop fee is $85. A $25 deposit must accompany registration with balance due two weeks prior. Cancellations more than two weeks prior are charged $10; deposit is forfeited thereafter.

Location: The School is situated in Door County Peninsula, the part of northern Wisconsin that juts out into Lake Michigan. It's convenient to housing, restaurants, and outdoor and cultural activities.

Contact: Bonnie Oehlert Smith, Director, Peninsula Art School, P.O. Box 304, Fish Creek, WI 54212; (414) 868-3455.

PENLAND SCHOOL
Penland, North Carolina

Two-month residency from January-February; three-week classes from March-April; one and two-week classes from May-September; four-week classes from October-November

Founded in 1929, this nonprofit school for the arts and crafts is committed to providing students of all levels of ability with an environment in which they can exercise creativity and explore new ideas and techniques. The school offers a Winter Resident Program and spring, summer, and fall classes in clay, fiber, glass, metal, and wood. Other offerings may include iron, book and print arts, drawing and painting, basketry, clothing construction, and photography. Although the instructors shape the sessions according to their own styles, virtually all classes include lectures, demonstrations, slide shows, individual and group critiques, and field trips. Some classes are "experimental studios", in which students and instructor collaborate on an idea and create a group project. Students are encouraged to visit other studios in the complex as well as the nearly 100 working studios operated by local craft artists.

The spring program consists of two three-week sessions from March through April, the summer program consists of eight one and two-week sessions from mid-May through August, and the fall program's two four-week sessions run from mid-September through mid-November. Four to eight classes run concurrently during each session and a few extend over two sessions. Symposia and conferences are also scheduled from time to time.

The Winter Resident Program, initiated in 1990, offers an opportunity for more in-depth exploration of work than can be accomplished in a few weeks. The program does not provide instruction, but rather a time for experimentation and development of new ideas in clay, fibers, metals, surface design, and wood. A maximum of 40 artists/craftsmen are provided shared studio space and a weekly seminar program.

A two-year Residents Program is available to emerging professionals and one or two-year Fellowhips are awarded former students who study, live, and work at the school in exchange for room, board, and tuition.

Specialties: Clay, fiber, glass, metal, wood, and other disciplines.

Faculty: Has included clay artists Doug Casebeer, Angela Fina, Steve Howell, Yih-Wen Kuo, and Kirk Mangus; fiber artists B.J. Adams, Judith Ann Larzelere, Susan Leveille, and Lyn Perry; glass artists Hugh Jenkins, Steven Tatar, Bill Worcester, and Sally Worcester; metalsmiths Glen Gardner, Randall Gunther, and Mac McCall; woodworkers Jon Brooks, Jim Kirkpatrick, and Michael Pierschalla; and book artists Sas Colby and Diane Philippoff Mauer.

Costs, Accommodations: Tuition is approximately $200 for one week, $400 for two weeks, $570 for three weeks, and $680 for four weeks. A nonrefundable $25 fee plus $250 deposit must accompany registration. Credit card (VISA, MasterCard) registrations are accepted at an additional 4% nonrefundable surcharge. The studio fee (supplies and materials) can range from $5 to $60. Cancellations received at least three weeks prior to workshop forfeit the $25 fee plus a $50 withdrawal charge; no refunds thereafter. Room and board (available only for students) at Penland ranges from $145 (dormitory) to $410 (single room with bath) for one week, from $285 to $700 for two weeks, and from $395 to $995 for three weeks. Students who live off grounds pay an administrative fee of $50 per week, which covers lunch. Undergraduate and graduate credit is available through East Tennessee State University for an additional charge. A limited number of work-study scholarships are awarded each session based on need. Scholarship students earn tuition and partial room and board in exchange for providing three hours a day in assistance with kitchen and housekeeping. Assistantships are available to applicants who are equivalent to graduate level students with a full knowledge of a working studio. The fee for the Winter Resident Program is $1,000 per month, which includes meals, housing, and utilities.

Location: Penland's 500 acres of Blue Ridge Mountain land and about 50 old buildings are located 65 miles northeast of Asheville Airport and can be reached by car from either U.S. 19E or N.C. Rte. 226. The school provides van service between the airport or bus terminal and Penland for $25 one way. Swimming, tennis, golf, movies, and scenic areas are nearby.

Contact: Penland School, Penland, NC 28765; (704) 765-2359.

THE PENNSYLVANIA GUILD OF CRAFTSMEN
Various locations in Pennsylvania
One to four-day weekend workshops from February-April

The nonprofit Pennsylvania Guild of Craftsmen sponsors more than a dozen spring weekend workshops that feature lectures, demonstrations, and, in some cases, hands-on experience. While most workshops are for all levels, some are geared to the experienced craftsperson and students are encouraged to bring samples of their work for discussion and critique. Typical workshop titles are Advanced Glass Fusing & Slumping (Gil Reynolds), Sprayed and Cast Paper (Elaine Koretsky), Advanced Stained Glass Design (Narcissus Quagliata), Shibori (Japanese Bound Resist) (Joyce Fogle), Pennsylvania Potato Basket (Darryl & Karn Arawjo), Mold Making for the Studio Potter (Barbara Bauer), Glass Blowing (Joel Bless), Clothing Construction for Weavers (Daryl Lancaster), Furniture Design and Construction (Tage Frid), Advanced Tinsmithing (Jim Eisenhart), and Kaleidoscopes (Frank Gallagher), in which each participant produces a brass and glass kaleidoscope.

Specialties: A variety of crafts topics.

Faculty: Instructors are all prominent professionals.

Costs, Accommodations: Workshop tuition ranges from $60 to $265. Full payment must accompany registration.

Location: The workshops are held at arts and crafts centers and colleges in such Pennsylvania cities as Richboro, York, East Berlin, Johnstown, State College, Everett, and Perkasie.

Contact: The Pennsylvania Guild of Craftsmen, P.O. Box 820, Richboro, PA 18954; (215) 860-0731.

PETER ALLRED GRANUCCI PAINTING WORKSHOPS
Gilsum, New Hampshire

Five-day summer and weekend fall workshops

Since 1982, Peter Granucci has offered drawing and painting workshops for artists of all levels. Each class is limited to ten students, who are taught to understand what they are seeing and taken from concept to final composition. Two five-day summer workshops, Landscape and Portrait & Landscape, emphasize drawing skills, value, shape, and color, and include critiques, lectures, and discussions of relevant art history. Each day begins at 9 am and concludes at 4 pm, with an evening session on figure drawing and sunset painting also scheduled. Weekend workshops are also offered in the fall and private or semi-private instruction may be arranged.

Specialties: Landscape and portrait painting.

Faculty: Experienced portrait and landscape artist Peter Allred Granucci received the M. Grumbacher Award Medallion, the American Artists Professional League Award, and the Tom Picard Award from the Salmagundi Club. His work has been exhibited in museums and galleries in New York and New England and is in the corporate collections of Exxon and AT&T.

Costs, Accommodations: Tuition for the five-day workshop is $175. A $50 deposit is required with balance due upon arrival. Full refund is granted cancellations more than one week prior. A list of nearby motel, bed and breakfast, and camping facilities is provided.

Location: Classes are held in a finished barn studio at the 150-year-old Riverrun Farm, situated in the Monadnock region of southwest New Hampshire. The scenic 186-acre farm includes fields, forests, outbuildings, a swimming pond, and a river.

Contact: Peter Allred Granucci, 66 Hammond Hollow, Gilsum, NH 03448; (603) 352-6828.

PETERS VALLEY CRAFT CENTER
Layton, New Jersey

One to nineteen-day workshops from May through August

Established in 1970 as a nonprofit craft education center, Peters Valley strives to promote appreciation of crafts by sponsoring workshops, demonstrations, exhibitions, and educational outreach programs. During the summer months, 10 to 15 workshops are offered in each of six disciplines: blacksmithing, ceramics, photography, textiles, woodworking, and fine metals. Most workshops range from one to eight days in length with a few somewhat longer. Sessions meet daily from 9 am to 5 pm and include lectures, demonstrations, and practical work. While most programs are open to all levels, some are specifically for beginning, intermediate, or advanced students. Children's and parent-child workshops were instituted in 1989.

Blacksmithing workshops cover such topics as Early American Hardware, Pattern Welded Steel, and Making Tools for the Shop. Typical ceramics workshop titles include Clay Sculpture About Pots, Not the Usual Pitfire, Restoring Ceramics, and The Potter's Wheel: An Expressive Tool. During the 19-day anagama workshop students live together, share the same cooking facilities, and work together for six days making pots for a four-day firing in the anagama kiln. Demonstrations, discussions of various philosophies of wood firing, and evening slide shows are also featured. Fine metals workshop titles include Jewelry and Metalsmithing Techniques, Sheet Metal Forming, Mixed Media for Metalsmiths, and Combining Metal for Patterned Imagery. Textile workshop topics are The Art of Hand Papermaking, Colorful Silks, Airbrush and Embroidery, and Color/Image Through Painted Warp, and woodworking workshops may focus on such topics as Cedar/Canvas Canoe Building, 18th Century Chairmaking, and Painted Surface Treatment in Furniture Design. General interest workshops cover such topics as marketing strategies and creative blockbusting. Children's programs, each limited to ten students from ages 7 to 10 and 11 to 13, meet for two hours on three consecutive Saturdays in May. Topics include ceramics, jewelry, weaving, and tie-dye and painting on silk.

Visitors to Peters Valley can observe workshops in progress and craftspeople at work in the studio from 2 to 4 pm daily, June 1 through August 31. An annual craft fair the last weekend in July features the work of more than 100 juried craftspeople, as well as demonstrations and live music. Peters Valley Craft Store sells the handmade work of artists from all over the U.S. and the Doremus Gallery features the work of past and present residents and summer instructors. Membership in Peters Valley offers such benefits as reduced workshop tuition, waiver of fees for children's programs, and a quarterly newsletter.

Specialties: Blacksmithing, ceramics, photography, textiles (basketry, papermaking, surface design, weaving), woodworking, fine metals.

Faculty: One accomplished, professional craftsperson in each discipline is selected for a year-round residency position. Residents receive studio and a home at a reasonable monthly rate and have the opportunity to manage a studio, plan programs, and earn a living at their craft. Blacksmithing instructors have included full-time blacksmiths Gary Gilmore, Jonathan Nedbor, Daryl Meier; blacksmith resident John Graney; and Jay Burnham-Kidwell. Ceramics instructors have included restorer Shirley Koehler; sculptor and artist Bennett Bean; ceramics resident Jim Jansma; and Tony Hepburn. Fine metals instructors have included resident metalsmith and platinum specialist Debra Stark; Chuck Evans, Frederick Marshall, and former fine metals residents Bob Natalini and Michael Leiber. Textile instructors have included textile resident Sandra Ward; basket artist Bryant Holsenbeck, papermaker Jennie Frederick; and full-time paper marbler Iris Nevins, author of *Traditional Marbling*. Woodworking instructors have included Horace Strong and David Finck; chairmaker Eugene Landon; and woodworking resident David Van Hoff.

Costs, Accommodations: Adult (member) tuition ranges from $55 ($40) for a one-day workshop to $370 ($350) for the 19-day anagama workshop plus a $15 nonrefundable application fee and materials fee. Children's workshops are $30 with a $5 nonrefundable registration fee and the one-day parent-child workshop tuition is $50 ($40). Studio assistantships are also available to qualified persons. Workshop application must be accompanied by a 50% tuition deposit, refundable if cancellation is postmarked at least three weeks prior; no refunds thereafter. Limited double occupancy housing is available in one of the Center's historic houses for $20 per night. Tickets may be purchased for three meals daily (lunch is offered for one-day workshops) and range from $27 for two days to $81 for five days. Annual Peters Valley membership dues are $25 regular, $40 couple.

Location: Peters Valley is situated in the Delaware Water Gap National Recreation Area in the Kittatinny Mountains bordering the Delaware River in northwest New Jersey, 70 miles from Newark airport. The area terrain is natural with unpaved driveways. Special assistance, if needed, may be arranged with the office. No direct public transportation is available but there is bus service to Newton Bus Station, 12 miles away, and prior arrangements may be made through the office to reach the school.

Contact: Peters Valley Craft Center, Layton, NJ 07851; (201) 948-5200.

PEWABIC POTTERY
Pewabic Society, Inc.
Detroit, Michigan

One and two-week workshops in June and July

Pewabic Pottery, a ceramic arts learning center, museum, gallery, and producer of hand-crafted architectural pottery and tile, founded in 1903, offers three or four summer workshops that are designed to bring the serious student and professional artist together to develop new skills and explore new ideas. Typical courses, limited to 14 students, include Ceramic Sculpture: Form & Content, a two-week workshop that utilizes slides, discussions, and hands-on practice to explore the potential of clay as a medium and a variety of construction techniques and firing methods; Useful Pots: Aesthetics & Process, which emphasizes the construction of salt and wood fired stoneware for the household and the development of thrown and altered shapes using the potters wheel; and Glaze Theory & Surface Development, which includes investigation of materials, molecular formation, glaze defects, and solutions, as well as discussions of historical pots, museum visits, and presentations by guest potters.

A two-year residency program, begun in 1987, is open to the talented, emerging ceramist whose focus lies in making functional pottery and/or architectural tile and who hopes to establish a successful studio. The resident is taught writing skills and how to deal professionally in the arts and in business and spends 20 hours weekly working for the pottery in one of its on-going programs. Each resident pays a $100 monthly studio fee and receives a $600 monthly living stipend, plus health insurance benefits. Applications are reviewed in the fall and spring.

The Pottery, which has been owned and operated by the nonprofit Pewabic Society, Inc., since 1981, also sponsors workshops and lectures by visiting ceramic artists, a two-year residency program for emerging craft artists, a residency for nonclay artists doing experimental work, community adult and children's classes, and gallery exhibitions. Pewabic's Museum houses an extensive permanent ceramics collection as well as historical documents that are available for research.

Specialties: Ceramics.

Faculty: Includes such prominent clay artists as Kathy Dambach, head of the Ceramic and Sculpture Departments at Henry Ford College, who earned her MFA from Ohio State University and whose sculpturally oriented clay work has been exhibited internationally; Joseph Bennion, a studio potter since 1977 and instructor at Brigham Young University, whose work has been exhibited in both juried and invitational shows; and Angela Fina, an experienced studio potter and board member of NCECA, who earned her MFA from the School of American Craftsmen and specializes in glaze theory and development.

Costs, Accommodations: Tuition (deposit), which includes daily lunch and one dinner, ranges from $250 ($100) for a one-week workshop to $400 ($200) for two weeks. Deposit plus a nonrefundable $15 application fee must accompany registration. Full deposit refund, less $50 withdrawal fee, is granted cancellations received more than 30 days prior. Housing is arranged on an individual basis within the community.

Facilities: Include electric, gas, wood, raku, and salt kilns and various types of tile-making equipment. All clay is made on-site.

Contact: Pewabic Pottery, 10125 E. Jefferson Ave., Detroit, MI 48214; (313) 822-0954.

PICTURE FRAMING ACADEMY
South San Francisco, California
Five and ten-day courses year-round

Founded in 1973, the Picture Framing Academy offers two courses in picture framing, each limited to six students and scheduled from 10:30 am to 5 pm, Monday through Friday. The five-day Basic Course, which is given approximately 15 times each year, covers conservation, matting, design, mounting techniques, frame making, glass cutting, fitting, and business theory. Advanced Framing, a ten-day course that is offered five times a year, covers such subjects as decorative matting, frame finishing, ornamentation, toning, antique frames restoration, liners, polygon frames, and shadow boxes. Students may enroll in both courses consecutively over a three week period. Classes are conducted in a relaxed atmosphere and a flexible schedule enables the teacher to adapt to each participant's knowledge and ability. A certificate of completion is awarded following successful course completion.

Specialties: Picture framing.

Faculty: Founder/director/instructor Paul Frederick, a framer with more than 30 years of experience, is a former education committee chairman of the Professional Picture Framers Association and editor of their monthly publication. He is currently a framing consultant for *Decor* and is author of *The Framer's Answer Book* and *More Answers for the Framer*.

Costs, Accommodations: Tuition is $500 for the Basic Course; $900 for the Advanced Course; and $1,200 for both courses. A nonrefundable $50 registration fee, which is not included in tuition, must accompany registration. Full refund, less registration fee, is granted cancellations more than three days prior; once classes have begun, refund depends on attendance time. Individual instruction can be arranged for an hourly fee. A list of nearby motel accommodations is provided.

Location, Facilities: Located in the center of South San Francisco opposite City Hall, the Academy is four blocks from the freeway ramp and 15 minutes from both the airport and downtown San Francisco. Facilities consist of a 1,200-square-foot workshop furnished with various makes and models of up-to-date equipment.

Contact: Picture Framing Academy, 435 Grand Ave., South San Francisco, CA 94080; (415) 588-4717.

PILCHUCK GLASS SCHOOL
Stanwood, Washington

18-day workshops from May-September

Established in 1971, the Pilchuck Glass School offers a wide variety of summer workshops for beginning to experienced students. Five 18-day sessions are scheduled from the end of May to the beginning of September, with five workshops offered during each session. Most workshops are open to serious beginners and more experienced students with advanced and masters class workshops requiring submission of slides, which are juried. Each workshop is limited to ten students, who are taught by one or two instructors and one to three teaching assistants. Sessions begin on Sunday afternoon with registration, supper, and orientation and conclude the third Wednesday at 4 pm. The daily schedule begins with breakfast at 7:45, followed immediately by class according to the instructor's format, lunch at noon, and dinner at 6 pm. Evenings are reserved for slide lectures presented by an instructor, artist-in-residence, teaching assistant, or staff member. Saturday classes are held at the discretion of the instructor and Sundays are free. Most studios and facilities are open 24 hours daily. Workshop titles may include Neon, Pate de Verre, Lampworking, Vitreography, Hot Glass, Kiln Formed Sculpture, Painting on Glass, Cold Working, Hot Glass Sculpture, Casting and Sand Mold Blowing, Stained Glass, Surface Decoration, Casting, Illusory Space in Glass, Engraving, and Hot Glass Design, Art and Craft.

The Pilchuck Society, a nonprofit, membership organization that represents a wide range of individuals and corporations interested in glass art, offers such benefits as an annual picnic, a semi-annual newsletter, discounts on books and posters, free admission to open houses, and opportunities to visit the school during the summer. Annual dues begin at $10 student/retired, $35 individual.

Specialties: Glass.

Faculty: Includes such prominent glass artists as Flora C. Mace, Joey Kirkpatrick, Fred Tschida, Henner Schroder, Susie Krasnican, David Reekie, Dana Zamecnikova, Marian Karel, Richard Royal, Dante Marioni, Ginny Ruffner, Liz Mappelli, Amy Roberts, Jose Chardiet, Jan Mares, Paul Stankard, Pino Signoretto, William Morris, Frantisek Vizner, Abinas Elskus, Susan Stinsmuehlen-Amend, Michael Scheiner, Robert Carlson, Dan Dailey, Klaus Moje, and Hans Gottfried von Stockhausen. Masters class instructors have included Stanislav Libensky, Jaroslava Brychtova, and Henry Halem and artists-in residence have included Judy Pfaff, William Wiley, Laddie John Dill, Michele Blondel, Dennis Oppenheim, Donald Lipski, John Torreano, Geralyn Donohue, Joan Wallace, Italo Scanga, and Tom Marioni.

Costs, Accommodations: Cost, which includes dormitory (student cottage) lodging, ranges from $1,125 ($1,375) to $1,450 ($1,700) per session. Application to all workshops must be submitted with a $25 nonrefundable application fee and advanced, graduate, and masters workshops require submission of slides and resume (plus letters of recommendation for masters workshop). A $250 deposit is required within two weeks of acceptance with balance due by May 15. MasterCard and VISA are accepted. Full refund, less $50 fee, is granted cancellations more than four weeks prior. Limited scholarship assistance is available, based on competitive application, and Teaching Assistantships, which cover payment for tuition, housing, meals, and some travel expense, are awarded to young professionals of unusual promise. A limited number of work/study positions enable students to pay a portion of their room and board by working 20 hours per week in the kitchen. Undergraduate and graduate college credit may be available.

Location, Facilities: The school is located at an elevation of 1,000 feet in the foothills of the Cascade Mountains, 50 miles from Seattle and 35 miles from Anacortes, where visitors can board ferries to the San Juan Islands. Nearby towns include Mt. Vernon and Bellingham. The extensively equipped studio complex, designed by Thomas Bosworth, FAIA, consists of a hot glass studio, a studio building, a cold working studio, a flat glass studio, and a wide variety of equipment. The Lodge contains the dining room, kitchen, and library.

Contact: Pilchuck Glass School, 1201 316th St. N.W., Stanwood, WA 98292; (206) 445-3111. From September 15 to May 15: Pilchuck Glass School, 107 S. Main #324, Seattle, WA 98104; (206) 621-8422.

PIPE SCULPTURE WORKSHOPS
Logan, Ohio and Fremont, California

Five-day workshops in July

First offered in 1973, these summer workshops for 12 to 18 students offer instruction in the techniques of sculpting with terra cotta sewer pipe extrusions, each six-feet in length and varying from four to twelve inches in diameter. The programs, which are held at clay pipe manufacturing plants in Ohio and California, begin with Sunday evening orientation and slide lecture followed by five days (and nights if desired) of hands-on experience using an unlimited supply of pipe. Work space in each plant is made available to participants and some of their completed pieces are fired by the host company along with its regular production ware. Applicants are required to submit slides of recent work for evaluation by a selection committee.

Specialties: Terra cotta pipe sculpture.

Faculty: Workshop director/instructor Jerry L. Caplan, who discovered the technique of using terra cotta pipe extrusions in 1955, holds a BFA and MFA from Carnegie Mellon University.

Costs: Fee for the entire workshop session is $250, which is payable upon acceptance. A list of tools and specific instructions are supplied.

Location: Workshops are held at the Logan Clay Products Co., located in the heart of Logan near Hocking State Park, and at the Mission Clay Co. in Fremont.

Contact: Jerry L. Caplan, Director, 5819 Alder St., Pittsburgh, Pa 15232; (412) 661-0179.

THE PLUM TREE SUMMER WORKSHOPS
Pilar, New Mexico

Five-day summer workshops

This bed and breakfast hostel sponsors a summer fine arts program that includes approximately five arts and crafts workshops, each limited to 12 participants. Typical workshop titles include Life and Landscape Drawing, a program devoted to drawing from a nude model and sketching along the Rio Grande; A Collaborative Sculpture, in which participants create a site specific sculpture that will become a permanent part of the Plum Tree grounds; Landscape Painting, for the intermediate to advanced student, which explores the color and space of the local countryside using oils and/or acrylics supplemented by discussions on color theory, composition, and content; The Gazebo: An Art Project, which involves the building of a traditional New Mexico-style gazebo; and Artforms: Handmade Papermaking, in which local plants are used for forming sheets and creating sculpture.

Specialties: A variety of topics, including painting, sculpture, papermaking.

Faculty: Instructors have included Gendron Jensen, Christine Taylor Patten, Raymond Tomasso, Rachel Stevens, Larry King, David Barbero, and Nadine Low.

Costs, Accommodations: Tuition ranges from $150 to $250. A 50% deposit must accompany application with balance due on arrival. Full refund, less 15% booking charge, is granted cancellations more than 20 days prior; deposit is forfeited thereafter. The hostel facilities consist of private rooms for couples and families, a women's dorm, bunkhouse, fully-equipped kitchen, and common get-together area. Accommodations, which include breakfast, range from $9.50 to $37.50 for one, $22 to $45 for two. A deposit of the greater of first night's rent or 50% of total is required and cancellations at least 48 hours prior receive full refund. Credit cards (MasterCard, VISA) accepted.

Location: Pilar, a centuries-old village along the banks of the Rio Grande, is 16 miles south of Taos. Airport shuttle and Greyhound bus service are available. The ski resorts of Taos Ski Valley, Angel Fire, and Sipapu, and the Indian pueblos and natural hot springs are all within driving distance. Other activities include hiking, cycling, and whitewater rafting.

Contact: The Plum Tree, Box 1A, Pilar, NM 87531; (800) 678-7586 *or* (505) 758-4696.

POINT REYES FIELD SEMINARS
Point Reyes Station, California
One to four-day seminars year-round

This self-supporting year-round program, sponsored by the Point Reyes National Seashore Association since 1976, offers courses in the arts, natural history, environmental education, and programs especially designed for families and teachers. Approximately 25 to 30 one to four-day arts and crafts seminars are scheduled each year.

The mostly one-day seminars, which are limited to 18 to 24 participants of all levels, include such titles as "Gyotaku" Japanese Fish Printing, which covers the use of these techniques on local fish and plants; Natural Materials Baskets, which emphasizes the use of palm leaves, moss, bark, sticks, and vines to fashion a free-form basket and a palm leaf fan; Drawing Nature Close-up, a day of pencil sketching that focuses on drawing seedpods, grasses, seashells, and other intricate forms of life; Illustrating Wildflowers, which stresses close-up work in pencil, ink, and scratchboard to capture the intricate forms of local wildflowers; and Drawing From Photographs, Drawing Natural Forms in Color, Pine Needle Baskets, and Illustration and Perception in Nature. Two to four-day seminars grant one or two credits from Dominican College of San Rafael to those who submit a paper or project.

Specialties: Outdoor and nature arts and crafts.

Faculty: Includes biologist Chris Dewees, marine fisheries specialist at UC-Davis, a fish printer since 1968; biological illustrator Chuck Stasek, a teacher at the California Academy of Sciences, Oregon Institute of Marine Biology and the Yosemite Association; Ana Rovetta, formerly director of Slide Ranch Environmental Education Center and education specialist at Audubon Canyon Ranch; and fiber artist Kathleen Hubbard.

Costs, Accommodations: Cost, which includes lodging, ranges from $30 to $55 per day, depending on instructor. College credit is $30 per unit. Bunkhouse accommodations are provided at the Clem Miller Environmental Education Center. Full refund less $10 fee is granted cancellations more than 15 working days prior to seminar; 50% refund less $10 is granted 11 to 15 working days prior; no refund thereafter. Those who cancel more than 10 days prior can opt for a seminar credit, good for one year, in lieu of refund.

Location: Point Reyes National Seashore is 50 miles north of San Francisco.

Contact: Point Reyes Field Seminars, Point Reyes National Seashore Assn., Bear Valley Rd., Point Reyes Station, CA 94956; (415) 663-1200.

PRISCILLA HAUSER SEMINARS
Panama City, Florida and other locations in the U.S. and Canada
Five-day seminars year-round

Since 1966, Priscilla Hauser has taught tole and decorative painting seminars that will give the novice or the experienced artist a foundation in method painting and techniques for painting a variety of fruits, flowers, leaves, Country French, and other subjects on wood, metal, glass, and fabric surfaces. The seminars cover brush strokes, dry-brush blending, back-grounds, and surface preparation and include critique sessions and discussions relating to business and teaching practices, store management, advertising, and promotion. Each seminar begins with an orientation from 4 to 9 pm on Sunday and classes meet from 9 am to 5 pm, Monday through Thursday, and from 9 am to 4 pm on Friday.

In the Basic I and II seminars, limited to 20 attendees per instructor and one assistant, students learn the fundamentals of surface preparation, back-grounds, staining, antiquing, and special effects, and complete several projects. Those who complete the Basic II qualify to become Priscilla Hauser Accredited Teachers. Basic III, limited to 12 students, covers advanced and creative painting, fine art realism, and color coordination. Special seminars include Roses and Advanced Roses, Priscilla's specialty; Paint a Merry Christmas, devoted to creating holiday items; and Wet Into Wet Oil Painting, which covers floral techniques on canvas and other frameable surfaces.

Specialties: Tole and decorative painting.

Faculty: Priscilla Hauser is the founder of the National Society of Tole and Decorative Painters and is featured in a public television series, *The Joy of Tole Painting.*

Costs, Accommodations: Tuition is approximately $275 for each seminar, with the exception of the Basic III and Roses, which are $300 each. The cost of projects averages from $100 to $160, depending upon projects. A nonrefundable $100 deposit must accompany registration with balance payable the last day of the seminar.

Location: Several seminars each year are held at Priscilla's Studio by the Sea, located on the Gulf of Mexico approximately ten miles from Panama City

Beach, which is in the northern Florida Panhandle. Other locations include Oklahoma, Georgia, Michigan, California, Ontario, and Quebec.

Contact: Priscilla's, P.O. Box 521013, Tulsa, OK 74152-1013; (918) 743-6072/5075.

PRUDE RANCH SCHOOL OF ART
Ft. Davis, Texas
Five-day workshops during two weeks in October

This annual two-week summer program, first offered in 1979, features a variety of five-day classes for artists of all levels. The school runs from Monday through Friday on two consecutive weeks, with a trip to Big Bend, Mexico, scheduled the weekend in between. Students can enroll in one of six classes that are offered each weekday morning, devoted to such topics as watercolor and oil painting, drawing, and portraiture. A two-hour afternoon caricature class may also be available. The weekend trip features a tour of Big Bend, a Rio Grande river rafting trip, a night in Lajitas, and a Sunday morning market visit.

Specialties: Landscape and portrait painting.

Faculty: Instructors, which change each year, have included Texas landscape painter Loveta Strickland, portrait painter John Squire Adams, impressionist painter Ann Templeton, and watercolorists John Carter, Ken Hosmer, and Carolyn Utigard Thomas.

Costs, Accommodations: Five-day tuition is approximately $125 and room and board ranges from $15 per day for three meals only to $50 per day for three meals and double occupancy motel room. Family units and recreational vehicle hookup are also available. The afternoon workshop is $25 per week additional. The weekend trip, which includes double occupancy lodging and raft trip, is $125. A $25 deposit must accompany registration with balance due on arrival.

Location, Facilities: Prude Ranch is situated in the Davis Mountains of West Texas, on the north border of the Chihuahuan Desert and near historic Ft. Davis and the McDonald Observatory. Ranch facilities include a swimming pool, tennis courts, horseback riding, and hay rides.

Contact: John Carter, Prude Ranch School of Art, 1700 Mockingbird Ln., Killeen, TX 76541; (817) 526-6413.

PYRAMID ATLANTIC
Washington, D.C. and Baltimore, Maryland
One to five-day workshops year-round; three-week summer intensive

Founded in Baltimore in 1980 and expanded to Washington, D.C., in 1986 as a nonprofit center for hand papermaking, printmaking, and the art of the book, Pyramid Atlantic provides access to equipment and technical expertise; sponsors workshops, master classes, lectures, demonstrations, and exhibitions; offers studio rental, residency, and publishing programs; and acts as a resource center. More than 50 workshops for adults and children of all ages and levels are offered during the year and a three-week summer intensive is held during July. Most workshops are scheduled from 10 am to 4 pm.

Workshops and master classes focus on the major areas of papermaking, printmaking, making of the book, offset printing, and photography and may be taken individually or in a sequence of four to six courses over a period of three to four months. Course content ranges from introductory level to specialized topics and master classes by prominent artists. Typical titles include Making Paper Moulds, in which students construct moulds and then use them to make paper; Binding Handmade Papers, which includes the construction of several books; Relief Printing, in which participants cut and print their own woodcuts using a variety of techniques; and One-of-a-Kind Artists' Books, which explores alternative structures and concepts. Introductory and young people's workshops are held at the Baltimore facility.

The summer intensive consists of two, three, and four-day workshops devoted to the making of paper and to papermaking equipment, letterform design, letterpress, bookbinding, and offset printing. The program also features prominent visiting artists, open access studio hours, lectures, discussions, and private tours of book collections. Participants can enroll in individual workshops, in a one-week session of workshops, or in the full three-week program. A series of short-term residencies for talented visual artists desiring to work in paper, prints, and books is available.

Specialties: Papermaking, bookmaking, printmaking.

Faculty: Founder/director Helen Frederick is a prominent artist who works in paper, prints, mixed media, and facilitates collaborative projects. Other instructors include Kathy Amt, Ed Bernstein, Doug Beube, Linda Blaser, Eileen Canning, Don Carrick, Karen Cunc, Ruth Faerber, Lynn Forgach, Brad Freeman, Miriam Hendel, Mary Holland, Rick Hungerford, Julia Kjelgaard, Lee S. McDonald, Jan Mehn, Kenneth Polinskie, Tanya Schmoller, Keith Smith, and Martie Zelt. Guest instructors include Neil Bonham, Hiromi Katayama, Rohn Risseauw, Jan Subota, Takeshi Takahara.

Costs, Accommodations: Workshop fees are approximately $60 ($45 for members) for one day, $95 ($80) for two days, $275 ($250) for five days. The cost of the summer intensive ranges from $25 to $400 per week, $1,000 for the entire three weeks. Payment, which must accompany registration, is 90% refundable for cancellations more than two weeks prior; 75% refundable two days to two weeks prior; no refunds thereafter. Housing for the summer intensive is available at George Washington University Intern Halls for $15 per night and nearby hotels and motels. Annual membership dues begin at $20 for donors, $35 for friends, who are entitled to workshop discounts.

Location, Facilities: The Baltimore location, which offers papermaking classes and studio rentals, is located on Guilford Avenue. The 4,000-square-foot Washington workshop, near the Takoma Metro stop, offers papermaking facilities and a wide range of printing equipment.

Contact: Pyramid Atlantic, 6925 Willow St., NW, #226, Washington, DC 20012; (202) 291-0088.

QUILT CAMP
Shaver Lake, California
Six-day seminars in July and August

First offered in 1977, this program for women who are interested in working with fabric provides the opportunity to learn new techniques of fabric design, renew skills in embellishment, start a quilt, or explore approaches to designing with a new material. Three intensive six-day seminars are scheduled during the summer, each limited to 26 students of all levels of experience. The seminars begin with Sunday reception, dinner, and evening session and the next five days consist of morning and afternoon classes, demonstrations, reviews, open studio time, and evening presentations. Typical activities include Silk Screen Printing, which covers the use of stencils and photo emulsion on fabric for special projects, quilt blocks, or clothing; Wood Appliqué, which focuses on using small electric jig saws and creating designs in wood for panels, puzzles, or free standing figures; and Cyanotype, which involves blue printing on fabric and the creation of permanent images from found objects, photographs, or drawings. One semester unit of college credit is available through CSU-Fresno.

Specialties: Quilting.

Faculty: Jean Ray Laury, author of *Ho for California: Pioneer Women and Their Quilts,* and Joyce Aiken, Professor of Art at CSU-Fresno.

Costs, Accommodations: Fee, which includes lodging, most meals, and supplies, ranges from $280 to $455. A $50 deposit must accompany application; balance due June 1. Cancellations after June 15 receive up to 50% of balance. Lodging includes individual and shared cabins and chalets.

Location: The camp is held at the Shaver Lake Community Center, at an elevation of 5,000 feet in the High Sierras, one hour east of Fresno.

Contact: Jean Ray Laury, c/o Bea Slater, 18994 Auberry Rd., Clovis, CA 93612; (209) 299-6327 *or* (209) 297-0228.

RIVERBEND ART CENTER (RAC)
Dayton, Ohio
One to five-day workshops

Established in 1965 as part of the Cultural Arts Complex at DeWeese Park, the nonprofit Riverbend Art Center is operated by the City of Dayton, Division of Recreation and Parks, and the Riverbend Arts Council. RAC sponsors nine-week courses, classes for young people, and art and craft workshops for adults of all levels. Class size ranges from 5 to 25 and sessions usually are held from 9:30 am until 3:30 to 4:30 pm. Typical titles include Painting Techniques, Introduction to Airbrush, Anticlastic Raising for Jewelers and Sculptors, Basketry, Marbleizing, Paper Making, Selling Methods for Artists and Craftsmen, and Exploring Color (page 70).

Specialties: A variety of subjects, including painting and drawing, enameling and metals, textiles, book arts, pottery, calligraphy, and gem cutting.

Faculty: Professional artists and craftsmen.

Costs: Nonrefundable tuition ranges from $15 to $35 for a one-day workshop, $55 to $100 for five days, plus materials fee of $5 to $10. General Membership fee of $10 is payable once a year and required for class enrollment. Full tuition and membership fee must accompany registration.

Location: The Center, which is handicapped accessible, is six minutes from central Dayton near I-75. Nearby attractions include the Air Force Museum, Museum of Natural History, and the Dayton Art Institute.

Contact: Riverbend Art Center, 1301 E. Siebenthaler Ave., Dayton, OH 45414; (513) 278-0655/0656.

RIVERSIDE — THE INN AT CAMBRIDGE SPRINGS
Cambridge Springs, Pennsylvania
Two-day spring and fall workshops

Since 1986, Riverside has sponsored Friday evening to Sunday afternoon workshops for all levels in watercolor (limit 15 students), drawing, oil and acrylic painting (limit 10), and sculpture (limit 5). Landscape and still life watercolor classes emphasize design, mood, color and critiques.

Specialties: Painting, drawing, sculpture.

Faculty: Riverside artist-in-residence William Wesley Wentz (watercolor) teaches at Valley Arts Guild and Thiel College; Charlie Pitcher (drawing, oil painting), Pittsburgh's 1987 Artist of the Year, studied at the Pratt Institute; George Christy (acrylic painting, sculpture), was a nominee for one of ten Pennsylvania Governors' Awards for excellence in arts.

Costs, Accommodations: The $160 fee includes double-occupancy lodging and meals. A $50 deposit secures reservation; balance due on arrival. Deposit is refundable more than four weeks prior if space can be filled.

Location: Riverside, an inn first opened in 1885 and now enrolled in the National Register of Historic Places, overlooks French Creek. Cambridge Springs is in northwest Pennsylvania, between Pittsburgh and Erie. Activities include golf, tennis, swimming, canoeing, and riding.

Contact: Cambridge Springs Workshops, Riverside Inn, Cambridge Springs, PA 16403; (814) 398-4645. Winter Address: Michael Halliday, 273 Main St., Greenville, PA 16125; (412) 588-8995/8300.

THE ROBERT LOEWE WEAVING SCHOOL
Divide, Colorado
Six-day courses year-round

Opened in 1987, the Robert Loewe Weaving School offers Monday to Saturday intensive courses devoted to the art of weaving rugs and tapestries on a two-harness floor loom. Each course is limited to three beginning students, who receive instruction in dyeing wool, methods of finishing a weaving after it's off the loom, winding the warp onto the loom, and marketing. Emphasis is on learning a variety of lines and shapes for weaving designs and students practice the rhythm of moving hands and feet to build up speed while obtaining straight edges. Instruction is scheduled from 9 am to 1 pm on three 2-harness floor looms and the studio stays open with the instructor available from 2 to 8:30 pm. Evening activities include an informal musicale and traditional matzo brei supper.

Specialties: Rug and tapestry weaving using two-harness floor loom.

Faculty: Robert Loewe, a former teacher, scout master, professional piano player, and author holds degrees from Western State College, Stanford University, and the University of Colorado. He has been a self-employed professional weaver since 1978.

Costs, Accommodations: Cost, which includes housing and wool, is $295. A 50% deposit must accompany application with balance payable upon arrival. Full refund is granted cancellations more than 14 days prior. Lodging, located 200 feet behind the main house/studio, is in a small, solar-heated guest house with refrigerator and cooking facilities. Students prepare their own meals and should bring provisions.

Location: The rustic mountain setting, 35 miles west of Colorado Springs, is situated at an elevation of 9,200 feet in a forested area that offers hiking and cross-country skiing. Ground transportation from the Colorado Springs Airport may be arranged for a fee of $15 plus $5 for each additional person.

Contact: Robert Loewe, Box W-26, Divide, CO 80814; (719) 687-3249.

ROCKFORD SCHOOL OF WEAVING
Rockford, Michigan
One to five-day workshops year-round

Established in 1968, this school, part of The Weavers Shop & Yarn Co., offers weekend and five-day workshops covering a variety of subjects and methods that are tailored to individual needs and experience. The five-day workshops, geared to all levels, are held daily from 9 am to 4 pm in July and August. Beginners learn such techniques as warping, dressing the loom, and weaving a mohair scarf, rug in boundweave, and lockweave wallhanging or pillow; intermediates work on pattern weaving, overshot, summer and winter, textile analysis, and rug and other techniques; and advanced students explore double and tubular weaving, pick up and swivel weaving, brocade, pique, and multiharness weaves. Classes-by-the-day allow students of all levels to practice and enhance their skills in the area they choose. A typical weekend course such as Weaving Pictures But Not Tapestry is limited to 15 students and covers such topics as the Moorman Technique, shaft switching, pick-up pique, brocade, Swedish inlay, and lock weave.

Specialties: Weaving.

Faculty: Jochen Ditterich began weaving in Finland and studied with commercial weavers in Germany and at the University of Michigan with Robert Sailors and Theo Morman. He has taught weaving since 1968.

Costs, Accommodations: Cost of each five-day workshop is $80; a $30 deposit must accompany application with balance due two weeks prior. Classes-by-the-Day are $30 per day ($30 deposit). Cost of the three-day weekend workshop is $40 ($20 deposit). Materials are extra. All deposits are refundable for cancellations received more than four weeks prior. Floor looms, both 36" and 45", are furnished. Lodging is available in nearby motels and private homes.

Location: Rockford is 20 minutes north of Grand Rapids. Local attractions include Squires Street Square, a community of shops in restored buildings of the 1800's, an historical museum, and a factory outlet mall.

Contact: The Weavers Shop & Yarn Co., 39 Courtland St., P.O. Box 457, Rockford, MI 49341-0457; (616) 866-9529.

THE ROCKPORT APPRENTICESHOP
WOODEN BOATBUILDING CENTER
Rockport, Maine

Six-week internships year-round; one-day to two-week summer workshops

This nonprofit educational institution, founded in 1982 by Lance R. Lee to sustain manual skills and preserve the the technology of constructing and using wooden boats, offers 18 to 24-month apprenticeships, six-week internships and volunteerships, and summer workshops during the two-week apprentices' vacation . No previous boatbuilding experience is required for any of the programs except the apprenticeships, which are filled by staff selection from those who have completed an internship or volunteership.

Two new interns start every three weeks throughout the year, pairing up with the two interns who started three weeks before to build two skiffs that are selected for the techniques they teach. Interns learn from instructors, apprentices, and a manual, but most learning is self-motivated. Between April and November, volunteers work on a variety of projects to improve the facility, grounds, and programs. Apprentices assist volunteers in building repairs and improvements, road maintenance, and boat painting.

About a half dozen workshops for adults and two or three for children are offered during summer break, including a two-week workshop, Build Your Own & Take It Home, in which participants build a 9' Norwegian Pram; Boatbuilding for Women, a five-morning course that covers the basics of tool sharpening, setting up, planking, framing, interior work, and finishing; and Traditional Decorative Marine Carving, a five-morning course that focuses on marine symbols. Five-afternoon courses for children, ages 8 to 12, include Wow, I Made That! An Introduction to Woodworking and Little Boats That Float, a model boatbuilding course. Enrollment ranges from 6 to 10 students.

Specialties: Boatbuilding and related crafts.

Faculty: The school has fourteen apprentices, three instructors, and four interns at a time. Instructors are master boatbuilder Dave Foster, who attended Harvard and owns Ponset Harbor Boatshop; Kevin Carney, who has worked for several boatyards and had his own boatbuilding shop; and Bruce McKenzie, who started the program at Cape Fear Technical Institute.

Costs, Accommodations: Cost of the internship is $900 and there is no cost to volunteer program. The two-week boatbuilding workshop is $765 ($750 for members); five-day courses are about $120 ($115); and children's courses are about $70 ($65). VISA and MasterCard are accepted. A $300 nonrefundable deposit is required for the internship, full tuition for the workshops. Workshop cancellations more than two weeks prior receive full refund less $25. A list of nearby accommodations is provided. Annual membership dues of $35 provide such benefits as a journal, newsletter, and workshop discounts.

Location, Facilities: The Apprenticeshop is on the waterfront in Rockport, a seaport resort halfway down the Maine Coast on Penobscot Bay. The closest airport is in Rockland, which has flights to Portland and Boston. Facilities include two boatbuilding bays, an office, and the Visitor's Loft, from which guests can view the activity and changing exhibits and purchase books, prints, and other items. The work area is wheelchair accessible.

Contact: The Rockport Apprenticeshop, P.O. Box 539, Sea St., Rockport, ME 04856; (207) 236-6071.

ROCKPORT ART ASSOCIATION
Rockport, Massachusetts
Three to five-day workshops from June-October

Founded in 1921, the Rockport Art Association offers a summer program of indoor and outdoor workshops and classes for artists of all levels as well as workshops and classes for children. Approximately eight to ten workshops are held annually, each taught by a prominent artist/instructor and including lectures, demonstrations, and individual critique. Typical workshop titles include Indoor Marine Painting in Oil (Charles Vickery), Indoor Portrait Workshop (Paul Leveille), Outdoor Oil Painting Workshop (Charles Movalli), Oil Still Life Workshop (Rudolph Colao), and Watercolor — Face & Figure (Roberta Carter Clark).

Specialties: Painting.

Faculty: Instructors change each year. In addition to the above, they have included Rockport Art Association members T.M. Nicholas, Pamela Fox, Ferdinand Petrie, and Frank Federico.

Costs, Accommodations: Tuition ranges from $150 for a three-day workshop to $225 for five days. A $50 deposit secures reservation with balance due two weeks prior. Deposit refunded cancellations at least one week prior.

Location: The Association is situated a block from the sea in the Old Tavern building, which was built in 1787 and has been a private home, an inn, a tavern, and a stagecoach stop. Rockport is 55 minutes north of Boston on Rtes. 128 and 127.

Contact: The Rockport Art Association, 12 Main St., Rockport, MA 01966; (508) 546-6604.

ROUND TOP CENTER FOR THE ARTS (RTCA)
Damariscotta, Maine

Five to seven-day workshops in June, July, and September

Round Top Center for the Arts, a nonprofit community resource center for the visual and performing arts and humanities, founded in 1988, sponsors a series of approximately ten summer workshops for artists of all levels. Typical subjects include egg tempera and egg tempera portrait, a hands-on exploration of the egg emulsion technique as practiced by the sixteenth and seventeenth century masters; Gyotaku-fish printing, a study of the layering of colors on rice paper using soft silk and unbleached cotton tampers; and watercolor, watermedia, and drawing. Each workshop begins with an evening reception and orientation and formal classes meet daily from 9 am until 3 or 4 pm with a final critique and dutch treat dinner scheduled the last day. The Center also offers year-round art classes and gallery shows and sponsors an annual summer arts festival.

Specialties: Painting.

Faculty: Has included Naomi Brotherton (Watercolor), an experienced commercial artist and past president of the Southwestern Watercolor Society, whose work has been featured in *Variations in Watercolor*, published in 1981; Frank Havlicek (Gyotak-Fish Printing), a former student of Yoshihiko Takahashi, whose prints have been exhibited at Chicago's Shedd Aquarium and the Walker Art Gallery; Al Brouillette (Watermedia), a member of the National Academy of Design, American Watercolor Society, and Allied Artists of America and author of *The Evolving Picture*; Stanley Maltzman (Drawing), a graphic artist and recipient of awards from the Hudson Valley Art Association, Ball State University, and the American Artists Professional League; Bradford Voight (Watercolor), a member of Academic Artists, Southern Vermont Artists and past president of the Connecticut Watercolor Society; Maxine Masterfield (Watermedia), a graduate of the Cleveland Institute of Art and author of *Painting the Spirit of Nature*; Morris Shubin (Watercolor), a purchase award-winner at the 1985 AWS annual exhibit and an electee to the Watercolor, U.S.A Honor Society; and Alex Gnidziejko (Egg Tempera), who studied at New York's Pratt Institute and has received awards from The Society of Illustrators, Graphic Design U.S.A., and the American Society of Business Editors.

Costs, Accommodations: Course fees range from $135 to $275. Lodging is available at local bed & breakfasts with daily rates from $45. Members of RTCA receive such benefits as workshop discounts, newletters, bulletins, and invitations to openings and receptions. Annual dues begin at $10 student, $15 individual, and $25 family.

Location: The Center is in Damariscotta at the site of a former dairy farm and the present Round Top Ice Cream Co. on Business Rte.1. Nearby recreational facilities offer swimming, boating, fishing, tennis, golf, bird-watching, and hiking and other area attractions include galleries and museums.

Contact: Round Top Center for the Arts, P.O. Box 1316, Damariscotta, ME 04543; (207) 563-1507.

SAGAMORE LODGE AND CONFERENCE CENTER
Raquette Lake, New York

Three to five-day workshops from May-October

This historic "Adirondack Great Camp" resort, built by William West Durant in 1897 and for 50 years a Vanderbilt family retreat, is run by Sagamore Institute, a nonprofit organization dedicated to the preservation of history and the environment, social concerns, personal growth, and arts and crafts. During the summer season Sagamore offers a variety of weekend and five-day programs on such topics as arts and crafts, photography, fishing, storytelling, mountain music, and llama trekking. Typical workshop titles include Painting and Illustrating Nature, Rustic Furniture, Basketry, and Woodcarving.

Specialties: Painting, woodcarving, basketry, and other topics.

Faculty: Includes Bill Smith (basketry), Tom Philips and Jackson Smith (rustic furniture), Wayne Trimm (painting and illustrating nature), and Rick and Ellen Butz (woodcarving).

Costs, Accommodations: Rates, which include double occupancy accommodations in guest lodges and meals in the dining room, range from $140 to $190 for two-night weekends and $350 to $400 for five nights. An $80 deposit must accompany reservation and telephone credit card (VISA, MasterCard) registrations are accepted. Cancellations more than one month prior to workshop are granted a $40 refund.

Location: Sagamore is near Raquette Lake in the central Adirondack mountains, 2 1/2 hours north of Albany, 1 1/2 hours north of Utica and 3 hours south of Canada.

Contact: Sagamore Lodge and Conference Center, Sagamore Rd., Raquette Lake, NY 13436; (315) 354-5311.

SAN MIGUEL WORKSHOPS
San Miguel de Allende, Mexico

Year-round workshops of two days or more

San Miguel Workshops, sponsored by Waterleaf Mill & Bindery (founded in 1978) and Pequeno Press (founded in 1984), offers private and small group (limit 6 participants) instruction in book crafts for students of all levels. Students may also elect to work privately on special projects, using the studio and facilities, and receive instruction part time. The workshops include Papermaking, both basic and advanced-experimental, which covers linter and botanical papers and dimensional paperworks; Marbling, a two-day intensive which focuses on traditional, experimental, Suminagashi, fabric, and leather as well as paste papers; Bookbinding, a four-day instructional program in basic (four book structures and slipcase) or advanced (traditional fine binding or boxes, or eccentric contemporary bindings) techniques ; and Letterpress, which offers printing instruction and use of the Pequeno Press facilities.

Specialties: Book crafts, including papermaking, marbling, bookbinding, letterpress.

Faculty: Pat Baldwin, workshop director, and papermaking instructor Jaime Gonzalez, who specializes in limited edition and miniature books.

Costs, Accommodations: Instruction in papermaking and letterpress is $75 per week; two-day marbling workshop is $50; four-day bookbinding workshops are $160 each. Studio rental (marbling and bookbinding) is $20 per day; papermill rental (papermaking), which includes use of Hollander beater, 20-ton hydraulic press, vats, moulds, and vacuum table, is $20 per day; and letterpress studio rental, which includes instruction, is $35 per day. Inexpensive lodging can be arranged locally in small posadas or pensions.

Location: San Miguel de Allende, a colonial hill town and artists' and writers' colony, is accessible from Mexico City.

Contact: Pat Baldwin, Waterleaf Mill & Bindery and Pequeno Press, Apdo. 96, San Miguel de Allende 37700, Mexico; (52) 465-20426.

SARS-POTERIES SUMMER SCHOOL
Musée-Atelier du Verre
Sars-Poteries, France

Five to nine-day summer workshops

Established in 1985, this center for experimental glass art offers about a half dozen workshops each summer for glass lovers of all levels of ability and experience. The workshops are limited to 10 to 12 students and cover a variety of glassworking techniques, including: Cold Working, which concentrates on cold technique and the design aspects of laminated and fabricated glass as well as kiln forming; Hot Glass Glass-Forming, a beginners session focusing on theoretical and practical glass forming possibilities and restraints and such techniques as kiln-forming, blowing, casting, and coating; Kiln Forming, which encourages a non-traditional and innovative approach and covers fusing, slumping, casting, and pate de verre; Hot Glass Blowing and Casting, which combines blowing and sand casting with cutting and polishing; Synergetic Research, a multi-disciplinary workshop originally intended as two parallel courses, covering the range of hot and cold techniques; and Pâte de Verre, which deals with the various techniques for kiln forming glass into molds and finished pieces.

Specialties: Glassworking.

Faculty: Durk Valkema (Cold Working), a studio artist living in Amsterdam, is an experienced furnace and kiln designer; Jean-Pierre Umbdenstock (Hot Glass Glass-Forming); Warren Langley (Experimental Kiln Techniques), a studio artist from Sydney, is involved with large scale projects of artworks in architectural spaces; Claude Monod (Hot Glass Blowing, Casting), a former student of Bertil Valien; Peter Layton and Edward Leibovitz (Synergetic Research); and Etienne Leperlier (Pâte de Verre), grandson of François Décorchemont.

Costs, Accommodations: Tuition ranges from 3,000 FF to 4,000 FF and a 250 FF fee must accompany application. Accommodations include local hotel rooms at 180 FF per night, bungalows shared by six students at 50 FF, and a nearby camping site. Meals (cold lunch, hot dinner) are shared at the Museum and cost approximately 60 FF daily. Students are requested to bring samples of work, portfolios, and slides as well as drawing materials and any favorite tools. Several half-grants are available.

Location: The northern French village of Sars-Poteries, once the site of an important glass industry, is now one of the major European centers for experimental glass art. It is located close to the Belgian border, several kilometers east of the Paris-Brussels road between Avesnes and Maubeuge, and is the site of a well-known glass museum that houses one of the most important contemporary collections in France.

Contact: Musée-Atelier du Verre, 1, rue du General de Gaulle - B.P.2, 59216, Sars-Poteries, France; (33) 27-61-61-44.

SAWMILL CENTER FOR THE ARTS
Cook Forest State Park
Cooksburg, Pennsylvania
One to five-day workshops from May-October

Established in 1974 by administrator Verna Leith, this nonprofit arts organization each year offers more than 130 workshops in the visual arts, including woodcarving, basketry, spinning, drawing and painting, quilting, weaving, rug braiding, calligraphy, block printing, picture framing, and origami. Most workshops meet from 9 am to 4 pm daily and are open to all levels with a few geared to experienced artists and craftsmen. Enrollment is usually limited to 12 students per instructor. The Center also sponsors an eight-week craft program for children, Elderhostel weeks, and a variety of other activities, including demonstrations, exhibits, a Craft Market, festivals, and live theatre performances at the Verna Leith Sawmill Theatre.

Typical woodcarving workshops include Relief Woodcarving (carving a picture in wood), Woodcarving in the Round (wood sculpture), Realistic Bird Carving, and Advanced Woodcarving, in which students carve a miniature carousel horse. Other workshop titles may include Big Brush Painting, Sculpting With Clay, Caricatures, and Linoleum Block Printing.

Specialties: Woodcarving, basketry, and other arts and crafts.

Faculty: Includes woodcarvers Joe Dampf, Wayne Edmondson, Larry Groninger, Nancy Jones, Robert Butler, and Robert Wilson; spinners Persis Grayson and Sue Beevers; block printer Mary Hamilton; and caricaturist John Johns.

Costs, Accommodations: Tuition ranges from $10 to $25 for a one or two-day workshop, from about $100 to $130 for five days. Materials are extra. A 50% deposit must accompany registration with balance due 15 days prior to class. Cancellations more than 48 hours prior receive full refund. Accommodations in nearby cabins, lodges, campgrounds and motels range from approximately $100 to $250 per week.

Location: This rural arts center, which is handicapped accessible, is located three hours from Pittsburgh and Cleveland in Cook Forest State Park, which covers more than 6,000 acres in northwestern Pennsylvania. Bordered by the Clarion River, the park has 30 miles of hiking trails and a virgin forest that is a Registered National Natural Landmark. The nearest city is Clarion, home of Clarion University.

Contact: Sawmill Center for the Arts, P.O. Box 180, Cooksburg, PA 16217; (814) 927-6655 *or* (814) 226-1947 (Nov.-May).

SCHOOL OF AIRBRUSH ARTS
Villa Park, Illinois

Five-day seminars in January, February, July, and August

Established in 1982, the School of Airbrush Arts offers three courses of instruction that lead to a mastery of the airbrush: Airbrush Painting, Photo-Restoration, and Photo-Retouching. The Airbrush Painting course consists of three 40-hour seminars (Beginning, Intermediate, and Advanced Airbrush) that are scheduled from 8 am to 4:30 pm, Monday through Friday; from 6:30 to 10:30 pm twice weekly for four weeks; and from 9 am to 3:15 pm three times a week for seven sessions. The Photo-Restoration and Photo-Retouching courses follow a similar format, with the Beginning Airbrush seminar preceding the three seminars specific to each course. Class size is limited to 20 students, who each have their own airbrush station.

The Airbrush Painting course emphasizes both technical and creative approaches and allows students to apply instruction to their own disciplines. The Photo-Restoration course covers montage techniques, creating formal portraits from snapshots, removing a person from the group without it being noticable, restoring damaged color photographs, and hand-tinting. The Photo-Retouching course teaches the fundamentals of retouching transparencies and black and white and color prints. Students are given a diverse selection of assignments that are designed to round out their portfolio.

Specialties: Airbrush techniques, including photo-restoration and photo-retouching.

Faculty: Airbrush painting and photo-restoration instructor Dennis D. Goncher received his BS in art from the University of Wisconsin-Madison and his MFA degree from the Rhode Island School of Design. Photo-retouching instructor Albert J. Corke has more than 30 years of experience as a photo-retoucher.

Costs, Accommodations: The cost of each 40-hour seminar or class is $385. The three-seminar (120 hour) Airbrush Painting course is $1,155 and the four-seminar (160 hour) Photo-Restoration and Photo-Retouching courses are $1,540. Materials for the Beginning Airbrush Painting seminar are provided by the school; for the other seminars the cost ranges from $40 to $75. Students can enroll in the complete course or individual seminars. The per-seminar registration fee is $25, up to a maximum of $75 for three or more seminars. Full payment of registration fee and tuition are due prior to the first session. A full refund is granted cancellations within seven days of acceptance and a tuition refund is granted those who cancel prior to the end of the first day of class. A refund schedule is in effect thereafter. Those who enroll as vocational students must have a high school diploma or equivalent, art experience, or professional experience. Those who enroll as avocational students may not be minors or enrolled in high school. A list of nearby accommodations is provided.

Location: The school is in a handicapped accessible one-story building that is located in the Chicago suburb of Villa Park, accessible by major thoroughfares with exits off the Eisenhower Expressway, Illinois Tollway, and Route 83. Villa Park borders on Elmhurst and Oakbrook and is 19 miles from downtown Chicago, which can be reached by rail from the Villa Park station.

Contact: School of Airbrush Arts, 1330 S. Villa Ave., Villa Park, IL 60181; (312) 834-7333.

SCHOOL OF THE ARTS AT RHINELANDER
University of Wisconsin-Madison
Rhinelander, Wisconsin
Five days in July

Held annually since 1964, this five-day school offers courses in visual and folk arts, writing, music, and theatre. Students of all levels may select up to three courses, some half and some full-day. A variety of special events, including lectures, photography and art exhibits, and an arts festival, are scheduled daily and in the evenings. Recreational activities such as fishing and boating are nearby.

Approximately 15 visual and folk arts courses are offered, most open to students of all levels. Typical visual arts courses include Beginning and Advanced Painting, Basic Drawing, Colored Pencil Drawing, and From Sketch to Watercolor Painting, for those who like to paint from their on-location drawings. Folk art workshops may include Rosemaling, Basic Woodcarving, Indian Crafts, and Introduction to Blacksmithing.

Specialties: Painting, drawing, and folk arts.

Faculty: Courses are taught by a staff of instructors who are also accomplished artists. The Artist-in-Residence and Folk Artist-in-Residence program features prominent artists each summer. Other instructors may include Susan Farmer, Barbara Manger, Donald H. Ruedy, Virginia Huber, Norwegian rosemaler Egil Dahle, woodcarver Lawrence E. Marten, and blacksmith William Kaul.

Costs, Accommodations: A nonrefundable registration fee of $15 is paid by all students. Tuition for the whole week (three 110-minute workshop sessions each day for five days) is $115, with a $30 fee for each additional 110-minute session. A limited number of scholarships are available to Wisconsin residents. One CEU or 10 DPI equivalency-clock hours is granted for each ten class-hours. Participants are responsible for their own housing at nearby motels, cottages, cabins, or campgrounds, and continental breakfast and light lunch may be purchased at the school.

Location: Courses are held at James Williams Jr. High School in Rhinelander, located in the Wisconsin Northwoods. Rhinelander can be reached by bus and by direct and connecting flights from Green Bay, Milwaukee, Madison, Chicago, and Minneapolis.

Contact: University of Wisconsin-Madison, School of the Arts at Rhinelander, 726 Lowell Hall, 610 Langdon St., Madison, WI 53703; (608) 263-3494.

SCHOOL OF SACRED ARTS
New York, New York
One-day workshops

Founded in 1983, the nonprofit School of Sacred Arts is dedicated to teaching, preserving, and perpetuating sacred art traditions from religions and cultures throughout the world. The school sponsors such weekly hands-on classes as Byzantine Icon Painting, Embroidery, and Vestment Making; Hebrew, Islamic and Medieval Calligraphy; Manuscript Illumination, and Egyptian Hieroglyphic Painting; as well as lectures, courses for youngsters, travel programs, an art show and bazaar, apprenticeships, a certificate program in medieval sacred arts, and workshops. Classes and workshops are each limited to ten students of all levels, with a student to teacher ratio of six to one. Gold Leafing, a typical one-day workshop running from 10 am to 6 pm, teaches several methods of laying both precious and common metal leaf and powders, the use of modern materials and traditional bole to burnish 23k gold, and methods of leafing on such surfaces as paper, fabric, metal, glass, and wood. A slide illustrated lunch time lecture emphasizes a variety of leafing materials and techniques, proper surface preparation, subtleties of toning and aging patinas, parcel gilding, and the restoration of gilded artifacts and frames.

Specialties: Sacred arts.

Faculty: Includes Ina Brosseau Marx and Allen Marx, directors of the Finishing School, Inc., who have restored objects for such institutions as the Cooper-Hewitt Museum, the Metropolitan Museum of Art, and the New York Historical Society, as well as for dealers and collectors. Other faculty includes Mark Hasselriis (Egyptian Hieroglyphics), Es Rouya (Islamic Calligraphy), John Nussbaum (Medieval Stained Glass), Karen Gorst (Medieval Calligraphy), Barbara Meise (Medieval Illumination), Vladislav Andreyev (Byzantine Icon), Antonina Kozlova (Byzantine Embroidery and Vestment Making), and Sigmund Laufer (Hebrew Calligraphy).

Costs: Workshop fee, including lunch is $175. A nonrefundable $10 fee must accompany registration. Full-time students and senior citizens receive a 25% discount.

Location: The school is located in a brownstone off Washington Square, in the heart of New York's Greenwich Village.

Contact: School of Sacred Arts, 133 W. Fourth St., New York, NY 10012; (212) 475-8048.

SCOTTSDALE ARTISTS' SCHOOL, INC. (SAS)
Scottsdale, Arizona
One and two-week workshops and master classes from October-May

Established in 1983 as a nonprofit educational institution, the Scottsdale Artists' School offers a wide variety of workshops conducted by working artists whose emphasis is on traditional art. The program is open to artists of all levels, with some workshops restricted to beginning, intermediate, or advanced level students. More than 60 workshops are held during the fall/ winter/spring, most limited to 20 participants and scheduled from 9 am to 4 pm, Monday through Friday, with an occasional two-day weekend session. One-week master classes are limited to 15 students and require permission of the instructor. Media include acrylic, alkyd, oil, pastel, and watercolor and subjects include anatomy, color, drawing, flower painting, life casting, figures, landscape, portrait, still life, studio with photographs, wildlife, scientific illustration, and sculpture. Such art-related topics as marketing and photographing the work are also covered. An annual art show and sale, "The Best and the Brightest", features the work of instructors and students. Ribbons and cash prizes are awarded in five categories and Best of Show.

Two five-day Forensic Art Workshops, sponsored by SAS and The Scottsdale Police Department, cover facial sculpture and composite drawing. Students in the Facial Sculpture Workshop are taught to develop the shape of the face and features directly on the skull, using plasteline, and also study the placement and function of the muscles in the head and neck. Previous experience with clay sculpture is helpful but not essential. The Composite Drawing Workshop is designed to enhance the practicing police artist's technical skill through hands-on practice and to give insight into the artist/ witness relationship. Lectures, slide presentations, and demonstrations cover facial anatomy, proportion, perspective, the biological variations of age, race, and sex, witness memory, interviewing techniques, courtroom testimony, and techniques and uses of art materials, equipment, and reference files. The workshop is also open to students who are competent in their drawing skills but have no knowledge of compositry.

Specialties: A wide variety of traditional art topics relating to drawing, painting, sculpture, illustration, and forensic art.

Faculty: The more than 60 instructors, all accomplished artists, include figure sculptors Nathan Cabot Hale and Wilfred Stedman, M.D., pastel portrait artist and author Leslie B. DeMille, animal artist Ken Bunn, watercolorists Irving Shapiro and Marilyn Simandle, bird sculptor Sandy Scott, life caster Willa Shalit, neo-realist Greg Wyatt, landscape artists Michael Lynch and Tom Nicholas, animal sculptor Gerald Balciar, and medical illustrator Gerald P. Hodge. Forensic art instructors are forensic sculptor Betty Pat Gatliff, who has been featured in *The Wall Street Journal*, forensic artist Karen Taylor Stewart, and Frank Domingo, a detective with the New York City Police Department.

Costs, Accommodations: Tuition (deposit) is $275 ($125) for one-week workshops, $150 ($75) for weekend workshops, $300 ($150) for the forensic workshops, and $375 ($175) for master classes. Balance is due 30 days prior to workshop. A full refund less $50 is granted cancellations more than 30 days prior, thereafter if space can be filled, and a $20 fee is charged transfers arranged more than 30 days prior. MasterCard and VISA are accepted. Tuition scholarships are awarded, based on merit, and applicants are required to submit a resume and slides in September for workshops from October through December and in December for workshops from January through May. Accommodations at the nearby Days Inn Scottsdale/Fashion Square Resort range from $43 to $47 per night, single or double.

Location, Facilities: The school is situated within walking distance of the Camelback Mall and Fashion Square, approximately ten miles from Sky Harbor International Airport. Facilities include three studio classrooms, a library, a lounge, a small art supply store, and a book store. Handicapped accessibility is provided, with an elevator to the second floor and specially equipped restrooms.

Contact: Scottsdale Artists' School, Inc., 7031 E. Camelback Rd., #201, Scottsdale, AZ 85251; (602) 990-1422.

THE SHEPHERDESS
San Diego, California
One to two-day workshops year-round

The Shepherdess, a retail store specializing in beads, has offered workshops since it opened in 1979 and more recently has expanded its program to operate full-time in the facility. A variety of craft subjects are taught in one or two-day formats, five hours per day, with emphasis on beadwork and jewelry (6 to 10 participants), as well as spinning and weaving (3 to 5 participants), basketry, and works with paper. Workshop topics include rigid heddle weaving, soft bodied bracelets, spinning with exotic fibers, wire bending for jewelry, various types of baskets and beadwork, jeweled leather necklaces, jewelry assemblage, solid bead and fashion bead embroidery, hand painted silk scarves, cards and soft-cover booklets, passementerie, and Zulu and multi-length necklaces. Each year, approximately 12 prominent artists are invited to conduct special guest workshops (limit 15 participants), which are held in a larger, rented space. Typical titles include Jewelry: From Crochet to Collage, The Beaded Necklace, and Making Extraordinary Fimo Beads.

Specialties: A variety of subjects with emphasis on beads and jewelry, spinning, weaving, and basketry.

Faculty: Includes San Diego artists and prominent guests.

Costs, Accommodations: Workshop fees range from $14 to $110. Advance registration is required and full payment must accompany application. Full refund, less $3 fee, is granted cancellations more than one week prior; no refunds thereafter. Special Guest Workshop fee, less $10, is refundable to those who cancel more than one month prior, no refunds thereafter. Registrants receive a 10% discount on the purchase of most items in the shop. Nearby motel accommodations are available at a 10% discount for out-of-town students.

Location: The school is in the Old Town area of San Diego. Most workshops, with the exception of guest workshops, are wheelchair accessible.

Contact: The Shepherdess, 2802 Juan St., San Diego, CA 92110; (619) 297-4110.

SIEVERS SCHOOL OF FIBER ARTS
Washington Island, Wisconsin
Two, three, and five-day courses from May-October

Established in 1979 as an outgrowth of a mail-order loom plan business, the Sievers School of Fiber Arts now offers more than 50 courses each year in weaving, spinning, dyeing, quilting, papermaking, and basketry. Most courses are open to all levels, with some geared to intermediate or advanced students. Student to instructor ratio is approximately eight to one. Weekend courses meet from 2 to 5:30 pm Friday, 9 am to noon and 2 to 5 pm on Saturday, and 9 am to noon on Sunday. Three-day courses begin with a Tuesday evening orientation and classes meet from 9 am to noon and 2 to 5 pm on Wednesday and Thursday and from 9 to noon Friday. Five-day classes meet from 9 am to noon and 2 to 5 pm from Monday through Thursday and from 9 am to noon on Friday. Evening hours are at instructor's discretion .

Typical weaving courses include Basic and Intermediate Weaving, Rag Rug Weaving, 8-Harness Weaving, Tapestry, Weaving Home Furnishings, and Design & Weave Wearable Art, an advanced course in which students use a variety of materials and techniques to create a unique garment. Basketry courses cover willow, rattan, ash splint, and wicker, as well as chair caning and seating. Other courses include beginning and intermediate level spinning, dyeing, and felting; beginning and advanced papermaking, quilting, patchwork, and appliqué; surface design and techniques such as batik, silk screen, fabric marbling, and machine embroidery; and creativity and design, utilizing brainstorming techniques.

Specialties: Weaving, spinning, dyeing, quilting, papermaking, basketry.

Faculty: The approximately 30-member faculty consists primarily of midwesterners who teach fiber arts in schools or colleges or are in a related business. Guest instructors teach their specialties.

Costs, Accommodations: Course fees (deposits) are $85 ($45) for a weekend, $120 ($60) for three days, and $180 ($90) for five days. Deposit must accompany registration and balance is due one month prior. Those who pay in full with registration can deduct $5 to $10 from the fee. Materials are additional. Cancellations more than four weeks prior receive full refund less $15; 50% of fee is refunded thereafter. Lodging in the school's dormitory ranges from $30 for a weekend to $75 for five days. A list of nearby motels, hotels, cottages, and campgrounds is provided.

Location, Facilities: Sievers School is in the refurbished Jackson Harbor School on remote Washington Island in Lake Michigan, six miles north of the Door County vacation area in northeastern Wisconsin. In addition to studios and the dormitory, facilities include a store that sells looms and supplies and a retail shop that sells work produced by students and teachers.

Contact: Sievers School of Fiber Arts, Shaw Rd., Washington Island, WI 54246-9723; (414) 847-2264.

SITKA CENTER FOR ART AND ECOLOGY
Otis, Oregon
One to five-day workshops from June-August

Founded in 1970 as a learning center for art, music and the ecology of the central Oregon coast, the Sitka Center for Art and Ecology offers more than 30 summer workshops and seminars in painting, fibers, book arts, printmaking, wood and metal, ceramics, and other creative media, including music, poetry, and photography. Workshop enrollment is limited to 10 to 20 participants of all levels and daily sessions are usually scheduled from 10 am until 4 pm. A varied program of evening events includes concerts, lecture/slide shows, demonstrations, films, and an annual open-house.

Typical workshop titles include Black on Black, Red on Red, a pottery workshop that explores the traditional techniques of Maria Martinez and the Native American artisans of the San Idelfonso Pueblo; Baskets From Nature, which focuses on basketry construction using a combination of gathered material and rattan; Painted and Machine-stitched Wall Quilts, including fabric painting, soft-edge machine appliqué, and machine quilting; as well as Sketches to Clay Sculpture, Drawing on Clay, Sketching on Location, Drawing in Color From Nature, Watercolor, Painting in Oils "en plein aire", Botanical Watercolor, Silkscreen Printmaking, Textile Painting, Lost Wax Casting, Expressive Letterforms Using the UNCIAL Alphabet, Marblizing and Bookbinding, The Grand Tapestry Weave, and Carving/Painting Mergansers and Sleeping Shorebirds, in which students carve and paint a decoy.

The Center also sponsors an Artist/Naturalist in Residence program during the winter, which provides housing and workspace in exchange for community outreach activities. Residencies are awarded on the basis of excellence and range in length from three to nine months. Applications for fall through spring are due June 1st.

Specialties: Painting, fiber arts, book arts, printmaking, wood and metal working, ceramics, photography, and other media.

Faculty: Instructors, who are accomplished artists, craftsmen, and teachers, have included artists Michael Gibbons, Suellen Johnson, Susan McKinnon Rasmussen, and Michael Schlicting, quiltmaker Vicki Johnson, fiber artists Marcy Hearing and Pam Patrie, metalsmith Lee Haga, ceramists Adrian Arleo and Frank Boyden, printmakers Andrew Larkin, R. Keaney Rathbun, and Margot Voorhies Thompson, book artist Pat Condron, and bird carvers Richard and Jinx Troon.

Costs, Accommodations: Class fee of $30 per day must accompany registration. Friends of Sitka family sponsors, which begin at $35, receive a 10% workshop discount. A full refund, less $5, is granted cancellations more than one week prior; no refunds thereafter. There is no on-campus housing, however accommodations for approximately $30 per day are available at nearby hotels, motels, and lodges.

Location: The Center, located in Otis along Oregon's central coast, is situated on the slopes of Cascade Head, bordering the Salmon River estuary.

Contact: Sitka Center for Art & Ecology, P.O. Box 65, Otis, OR 97368; (503) 994-5485.

SNAKE RIVER INSTITUTE
Jackson Hole, Wyoming
Three to five-day workshops from June-October

The Snake River Institute was founded in 1988 to offer workshops and seminars that explore connections between the arts and the natural world. Programs are tailored to the adult artist or writer who desires insight and critique from a nationally recognized expert within a scenic natural setting. Approximately 10 three to five-day workshops are offered from June to October, including at least two or three devoted to arts and crafts. Attendance ranges from 8 to 20 participants, who explore Western culture as it relates to their discipline. "Classroom" locations, selected to complement the subject, range from rustic pine lodges to hikes in national parks. Typical workshops include Understanding and Interpreting Light and Color in Outdoor Painting, a plein-air oil painting seminar that focuses on the essentials of color mixing in the field to represent effects of light and atmosphere; The Personal Language of Drawing: Outdoor Drawing as a Foundation for all Mediums, emphasizing development of personal style and an understanding and familiarity with the techniques and tools of drawing; and Cultural Diversity as Reflected in the Artist's View of Nature, which includes a review of the appropriate literary and visual arts and introductions to artistic expressions in writing, drawing, and sculpting.

Specialties: Various topics, with emphasis on the connection between the arts and the natural world.

Faculty: Has included Ned Jacob, a prominent artist and teacher whose work was the subject of the book, Sacred Paint; Skip Whitcomb, an experienced plein-air painter, draftsman, and printmaker, whose work has appeared in juried exhibitions by the American Watercolor Society and the National Academy of Western Art; and Tony Angell, recipient of the State University of New York's Fine Stone prize and the Oak Leaf Award from the National Office of the Nature Conservancy.

Costs, Accommodations: Tuition, which does not include lodging or meals, ranges from $250 to $425. A $100 deposit must accompany registration with balance payable prior to the start of the workshop. Cancellations at least 40 days prior receive full refund less a $30 handling fee; thereafter deposit is forfeited unless space can be filled.

Location: Workshops are held in Jackson Hole and surrounding areas, including the banks of the Snake River.

Contact: Snake River Institute, P.O. Box 7724, Jackson Hole, WY 83001; (307) 733-2214.

SOUTH HILL PARK ARTS CENTRE
Bracknell, Berkshire, England
Weekend workshops year-round

One of the largest art centers in England, South Hill Park Arts Centre has a year-round program of events and activities that include music, theatre, opera, and arts and crafts. Weekend workshops, which are open to all levels and usually scheduled all day Saturday and Sunday afternoon, typically include Woodcut, Jewelry/Silversmithing, Make Your Own Creative Jewelry, Pottery, Dyeing, Flax Spinning, and Paint & Dance, in which students create their own choreography, paintings, and sculptural costumes that relate to and contain movement.

Specialties: A variety of arts and crafts topics.

Costs: Two-day workshops are approximately £30. Full payment must accompany registration. VISA, Access, Diners Club, and American Express credit cards are accepted.

Location: The Centre is in the Birch Hill area of Bracknell, which is on the London Waterloo to Reading line.

Contact: South Hill Park Arts Centre, Bracknell, Berkshire, RG12 4PA, England; (44) 0344 427272.

SOUTHERN VERMONT ART CENTER
Manchester, Vermont
Two-day to two-week workshops in August and September

This nonprofit educational institution, founded in 1933 by a group of artists, offers a wide variety of activities relating to the visual and perfoming arts, including workshops, concerts, classes, and an annual film festival and fair. Four or five nature painting workshops are held during the summer months, utilizing such media as watercolor, pen and ink, oil, acrylic, pastel, and mixed media. Most programs are limited to 15 students of all levels and are scheduled from 10 am until 4 pm daily.

Specialties: Painting.

Faculty: Has included watercolorist Bradford Voight, whose paintings of New England have been exhibited at The National Academy, the Corcoran Gallery, and the San Francisco Palace of Fine Arts; Barbara Frey, who studied at the Art Institute of Chicago and with Roger Curtis, Franklin Jones, and Tony van Hasselt; botanical artist and illustrator Carol Ann Morley, who has taught for the New York Botanical Garden; and watercolorist Joan Rudman, who studied at the Art Students League with Arnold Blanch, Edgar A. Whitney, and Charles Reid.

Costs: Tuition ranges from $100 for a two-day workshop to $225 for two weeks. Full payment must accompany registration.

Location, Facilities: The Center is housed in Yester House, an historic Georgian mansion set on a hilltop above Manchester and surrounded by 375 acres of forest and pastureland. It's situated on West Road, between Rtes. 30 and 7A. Facilities include galleries with changing exhibits, a sculpture garden, and a botany trail with pool, waterfall, and unusual plants and trees.

Contact: Southern Vermont Art Center, West Road, P.O. Box 617, Manchester, VT 05254; (802) 362-1405.

SOUTHWEST CRAFT CENTER (SWCC)
San Antonio, Texas
Weekend workshops year-round

Incorporated in 1965 to provide visual arts and crafts education to adults and children of all levels, this nonprofit organization offers year-round courses and a visiting artists program of workshops, demonstrations, and slide lectures in the disciplines of ceramics, fibers, metals, painting, papermaking, and photography. Approximately ten workshops are offered each season, taught by guest and resident faculty and relating to their area of expertise. Enrollment is limited to 8 to 15 students of all levels. The Center also sponsors lectures, concerts, art exhibitions, and an artist-in-residence program that provides studio space to qualified local artists.

Typical workshop titles include Color Blending in Wearables, a two-day fibers workshop in which students work with six looms, each dressed in a different color, and learn the basics of changing a color; Paper: The Transitional Plane, which explores the two and three-dimensional potential of handmade paper through study of vacuum table operations; No Compromise With Gravity, a two-day ceramics workshop that emphasizes firing techniques and revision of fired surfaces by slowing down the forming process; and Color in Metals, in which students apply paints, pigments, and patinas to etched and textured metals. Other workshops may include The Decorated Teapot, Kasuri: Japanese Dyeing Techniques for Ikat Weaving, A Contemporary Approach to Metal Forming, and Marbling: Fabrics and Paper.

Specialties: Ceramics, painting, fibers, jewelry, papermaking, photography.

Faculty: Each year, 30 nationally recognized artists conduct programs at SWCC. They have included ceramists Linda Arbuckle, Bennett Bean, Linda Christianson, Michael Conroy, and Harvey Sadow; textile and fiber artists Cat Brysch, Robert Hills, John Marshall, Mariana Santiago, and Diane Varney; metalsmiths Claire Holliday, Enid Kaplan, Shari Mendelson, and Norman Taylor; and papermakers Sas Colby, Helen Frederick, Ted Ramsay, and Beck Whitehead.

Costs, Accommodations: Tuition ranges from $60 to $125; lab fees vary. A nonrefundable registration fee of 50% of tuition must accompany application. Refund, less registration fee, is granted written cancellations received prior to start of class. Senior citizens receive a 15% discount and scholarships are available. A nearby hotel offers participants a special rate of $55 per night (double occupancy) or accommodations may be arranged at other area hotels.

Location, Facilities: The Center is located downtown, on the grounds of the historic 142-year old Ursuline Academy and Convent, overlooking the San Antonio River. Facilities include a gallery that exhibits work of various well-known contemporary artists, a visitor/hospitality center, a luncheon restaurant, and a gift store/gallery.

Contact: Southwest Craft Center, 300 Augusta, San Antonio, TX 78205; (512) 224-1848.

SPLIT ROCK ARTS PROGRAM
University of Minnesota (UMD)
Duluth, Minnesota

Six-day workshops in July and August

Split Rock is a summer series of 45 six-day intensive residential workshops in the visual and literary arts and the nature and application of creativity. All workshops begin on Sunday evening and end the following Saturday at noon and are limited to 16 to 18 participants, most of whom have some background or experience. Workshops require approximately 60 hours, including assignments before arrival. Typical visual arts workshop titles include Pattern Design: Exploring Two Dimensions, for quilters and other craft artists, which focuses on spacial illusions, movement, tension, proportion, and scale and their manipulation to create overall patterns; Process and Discovery: A Painting Retreat at the Cloquet Forestry Center, an exploration of personally meaningful imagery that stresses the concept of "automatic" painting — working in a free, uncontrolled way in the early stages of a painting; Contemporary Chinese Landscape Painting, which employs such traditional techniques as the "broken ink" and "splash ink" methods to achieve nontraditional results, plus ways to portray perspective and treat negative space; Computer Visualization for Artists, which emphasizes the production of original and unusual artworks using "friendly" computers and software programs to create, copy, enhance, and animate images; Painted Sculpture, devoted to the role of painting in the development of three-dimensional forms and surfaces; and Shaman Sculpture: Making Objects of Strength and Empowerment, which combines guided meditation to identify and clarify the forms and images within one's deeper self with the construction of two and three-dimensional objects that embody these images. Other workshops may include Creative Knitting, Handbuilding With Clay, Paper Casting, Watercolor, Monoprints With Master Printers, Chinese Calligraphy, Basketry, Feltmaking: From Process to Image, and Japanese Woodblock Printing.

Specialties: A variety of visual arts topics, including drawing and painting, sculpture, basketry, calligraphy, printmaking, computer art, clay, knitting.

Faculty: Includes painters Chen-Khee Chee, David Feinberg, Herman Rowan, and Chen Xiang Xun; ceramist Thomas Kerrigan; fiber artists Morgan Clifford, Chad Alice Hagen, Ana Lisa Hedstrom, Mary W. Phillips, and Susan Wilchins; papermaker Zarina Hashmi; quilt artist Michael James; sculptor Nancy Azara; basketmaker Kari Lonning; calligrapher Wang Dong Ling; and printmakers Susan McDonald, Bernice Ficek-Swenson, and Jon Swenson.

Costs, Accommodations: Tuition ranges from $207 noncredit ($217 credit) to $252 ($262); some workshops charge an additional fee of $10 to $60. Full tuition and fees must accompany reservation. Credit cards (VISA, Master-Card) accepted. Full refund, less $30 fee, is granted cancellations more than three weeks prior; 50% refund two to three weeks prior; no refunds thereafter. Two undergraduate or graduate quarter-hour credits are available from the University of Minnesota. Apartments in the university's newest dormitory complex range from $75 per week for a shared bedroom to $130 per week for a private bedroom in a shared suite. On-campus cafeteria service is $35 for a ten-meal ticket. Motel, hotel, and camping options are also available.

Location, Facilities: Split Rock is held at the University of Minnesota's Duluth campus, overlooking the city, Lake Superior, and the St. Louis River. Campus facilities include a pool, tennis courts, tracks, the Tweed Museum of Art, and the Minnesota Repertory Theatre. Duluth, 150 miles north of the Twin Cities, offers such activities as sports, sailing, and trout fishing.

Contact: Split Rock Arts Program, 306 Wesbrook Hall, 77 Pleasant St. S.E., University of Minnesota, Minneapolis, MN 55455; (612) 624-6800.

STUDIO CAMNITZER
Valdottavo, Italy
Five-week sessions from June-August

Since 1975, Studio Camnitzer has offered graphics arts courses that are designed to assist the participant in maximizing expression through exploration or invention of appropriate techniques. The two five-week sessions (June-July, July-August) are each limited to ten artists and students, selected on the basis of motivation and commitment, who work with one faculty member and two assistants. Workshop activities, which are based on individual tutorials, include such printmaking techniques as intaglio (engraving, drypoint, mezzotint, aquatint, photo-etching), relief techniques (wood and linoleum cut), mixed media techniques (collagraphs), and photography (camera and darkroom work). All techniques are covered in each session: the first session concentrates on aesthetic problem-solving and photo-etching techniques, including color separation, and the second session stresses multiplate color etching and registration, non-acid techniques, and photo-etching. Classes are held weekdays, except Wednesday, from 10 am to 1 pm and 3 to 7 pm, and the studio is available as an open, informal workshop all day Sunday and from 10 am to 3 pm on Wednesday.

Specialties: Printmaking.

Faculty: Studio director Luis Camnitzer, who teaches the first session, is Professor of Art, SUNY-Old Westbury, and an Honorary Member of the Academy of Florence. His work is represented in such collections as New York's Museum of Modern Art, Metropolitan Museum, and Public Library, and the Bibliothèque Nationale in Paris. David Finkbeiner, an instructor at Pratt Institute, Parsons School of Design, and SUNY-Purchase, teaches the second session. His work is represented in the collections of the Brooklyn Museum, Smithsonian Institution, University of California, and Art Institute of Chicago and has been reproduced in *Printmaking Today* and *The Complete Printmaker*. The Studio is known for its work in four-color separation photo-etching and a textbook on the subject.

Costs, Accommodations: Tuition, which includes four lunches per week and general supplies, is $1,590 for one five-week session and $2,860 for both sessions. Applications, which must include a description of artistic background and proposed project, 10 slides of work, two character references, and a $150 deposit, are accepted until March 1. Balance of payment is due by April 15. Cancellations prior to April 15 receive full refund; deposit is forfeited between April 15 and May 15; tuition is forfeited therafter. Accommodations, which are rooms in local houses rented by the Studio, range from $360 double to $470 single. Free camping grounds are also available.

Location, Facilities: The Studio, originally an 18th century farmhouse, includes intaglio, relief, and photographic facilities. It's in the Tuscan village of Valdottavo, eight miles north of the medieval walled city of Lucca, one hour from Florence, and 3 1/2 hours from Milan, Venice, and Rome.

Contact: Luis Camnitzer, Studio Camnitzer, 124 Susquehanna Ave., Great Neck, NY 11021; (516) 487-8244/ 466-6975 (evenings), Sept. to May *or* Melchiade 1, Valdottavo, Lucca, Italy; (39) (0583) 835781, June to Aug.

STUDIO JEWELERS, LTD.
New York, New York
Five-day courses year-round

Established in 1979, Studio Jewelers, Ltd., offers four five-day jewelry courses that are designed to provide intensive instruction in a short time period. Each of the four courses is held one week a month and scheduled from 10 am to 5 pm, Monday through Friday. Class size is limited to five students of all levels per instructor. The course titles are Jewelry Repair, which includes ring sizing, re-tipping, chain repair, and repairing and replacing earring backs; Diamond Setting, "A" focuses on prone settings, both as center stones and in cluster settings, and channel settings on rings that consist of single and multi-row channels; Diamond Setting "B" covers bead work and pavé settings, how to prepare engravers, raise beads and bright cut, as well as fit stones on both flat metal and rings; and Wax Modeling, covering basic techniques to create rings and earrings using a variety of tools and waxes. Longer term two to six-month training courses in basic and specialized jewelry making as well as open workshops for experienced students are also available throughout the year.

Specialties: Jewelry making, design, and repair.

Faculty: Founder and Director Robert Streppone, an experienced teacher who holds degrees in industrial art education; Joseph Daboosh, an established commercial diamond setter; Maria Canale, head designer for Kerentz & Co.; Ann Parkin, recipient of a diploma from the Gemology Association of Great Britain; and Hiroko Miyachi Streppone, principal of Horoko Designs.

Costs: Tuition, which includes most tools and supplies, ranges from $450 to $595. A $50 deposit must accompany application with remainder due no later than two weeks prior.

Location, Facilities: The 4,500-square-foot workshop has spacious, well-lit work areas and is located close to Manhattan's Jewelry District and the Empire State Building. Facilities are handicapped accessible.

Contact: Studio Jewelers, Ltd., 32 E. 31st St., New York, NY 10016; (212) 686-1944.

SUMMER PAINTING STUDY ON MONHEGAN ISLAND
Monhegan Island, Maine
Minimum of three half-day sessions from June 1 to Labor Day

Since 1981, Monhegan Island resident artist Lawrence C. Goldsmith has been teaching small groups of experienced and advanced watercolorists and painters in other media who work on-site, weather permitting, or in the studio when necessary. Usually one to four artists are working at a session. The aim of the program is to assist the individual in progressing toward his or her goals and participants choose their own period of study — from two or three sessions a week to every day — depending on the length of stay.

Specialties: Painting, with emphasis on watercolor.

Faculty: Lawrence C. Goldsmith, a full member of the American Watercolor Society, is author of *Watercolor Bold & Free* and was featured in an article in the May, 1987, issue of *American Artist*.

Costs, Accommodations: Half-day sessions are $50 each and a $100 advance deposit is required. A list of nearby accommodations is provided.

Location: The artist's studio-house is located in Monhegan Island's Lobster Cove with easy access to a variety of scenic locales. The Island is accessible by boat from Port Clyde or Boothbat Harbor. No cars are permitted.

Contact: Lawrence C. Goldsmith, R.D. 2, Fairfax, VT 05454; (802) 849-6633 or Monhegan Island, ME 04852; (207) 596-6098 (from June 1 to Labor Day).

SUMMER SCHOOL OF PAINTING & DRAWING
Llangynyw, Welshpool, Powys, Wales
Six-day to three-week courses during June, July, and September

Established in 1982 by painter and printmaker David Millward and his wife, award-winning children's fiction writer Jenny Nimmo, this school offers courses for artists of all levels, with a 20-lesson structured program available for beginners or those desiring a refresher course. Students, limited to 12 per session, may enroll for six days, which run from Sunday afternoon until Saturday, or stay over for a two or three-week period. The daily schedule, from Monday through Friday, includes instruction for an hour or so in the morning and afternoon with assistance as needed during other times. Some mornings are devoted to life classes, usually with a live model, one day is spent working in the hills, alternate evenings are reserved for slide presentations, and one evening features a visiting artist who dines with the group and gives a lecture. Friday afternoon features a display of the week's work and critique. Specialized one-week courses in portraiture, drawing, and lithography are offered in May, July, and October.

Specialties: Landscape, still life, model; printmaking.

Faculty: David Wynn Millward studied at the Royal Academy Schools under the guidance of Peter Greenham, the Patron, who was Keeper of the Schools until 1985. He earned a Bachelor of Law degree and received his Art Teacher's Certificate from the University of London. A visiting artist is usually in residence during July.

Costs, Accommodations: Cost of the six-day course, which includes room and board at Henllan Mill, is £216. Those booking for two or three weeks can stay the weekend for no extra charge. Tuition for nonresidents is £75, which includes lunch. A nonrefundable deposit of 1/2 the cost secures reservation with balance due on arrival. One ground level room and studio are available for handicapped persons. Off-season bed and breakfast accommodations for non-artists and bookings for art groups of four or more are also available.

Location, Facilities: The school is situated in the country on the River Banwy, two miles from Llanfair Caereinion and seven miles from Welshpool. Facilities include two indoor studios and a portable outdoor studio. Recreation and nearby attractions include fishing, boating, swimming, golfing, pony trekking, logging, and visits to nearby castles.

Contact: Henllan Mill, Llangynyw, Welshpool, Powys SY21 9EN, Wales, Great Britain; (44) 0938 810269.

SUNBURY SHORES ARTS AND NATURE CENTRE, INC.
St. Andrews, New Brunswick, Canada
One to three-week summer courses; weekend workshops year-round

This nonprofit membership corporation, founded in 1967, offers a variety of art and craft, natural history, and conservation programs for adults and children of all levels. During the July and August summer program, the Centre sponsors one to three-week courses in such topics as drawing, oil painting, watercolor, wildlife illustration, printmaking, pastel painting, weaving, mixed media, art history, and photography. Class enrollment ranges between 6 and 20 students per instructor and special activities include whale-watching trips, beach walks, and illustrated talks. Workshops specifically for teenagers and morning programs for children are also offered. During the fall, winter, and spring, evening courses and weekend workshops cover such crafts as chair caning, weaving, stained-glass window construction, nature study, printmaking, painting, and pottery.

Summer course participants are members of Sunbury Shores. Benefits include a bi-monthly newsletter describing upcoming events, such as art exhibitions, illustrated talks, films, concerts, and other special events.

Specialties: Drawing, painting, wildlife illustration, printmaking, pottery, weaving.

Faculty: The instructors, all selected for their expertise, include wildlife artist Gary Low, watercolorists Robert Percival and Molly Lamb Bobak, Fredericton artist Noreen Carr, as well as Bridgett Grant, Sharon Yates, Denis Cliff, Nina Bohlen, Dorothea Hooper, Susan Judah, and Cathy Ross.

Costs, Accommodations: Sunbury Shores annual dues, which are tax deductible, begin at C$6 for student or senior, C$12 for individual, and C$20 for family. Summer course fees are approximately C$150 per week for adults, less for students. Membership fee and a C$50 to C$100 deposit, C$10 of which is nonrefundable, are due in mid-June. The remainder of deposit is refundable for cancellations more than two weeks prior. Scholarships covering tuition and most living expenses are available for New Brunswick students ages 15 to 23. A list of nearby accommodations is provided.

Location, Facilities: The home of Sunbury Shores is Centennial House, a refurbished old general store on the St. Andrews waterfront. It contains a gallery, two artists' studios, a library, a children's nature room, and a print studio. A wheelchair ramp accesses the first floor. St. Andrews is situated on Passamaquoddy Bay, an arm of the Bay of Fundy, and is the home of the Biological Station of Fisheries and Oceans Canada, the Huntsman Marine Laboratory and its public aquarium, and the Atlantic Salmon Federation.

Contact: Sunbury Shores Arts and Nature Centre, Inc., P.O. Box 100, St. Andrews, NB, EOG 2XO, Canada; (506) 529-3386.

TEMPLETON ART WORKSHOPS
Various locations in the U.S., Mexico, and Spain
Four to twelve-day workshops

Since 1974, Ann Templeton has taught oil painting workshops that emphasize the artist's own emotional input and utilize the rules and order of good art. Limited to 15 artists who should have at least a year of painting experience, the workshops stress sound design, color theory, and the dramatic impact possible in two-dimensional art. Different techniques and styles are explored, each designed to capture the mood and essence of the subject. Classes are held in the studio with a variety of subject matter and on-location for landscapes. Daily demonstrations and lectures are presented as well as one-on-one and group critiques.

Specialties: Oil painting.

Faculty: An artist-painter since 1969, Ann Templeton teaches approximately 15 workshops a year, lectures and demonstrates for art guilds and college classes, and juries several art shows. Her work is in the collections of the Brownsville Art Museum, ClayDesta Bank, Tacker Enterprises, Commerce Club, and Montjoy, Inc., and she is represented by galleries in Texas and New Mexico.

Costs, Accommodations: Costs and accommodations vary, depending on location and sponsor.

Location: Includes Texas, New Mexico, Indiana, Kentucky, Hawaii, Colorado, California, Idaho, Arizona, Mexico, and Spain.

Contact: Ann Templeton, Box 234, Alto, NM 88312; (505) 336-9687.

TEXTILE ARTS CENTRE (TAC)
Chicago, Illinois
One to three-day classes year-round

The nonprofit Textile Arts Centre offers a variety of short term workshops and one to eight-session classes devoted to weaving, hand and machine knitting, spinning, dyeing, surface design, constructed textiles, papermaking, and basketry. "Fastrack" classes, which meet for three sessions or less, are scheduled from 10 am to 4 pm weekends or 7 to 10 pm daily and most are open to all levels with some geared to the experienced textile artist. Weaving classes include Tablet Weaving, a very old form of warp-twined weaving; Inkle Weaving, also known as band weaving; and Rigid Heddle, using the two-harness rigid heddle loom. Hand knitting classes cover Multicolored Knitting, Knitting to Fit, and Finishing for Hand Knits, and machine knitting topics include interlacing and charting through mathematical formulas to design garments. Other classes include Handpainted Silk, Air-Brushed Textiles, Quilting, and Embellishing and Finishing Techniques for Fabrics. TAC also sponsors lectures, special events, and a textile gallery.

The Artists Series Workshops, which focus on a different theme each quarter, are generally one to three sessions taught by experienced fabric artists. A typical theme, East Meets West, covers such topics as Traditional Rug Hooking, in which students select a pattern, do color planning, learn dyeing techniques, and make a small rug in the traditional North American style; Japanese Clothing Design, which deals with designing and constructing unique garments based on traditional Japanese patterns and sewing techniques; Papermaking, which emphasizes sculptural form and the ritualistic qualities of handmade paper using cotton linter, color, collage, mixed media, and sheet forming techniques; and Chinese Knotting, Origami, and Shibori.

Specialties: Fiber arts, including weaving, knitting, spinning, dyeing, surface design and related crafts.

Faculty: Has included such artists as John Marshall, author of *Sew Your Own Japanese Clothing: Patterns and Ideas for Modern Wear*; Jacqueline Chang, Thomas Grade, Vivian Mak, and Joan Reckwerdt.

Costs: Class tuition ranges from $35 ($25 for members) to $80 ($70) and Artists Series Workshops range from $45 ($40) to $120 ($110). A $5 to $35 supply fee is charged for some sessions. A nonrefundable $25 deposit must accompany registration with balance due on first day of class. Full refund, less $25 fee, is granted cancellations more than three days prior; no refunds after start of class. Annual TAC membership is $15 for student/senior; $25 individual; and $35 family.

Location: TAC is located in Chicago's Lincoln Park area, nine blocks west of Lake Michigan and 10 minutes north of downtown by car or rapid transit.

Contact: Textile Arts Centre, 916 W. Diversey Pkwy., Chicago, IL 60614; (312) 929-5655.

THELIN WORKSHOPS, INC.
Ogunquit, Maine
One to four-day workshops from May-October

Established in 1970 by Valfred Thelin, these workshops offer instruction in watercolor, acrylic, and mixed media to artists of all levels. Most workshops run for four consecutive days — Monday through Thursday — and are limited to 12 students of all levels. The schedule includes a daily demonstration from 9:30 to 11:30 am and hands-on practice until 2:30 pm with the final afternoon reserved for a critique session. Students are asked to submit a brief resume outlining their experience so that they can be placed in a workshop with artists at a similar level. The four-day Magic Miniature Workshop, a miniature painting course held in the fall, offers students the opportunity to create holiday samplers. Three-day workshops for children meet on a once-a-week basis.

Specialties: Painting in watercolor, acrylic, and mixed media.

Faculty: Valfred Thelin studied at the Chicago Art Institute, the University of Wisconsin, and worked with Hans Hoffman and Georgia O'Keeffe. He is author of *Watercolor, Let the Medium Do It*, a series of twelve instructional video tapes, and has contributed to *Ford Times, Art in America,* and *Arts Magazine*. He serves as juror for many art organizations and his work is in museums and corporate and private collections.

Costs, Accommodations: The fee for instruction is $40 per day or $150 for a four-day workshop. A $50 deposit reserves a space and a 20% discount is granted full payment in advance for a four-day workshop. Cancellations more than 60 days prior receive a full refund. A list of accommodations is provided.

Location: The studio is on Shore Road in a building overlooking the ocean and across the street from the Ogunquit Museum of Art. With advance notice, handicapped persons can be accommodated. Ogunquit, a summer resort that's favored by artists, offers such attractions as the Ogunquit Playhouse, many diverse restaurants, and seven miles of beach. Ogunquit is north of Portsmouth and south of Portland.

Contact: Thelin Workshops, Inc., Box 473, Ogunquit, ME 03907; (207) 646-2616.

TOUCHSTONE CENTER FOR CRAFTS
Uniontown, Pennsylvania

Weekend and six-day workshops from June to August

Opened in 1983 as a summer arts center in a mountain retreat setting, Touchstone offers nearly 50 intensive workshops in six tracks: ceramics, fibers, drawing and painting, metals, wood and basketry, and glass and photography. The workshops, which stress lecture, demonstration, and hands-on experience, include programs for all levels as well as for beginning, intermediate, and advanced or professional artists, who have the opportunity to study with prominent faculty. Sessions specifically for children and teenagers are also offered. Group size is limited, with number of participants determined by the instructor. Weekend workshop schedule is 7 to 9 pm Friday and 9 am to 4 pm Saturday and Sunday, and the six-day workshop schedule is 9 to 4 pm from Monday through Friday, 9 am to noon on Saturday. Some workshops, such as White Oak Basketry and Beginning Pottery are offered consecutive weeks, allowing students to enroll in a two-week workshop. Touchstone also sponsors special summer events, including rotating exhibits of faculty work, open-to-the-public lectures by faculty and guest artists, and a Thursday evening performance in art, drama, or music.

Typical workshops for all levels include Bronze Casting — Glass Casting: The Ancient Lost Wax Method, Rugs and More, Monoprint and Creative Drawing With Introductory Etching, Japanese Furniture Making, Handmade Paper: The Fiber of Collage, Coloring Your Weaving: Ikat, Printing and Painting, and Rakú. Workshops for the intermediate to advanced student may include Stained Glass and Painting on Glass, 18th Century Ironwork, Nature Printing Explorations, Sculptural Jewelry in Acrylics, Self-Expressive Quiltmaking in Mixed Media, and Electric Kiln Ceramics. Typical workshops for teenagers include Oil Painting for the Young Artist and Intro to Stained and Etched Glass for the Young Artist.

Touchstone is operated by the Pioneer Crafts Council (PCC), a nonprofit membership organization that was founded in 1972 to promote traditional regional crafts. In addition to the summer program, the Council presents year-round exhibitions, workshops, and in-school projects.

Specialties: Ceramics, fibers, drawing, painting, metals, wood and basketry, glass, and photography.

Faculty: Instructors have included surface design artist Lee Bale, blacksmith Richard Guthrie, professor of drawing Herb Olds, wood sculptor Thomas Merriman, weaver Judith Bushyager, glass sculptor Stephen Day, portraitist Patrick Daugherty, ceramist Cynthia Bringle, master goldsmith Charles Lewton-Brain, metalsmith J. Robert Bruya, textile artist Bonnie Lee Holland, basket maker Estel Youngblood, watercolorist Frederick Graff, nature printer Robert Little, and stained glass artist Stephen Schuler.

Costs, Accommodations: Tuition ranges from $110 to $130, with additional lab fees of $5 to $35. PCC members receive a $5 discount. A $50 deposit must accompany application with balance due three weeks prior to workshop. Cancellations at least four weeks prior receive full refund; within four weeks an 80% refund is granted. Students are accommodated in rustic cabins, campsites, or nearby hotels or motels and can select from a variety of meal plans. A limited number of scholarships and work/study programs are also available.

Location, Facilities: This 63-acre mountain retreat is ten miles east of Uniontown, 1 1/2 hours from Pittsburgh, and 3 1/2 hours from Cleveland and Washington, D.C. Facilities consist of 29 buildings with a newly constructed dining hall and nine studios, including a darkroom. Regional attractions and historic sites include Frank Lloyd Wright's "Fallingwater", Fort Necessity National Battlefield, Friendship Hill, state forest preserves, and glass factories. Recreational opportunities include white water rafting, bicycling, fishing, swimming, and boating.

Contact: Pioneer Crafts Council, Touchstone Center for Crafts, P.O. Box 2141, Uniontown, PA 15401; (412) 438-2811.

TURLEY FORGE BLACKSMITHING SCHOOL
Santa Fe, New Mexico

Three and six-week courses

Since 1969, Frank Turley has taught blacksmithing to students of all levels. The three-week (105-hour) Blacksmithing Techniques course and the six-week (210-hour) Blacksmithing Techniques and Personal Project Planning course are each offered two or three times a year. Class hours are 8:30 am to 4:30 pm and enrollment is limited to six students, who are provided with an individual station equipped with forge, anvil, and leg vise. Blacksmithing Techniques is equally divided between demonstration/lecture and lab and includes instruction in use of the forge, anvil, and accessory tools and in the annealing, hardening, and tempering of the student's handmade tools. Essential techniques covered are drawing, upsetting, punching, hot splitting and hot rasping, fullering, bending, forge welding and forge brazing, and striking with sledge hammer. Class projects are devoted to the making of the student's fire rake and shovel, steel tools, strap hinges, scrollwork, and rivets. The six-week course, which includes the three-week curriculum, emphasizes hands-on experience and personal project planning and development. One-third of class time is devoted to demonstration/lecture, the rest to lab work. Ferrous Forging Forum For Farriers, a six-day (42-hour) combination seminar and flash course for professional horseshoers, focuses on forging shoes, calks, clips, and tools and addresses "corrective" and "therapeutic" shoeing. One or two-day on-site blacksmithing workshops can be arranged individually.

Specialties: Blacksmithing.

Faculty: Master Ironworker and Farrier Frank Turley, a graduate of Michigan State University, was conservator for the Museum of New Mexico specializing in the restoration of colonial ironware and firearms. He has presented lectures and workshops at universities and craft centers and is co-author of *Southwestern Colonial Ironwork*, winner of the State of New Mexico Award of Honor.

Costs: Tuition (deposit), which includes ironworking hand tools and floor equipment, is $900 ($300) for the three-week course, $1,800 ($600) for the six week course. Deposit is refundable for cancellations more than 14 days prior. Students make their own arrangements for accommodations, food, and transportation.

Location: Turley Forge is approximately five miles west of the center of Santa Fe, at an altitude of 7,000 feet. State and national camping grounds are available in the nearby mountains. Motel-kitchenettes are located three to four miles from the forge.

Contact: Turley Forge Blacksmithing School, Rte. 10, Box 88C, Santa Fe, NM 87501; (505) 471-8608.

THE TUSCARORA POTTERY SCHOOL
Tuscarora, Nevada

Two-week summer sessions; two to four-week spring and fall open studio workshops

The nonprofit Tuscarora Pottery School, an international ceramic arts study centre founded in 1966 by Dennis Parks, offers special emphasis pottery sessions and open studio workshops that are primarily for the advanced beginner to the professional potter. The summer schedule usually consists of one four-week open studio workshop and three two-week special emphasis workshops and the fall open studio workshop program is limited to experienced potters who are selected on the basis of slides and letters of recommendation. Enrollment in each workshop is limited to four students per teacher and instruction is given in dialogue rather than in a lecture format, supplemented by group slide presentations and demonstrations. In the open studio workshops, each participant decides upon a specific area of focus, such as a form or a technical question. Special emphasis workshops focus on a single topic, such as Throwing, Raw Glaze Composition and Application, and Firing With Diesel and Crankcase Oil. Clay possibilities start with local red earthenware and extend through blended stoneware and porcelain. Those interested in experimenting with local materials can utilize such resources as rocks, exotic earths, and sagebrush ash.

Specialties: Pottery.

Faculty: Dennis Parks, an electee to the International Academy of Ceramics and author of *A Potter's Guide to Raw Glazing and Oil Firing*, has been widely exhibited and examples of his work have been acquired by several public collections. Visiting artists have included Sana Musasama, Bennett Bean, Jean Biagini, Kari Christensen, Thanos Johnson, Doug Lawrie, Tamas Ortutay, Jim Romberg, and Mary Will.

Costs, Accommodations: Tuition of $590 for two weeks, $1,060 for four weeks, and $1,590 for six weeks includes room, board, and glazing and firing. A $15 fee must accompany application with a nonrefundable $100 deposit payable upon acceptance and balance due upon arrival. Applicants for the fall program should enclose six slides of their work and two letters of recommendation. Participants are housed in a rustic 19th century rooming house, one or two to a room. Two meals are served daily and students prepare breakfast.

Location, Facilities: Tuscarora, an old mining camp in northern Nevada with a population of less than 20, is situated at a 6,400-foot elevation on the side of Mount Blitzen. The site was chosen for the pottery school because of its isolation, quiet, clean air, and spring water. The studios, which remain open 24 hours, are equipped with individual momentum kick-wheels and handbuilding tables and various kilns that range in size from 4 to 120 cu. ft. Recreation includes fishing and swimming in a nearby pond and creeks, hiking, backpacking, and nature walks. Elko, the nearest town with air and bus service, is approximately 50 miles away and pick-up and transportation to the school can be arranged.

Contact: Tuscarora Pottery School, P.O. Box 7, Tuscarora, NV 89834; (702) 756-6598.

VERMONT STATE CRAFT CENTER AT FROG HOLLOW
Middlebury, Vermont
One to five-day workshops

Founded in 1971, this nonprofit educational organization offers a variety of one to five-day workshops as well as on-going classes for adults and children of all levels. Workshops for adults usually run from six to eight hours daily and are limited to 8 to 10 students. Typical titles include Surface Design — Painting On Silk, a one-day introduction to the various methods and applications of this technique in which each student completes the surface design of a scarf; Jeremiah Market Basket, which covers construction of this large, square-bottomed basket; Mold Making For Ceramics, a two-day hands-on workshop with demonstrations that focus on the use of plaster molds and slip casting to make ceramics; and Raku And Pit-Firing, a five-day workshop that involves the making and firing of various glazed and unglazed ceramic objects. The 60 to 90-minute children's classes include Origami, pottery glazing, storytelling and painting, and drawing and painting side-by-side, where parents and children work as partners. The Center also sponsors intensive workshops for professionals, special exhibits, and elementary school outreach programs.

Specialties: A variety of arts and crafts including basketry, ceramics, and painting.

Faculty: Has included Bob Green, Frog Hollow's potter-in-residence and recipient of the 1987-88 Vermont Council of the Arts Fellowship Award; Marcia Rhodes, a prominent New England fiber artist whose work has been featured in *American Craft*; Ellen Spring, a self-employed fabric painter; and Laurie Curtis, a contemporary twig basketmaker.

Costs: Tuition, which must be paid in full at time of registration, ranges from $30 to $100; materials fee ranges from $12 to $35. Members receive a 10% discount (annual dues begin at $15 student, $25 friend) and VISA and MasterCard are accepted. A limited number of scholarships are available.

Location: Middlebury is midway between Rutland and Burlington on Rte 7. The Center is located in the city's downtown historic Frog Hollow District.

Contact: The Vermont State Craft Center at Frog Hollow, Middlebury, VT 05753; (802) 388-3177.

VERROCCHIO ARTS CENTRE
Casole D'Elsa, Siena, Italy
Two-week courses from May-October

Established in 1984, the Verrocchio Arts Centre offers painting and sculpture courses concurrently during approximately a dozen two-week periods from early May through mid-October. The courses are open to adults of all levels, with painting classes limited to 15 students and sculpture classes limited to eight. Painting topics include Watercolor, Light and Color in the Tuscan Landscape, Developing a Personal Vision, Nature and Intervention, and Seeing the Particular. Sculpture courses may include drawing, modeling, ceramics, and/or art history lessons. Students may paint in any medium and can divide their time between painting and sculpture. The courses begin with Friday night supper and an introductory talk on Saturday morning and conclude after breakfast the second Thursday. Morning and afternoon three-hour instructional sessions are scheduled daily as well as informal slide lectures, discussions, optional trips, and a free day halfway through the course. The studios are open at all times as well as during the winter months, with the resident director available to teach privately.

Specialties: Painting, drawing, sculpture, ceramics.

Faculty: Resident director Nigel Konstam, a sculptor and author of *Sculpture, The Art & The Practice*, teaches the sculpting courses. His work has appeared in solo exhibitions in London, Madrid, Barcelona, and Salamanca and he has been published in *Apollo, The Burlington, The Artist, Leonardo*, and *Rembrandthuiskroniek*. The painting courses are taught by guest artists, most of whom are university lecturers.

Costs, Accommodations: Cost, which includes single (shared) room in the Centre and half board, is £750 (£650). Without meals, the cost is reduced by £78. Nearby hotel, apartment, and bed and breakfast accommodations can also be arranged. A £100 fee must accompany reservation with balance due on arrival. Cancellations at least six weeks prior receive a full deposit refund less £10; no refund thereafter. Students who register for more than one course receive a 10% discount on the second and subsequent courses and a fee reduction of up to £80 is offered two young students who help in the kitchen. Transportation from Florence on arrival day is £6.60.

Location, Facilities: Once a "fattoria", where harvests of grain, wine, and olives were processed and stored, the Centre stands on the ancient town walls between two round defense towers. The 600 square meters of studio space consists of painting, drawing, sculpture, and ceramics studios, a print room with etching press and darkroom, living quarters, a library/sitting room, farmhouse-style kitchen, and working terrace suitable for carving stone. The large village of Casole D'Elsa is a short drive from Florence, which is one hour from the nearest airports, in Pisa and Bologna.

Contact: Verrocchio Arts Centre, Via San Michele 16, Casole D'Elsa, Siena 53031, Italy; (39) 577 948312.

VESTERHEIM
The Norwegian-American Museum
Decorah, Iowa and Norway
Two to six-day summer workshops; two-week biennial workshop/tour

Since 1967, Vesterheim, a complex of historic buildings housing the largest collection of Norwegian and Norwegian-American arts and crafts in the U.S., has sponsored workshops and tours in which the materials in the collection are used as an inspiration for creative work. More than 30 workshops are offered each summer, most from June through September, in Norwegian rosemaling, fiber arts, and woodworking. Some programs are open to students of all levels while others are geared to beginning, intermediate, or advanced students.

Workshops in rosemaling — decorative painting on wood — cover techniques from Telemark, Rogaland, Hallingdal, Gudbrandsdal, Valdres, and other areas as well as lettering, drawing, pencil design and color, and borders and backgrounds. The fiber arts workshops, usually limited to eight students, include spinning, weaving, embroidery, rug hooking, knotless netting, felting, and knitting. Woodworking classes cover acanthus carving, chip carving, figure carving, bentwood and birchbark techniques.

A two-week summer rosemaling, woodcarving, and weaving workshop in Norway, scheduled in odd-numbered years, includes eight full days of instruction and six evenings of open classrooms augmented by visits to museums, craft shops, farms, and the homes and workshops of craft artists. Each trip features visits to different parts of Norway.

Specialties: Traditional Norwegian rosemaling, fiber arts, woodcarving, and knife-making.

Faculty: Instructors are from Norway and America. The Norwegians, who teach approximately half of the workshops annually, are chosen from established traditional craftsmen — decorative painters (rosemalers), woodcarvers, woodworkers, and textile artists. The American teachers are largely Gold Medal-winners at national traditional Norwegian arts and crafts exhibitions held in this country.

Costs, Accommodations: Tuition ranges from $40 for a two-day class to $120 for five days. A $40 deposit must accompany registration with the balance due the last two days of class. Cancellations more than 45 days prior receive full refund less $8; no refunds thereafter. Students may bring their own supplies and equipment, such as brushes, paints, woodworking tools, and scissors. Looms and spinning wheels are available for use and most equipment and supplies are available for purchase. A list of nearby motels and campsites is provided and moderately priced restaurants are within a one-block walk.

Location: Most rosemaling, weaving, embroidery, and woodcarving classes are held in the Vesterheim Center, east of the main museum building. Facilities include a large elevator, ramp, and restroom facilities equipped for handicapped persons. Some classes are held at the historic Jacobson Farm, six miles from Decorah and reached by car pool from the museum. Rug hooking classes are at Luther College. Decorah, a small town in a wooded valley surrounded by trout streams, caves, and scenic and historic attractions, is approximately 60 miles south of Rochester, Minnesota, and LaCrosse, Wisconsin and 160 miles south of Minneapolis, all of which have air service.

Contact: Vesterheim, Norwegian-American Museum, 502 W. Water St., Decorah, IA 52101; (319) 382-9681.

WATERCOLOR AND SCULPTING WORKSHOP CRUISE WITH LOREN KOVICH AND FRED BOYER
Cablo San Lucas, Mazatlan, and Puerto Vallarto, Mexico
One-week in April

Artists Loren Kovich and Fred Boyer host a week-long workshop cruise in watercolor and sculpting for students of all levels, with a planned student to instructor ratio of approximately 20 to 1. The sculpting workshop, which is geared to the beginner to intermediate and utilizes such additive mediums as modeling wax, plactilina clay, and polyform, begins with the development of armatures and progresses through the finished piece with emphasis on proper proportions and movement. Participants in the watercolor workshop furnish their own supplies; the sculpting materials are provided.

Specialties: Sculpting, watercolor.

Faculty: Loren Kovich is recipient of the 1988 Montana Watercolor Society Show Gold Medal and second place award at the 38th Annual Westwood Show in Los Angeles. Fred Boyer received the Doc Smith Achievement Award for artistic excellence at The Blackfoot Valley Art Show and first place for sculpture at the National Ghost Town Enthusiasts Juried Show.

Costs: Tuition is $75 for the watercolor workshop, $125 for the sculpting workshop. Cost of the cruise is to be determined. Tuition is waived for nonparticipant spouses and guests.

Location: The Princess Line cruise to the Mexican Riviera visits such ports as Cablo San Lucas, Mazatlan, and Puerto Vallarto.

Contact: Loren Kovich, 1931 9th Ave., Helena, MT 59601; (406) 449-2623 *or* Fred Boyer, 212 Evergreen, Anaconda, MT 59711; (406) 563-6937. Cruise information: Livery Travel, 25 Neil Ave., P.O. Box 147, Helena, MT 59624; (800) 823-2323.

WEAVING, SPINNING AND DYEING COURSES IN RURAL NORTHAMPTONSHIRE
Gretton, Northamptonshire, England
One-week courses year-round; shorter bookings on occasion

Professional teachers Malcolm and Elizabeth Palmer offer individualized courses in weaving, spinning, and dyeing for all levels, from beginners wishing to learn the basics to those desiring help with advanced techniques. Students live as a family with the Palmers and their two teenaged children and receive at least four hours of one-on-one instruction daily with free access to the studio at other times. The courses begin and end on Saturday and students are asked to write beforehand to provide details of their spinning and weaving experience and any particular aspects they wish to cover. Nonparticipant spouses and guests are welcome.

Specialties: Weaving, spinning, dyeing.

Faculty: Elizabeth trained at "Gospels" in Sussex, the workshop founded by Ethel Mairet. A weaver for more than 30 years, she works primarily with wool. Malcolm has been weaving for more than 20 years and prefers to spin and weave luxury fibres. Formerly a mechanical engineer, he helps students understand the spinning wheel and loom mechanics, to enable them to get the most from their equipment. The Palmers weave fabric yardage and do all of their own milling and fine spinning.

Costs, Accommodations: The cost for the one-week course, which includes twin-bedded room and meals prepared from home-grown fruit and vegetables, is £245 for one person, £450 for two people sharing a room and receiving instruction, and £385 for two people with only one receiving instruction. A nonrefundable £50 deposit secures booking with nonrefundable balance due four weeks prior. Shorter stays (a minimum of three nights) can be arranged, depending on time of year, and are charged on a pro rata basis. The cost of materials is additional and billed at the end of the stay.

Location, Facilities: Gretton is a village in the Welland River Valley, close to Stamford, Oundle, and Uppingham. Transportation is provided to and from Kettering Railway Station, one hour from London, or Corby Bus Station. Two studios are located in the cottage. Equipment includes a countermarch foot loom, two counterbalanced foot looms, a folding loom, and several four-shaft table looms; rectangular and circular tapestry frames; six spinning wheels, including an electric wheel and accessories; and a variety of fibers, including wool, silk, cashmere, and mohair. Smoking is not permitted in the studios.

Contact: Malcolm and Elizabeth Palmer, Crown Cottage, 46 High St., Gretton, Corby Northamptonshire, NN17 3DE, England; (44) 0536 770303.

WEAVING WORKSHOP
Madison, Wisconsin

One-day workshops

Opened in 1971, the Weaving Workshop offers three to six-hour one-day workshops and on-going classes in knitting, weaving, and basketry. Most sessions are open to all levels, while others require some experience. Typical knitting and weaving workshop titles include Feltmaking, which emphasizes greater control through hand manipulation and the production of tapestry-like imagery; Rag Rug, which takes the student through the entire process, from designing through material selection and preparation to weaving and finishing; Seaming & Finishing For Knitting, which features hands-on experience with different types of seaming and applications, shaping corners and curves, attaching bands, and edge trimming, plus a discussion of steaming, finishing, blocking, and pressing; Stranded Two Color Knitting, which covers color block (intarsia) and Fair Isle (two color) knitting; and Knit A Skirt, Pi (round) Shawl, Socks, Double Knitting, and Mittens. Basketry workshops teach the construction of such varieties as the twined wicker fruit, hen, melon/egg, cornucopia, Cherokee-style market, doll's cradle, and split wall. Beadwork workshops include beginning and intermediate techniques and hand-made FIMO beads and jewelry. The Workshop also sells a variety of yarns and fibers, books and magazines, and equipment.

Specialties: Weaving, knitting, basketry, spinning, and beadwork.

Faculty: Includes weavers and knitters Carol Anderson, Jenny Bagnell, Mark Nofsinger, Jan Sanger, Christine Thompson, Gloria Welniak (feltmaking and basketry), and Priscilla Wood (basketry).

Costs: Workshops range in cost from $15 to $45, which must be paid in full with registration.

Contact: Weaving Workshop, 920 E. Johnson St., Madison, WI 53703; (608) 255-1066.

WELLS STUDIO-GALLERY WORKSHOPS
Islamorada, Florida
Five-day workshops in February, April, and December

Founded in 1969 by watercolorist Millard Wells, A.W.S., three on-location workshops are held during the winter tourist season — the first week of December, the second week of February, and the last week of April. The workshops are limited to 15 participants who have a working knowledge of drawing and wish to paint outdoors in their preferred media with personal, professional instruction.

Specialties: Outdoor painting.

Faculty: Millard Wells received his art education at the Flint Institute of Art and Chicago Institute of Design. Active in several watercolor groups, he specializes in the subtropical areas surrounding the Florida Keys, as well as Grand Cayman, the Dry Tortugas, Cozumel, and the Yucatan Peninsula. His work has won awards in shows at the National Gallery of Art in Washington, D.C., the Detroit Institute of Art, and the Watercolor Societies of Florida, Alabama, and Louisiana. The Wells Studio-Gallery exhibits his work.

Costs, Accommodations: The tuition is $175, which does not include materials, meals, or lodging. A $50 deposit secures reservation and is refundable to those who cancel more than one week in advance. A variety of accommodations are situated nearby.

Location: Students paint in a variety of locations in the scenic Florida Keys, including Key West, Marathon, and Key Largo. Nonparticipant family and guests can swim, dive, fish, and sightsee. Islamorada is on Rte. 1 approximately 100 miles south of Miami and 90 miles northeast of Key West.

Contact: Wells Studio-Gallery, P.O. Box 152, Islamorada, FL 33036; (305) 664-4971.

WESLEYAN POTTERS, INC.
Middletown, Connecticut
One to five-day workshops

Established in 1948 by a small group of Middletown residents who were taught by a Wesleyan University professor, this nonprofit cooperative guild (which has no connection to Wesleyan University) comprises about 100 members who are active in pottery, jewelry, basketry, and weaving crafts. Wesleyan Potters offers once-a-week courses during four nine-week semesters as well as workshops between semesters and during the summer months. Special courses for children and teenagers are also offered. Enrollment is usually limited to eight to twelve students.

Members are accepted on a limited basis and are committed to volunteer work at the Pottery. Each member must have been a student at Wesleyan Potters, must show a certain degree of skill, and must be recommended by an instructor. Benefits include unlimited access to studio space and participation in the Annual Exhibit and Sale, a juried event.

Specialties: Pottery, jewelry, basketry, weaving.

Faculty: The more than 15-member faculty includes Soose Baker, Manon-Lu Christ, Thomas J. Cook, Fran Curran, Adele Firshein, John Frink, James Gorman, Jonathan Hewey, Anne Hyland, Jonathan Kline, John E. McGuire, David McLellan, Ron Meyers, David Rynick, Betsy Tanzer, and W. Joseph Washburn. Visiting craftsmen also conduct workshops from time to time.

Costs: Fees range from $25 to $125, materials are extra. Full payment, which includes a nonrefundable $5 fee, must accompany registration. Full refund, less $5 fee, is granted cancellations at least two weeks prior or if space can be filled. Scholarships and student aid are available to those who apply at least one week prior to course or workshop. Supporting membership, which is open to anyone and includes announcements of special events, begins at $15 (tax deductible).

Location, Facilities: Situated in a 9,000-square-foot building on the east side of Rte. 17, between Lake St. and Hunting Hill Ave., Wesleyan Potters' equipment includes three large gas kilns suitable for high-fire reduction stoneware and porcelain, a weaving studio with 20 looms, large classrooms, and Gallery Shop, which offers for sale work by members and other craftspeople.

Contact: The Wesleyan Potters, 350 S. Main St., Middletown, CT 06457; (203) 347-5925.

WEST DEAN COLLEGE
The Edward James Foundation
Chichester, West Sussex, England
Weekend to one-week courses year-round

Established in 1964, this residential college offers a large variety and number of short courses in antique care and repair, drawing and painting, basketry (cane and rush seating), blacksmithing, bookbinding and papermaking, creative writing, calligraphy and lettering, glass engraving and stained glass, photography, pottery, sculpture (carving, modeling, casting), print-making, silversmithing and jewelry, soft furnishing and upholstery, textiles (design, weaving, embroidery, lace), woodworking, music and dance, and archeaology, as well as one to three-year courses in antique furniture, ceramics, porcelain, and clock restoration; care of books and bookbinding; tapestry weaving; and the making of early stringed instruments. More than 150 short courses are offered during the months from April to September with most for students of all levels and a few for either beginners or those with intermediate to advanced skills. Most courses are limited to 10 students per instructor.

Specialties: A wide variety of courses in arts, crafts, and related subjects.

Faculty: Includes accomplished artists, craftsmen, and teachers.

Costs, Accommodations: Fees for weekend workshops, including accommodations and board, range from £88 to £103, depending on type of room; day student fees (lunch included) are £5. Fees for six-day summer school courses are £168 for day students and £240 to £249, including room and board. Limited specially-built accommodations for handicapped persons are available.

Location: West Dean College, located on the 6,000 acre West Dean Estate in southeastern England, is surrounded by ornamental gardens, farmlands, and woods. The workshops are equipped for a wide range of activities and all major tools and equipment are provided. A shop stocks materials and tools for sale to students. Recreational facilities include a cricket ground and tennis courts. The college is five miles north of Chichester and one hour from Heathrow and Gatwick Airports.

Contact: College Office, West Dean College, West Dean, Chichester, West Sussex, PO18 0QZ, England; Singleton (44) 024363 301.

WESTHOPE COLLEGE
Craven Arms, Shropshire, England
Two-day courses year-round

This privately run craft school, established in 1980, offers ten to twelve weekend residential and nonresidential courses in drawing and painting and textile crafts. Sessions are generally limited to 12 students of all levels, who attend class from 10 am to 5 pm daily. Typical courses include Curved Logcabin Patchwork, Drawing and Painting Flowers, Machine Embroidery, Painting on Silk, and Decorative Handmade Felt. On Tuesdays the studios are open for people to learn new crafts or experiment in embroidery and other textile crafts, basketry, chair seating, and toys. Aids are available for physically disabled students.

Specialties: Drawing, painting, embroidery, textile crafts.

Faculty: Most courses are taught by proprietor Anne Dyer.

Costs, Accommodations: Weekend cost, which includes accommodations and home-cooked meals (beginning with dinner the night before), is £50; tuition only is £12. Single supplement is £12. A £5 deposit must accompany booking with balance due on arrival. Cancellations more than a week prior may receive a refund of most of the deposit.

Location: The school is approximately 25 miles from Shrewsbury, 20 miles from Bridgnorth, and 35 miles from Hereford.

Contact: Anne Dyer, Westhope College, Craven Arms, Salop, Seifton 293, Shropshire, SY7 9JL, England.

WILD FIBERS PAPERMAKING WORKSHOP
Hawaii and U.S. Mainland
Three-day workshops

Wild Fibers Paper Mill, established in 1982, offers two weekend workshops a year devoted to papermaking with Hawaiian plant fibers. Each course is limited to 18 students with 3 instructors and begins with Friday evening dinner followed by a discussion and slide presentation on papermaking and plant identification and processing. Saturday morning is spent cooking and preparing the fiber for the vat and the remaining sessions cover forming, drying, and preparing the sheets of paper and discussions of the various ways they can be used in creative art works.

Specialties: Papermaking.

Faculty: Marilyn Wold, owner of Wild Fibers and a fiber artist since 1970, is represented in galleries and in Honolulu's State Foundation of Culture and the Arts and has been exhibited in juried and group shows. Her publications include *Papermaking for Basketry* and *Papermaking in Hawaii*. She is assisted by artists/papermakers Lee Christie Conn and Janice Matsumoto.

Costs, Accommodations: The $300 fee includes food, dormitory-style lodging, and supplies. Nonrefundable $100 deposit is required 60 days prior.

Location: The workshop location is a farm in Pu'uhonua O'Honaunau Mauka Gardens, an historical park on the coast of the Big Island of Hawaii. The area is rich in the native plants used in Hawaiian crafts and celebrations.

Contact: Marilyn Wold, Wild Fibers, P.O. Box 4590, Kailua-Kona, HI 96745.

WILDACRES WORKSHOPS
Ringling School of Art and Design
Little Switzerland, North Carolina
One-week summer and fall workshops

The Ringling School of Art and Design sponsors two one-week art workshops annually, one in the summer and one in the fall, at Wildacres, a retreat dedicated to the the development of better human relations. Participants in the program may take part in any of the classes offered, which include portrait study, landscape drawing, oil painting, pastels, monoprints/drypoint, figure drawing, and watercolor. Critique sessions are scheduled at varying times during the week and students can arrange to work with an instructor in an independent study program. Special activities consist of an opening reception, dinner and orientation, and evening slide presentations by the instructors. The program concludes with an exhibition of works completed in class, followed by dinner, awards presentations, and a farewell gathering.

Specialties: A variety of arts topics, including drawing, watercolor, oil, pastels, and monoprints/drypoint.

Faculty: Four faculty members from the Ringling School.

Costs, Accommodations: The program fee of $275 includes lodging and meals. A $50 deposit must accompany registration with balance due approximately six weeks prior. Full refund is granted cancellations more than 30 days prior; thereafter a $30 service charge is deducted. Accommodations are double occupancy rooms in recently completed lodge-type buildings.

Location: Wildacres retreat is situated at an elevation of 3,300 feet, 20 miles from Interstate 40, which is midway between Hickory and Asheville.

Contact: Wildacres Workshop, c/o Ringling School of Art and Design, 2700 N. Tamiami Trail., Sarasota, FL 34234; (800) 255-7695 *or* (813) 351-4614, ext. 117/118.

WINE COUNTRY WORKSHOPS
Calistoga, California
Five-day workshops from January-June

Approximately a half dozen five-day watercolor workshops are offered annually in this Napa Valley resort. Instructors include such prominent artists as Barbara Nechis, Marilyn Phillis, Morten Solberg, Frank Webb, Tom Hill, and Harley Brown. Tuition ranges from $200 to $250.

Contact: Bea Marlais, P.O. Box 497, Calistoga, CA 94515; (707) 942-6378.

WOMEN'S STUDIO WORKSHOP (WSW)
Rosendale, New York
Five-day summer workshops; weekend workshops

This multi-disciplinary nonprofit arts organization, dedicated to contemporary arts education, offers weekday classes, weekend workshops, and approximately 20 summer workshops in printmaking, papermaking, book arts, and photography. The workshops, limited to four to eight men and women of all levels of experience, are scheduled from 10 am to 4 pm each day and the studios remain open from 9 am to 10 pm to allow students to continue work on projects begun in class. WSW also sponsors exhibitions and one and two-day weekend workshops on such subjects as sculptural etching, fabric printing, Western and Oriental papermaking, and bookbinding.

Typical workshop titles include Pop-ups and Paper Engineering, which focuses on basic on-the-fold pop-ups, more complicated 3-dimensional constructions, decorative paper techniques, and the production of a book incorporating these dimensional elements; Everyday Fibers for Hand Papermaking, which begins with the collection of local plants — cattail, milkweed, wild flowers, and corn — then concentrates on the processing, use, and special characteristics of their fibers for papermaking; and Hanga: Exploring Japanese Woodblock Printing, which emphasizes proper tool handling, planning and transferring designs to blocks, types of pigments and colorants, and the completion of an edition of prints. Other workshops may include The Sculptural Etching Plate, Screenprinting on Fabric, Sculptural Paper, The Offset Printed Book, Monotype, Brush Books, Hand Bookbinding, and Waterbase Silkscreen Printing.

Specialties: Printmaking, papermaking, book arts, photography.

Faculty: Includes Carol Barton, Barbara Bash, Kathleen Caraccio, Martha Carothers, Betsy Damon, Amanda Degener, Susan Fateh, Leni Fried, Karla Hagen, Ann Kalmbach, Tana Kellner, Ann Kresge, Lisa mackie, Lucy Michels, Clarissa Sligh, Pamela Spitzmueller, Marilyn Sward, Martha Tabor, Joan Wolbier, and Zarina.

Costs, Accommodations: Five-day workshop tuition is $250 ($235 for members) and weekend workshops are $50 per day. Materials for some classes are additional. A $50 deposit must accompany application with balance due at first session. Cancellations more than one month prior receive full refund; deposit is forfeited thereafter. Lodging is available in nearby hotels, bed and breakfasts, and campgrounds. Membership in the WSW ranges from $25 for an individual ($35 family) to $100 for a sponsor.

Location, Facilities: The Workshop is situated in the Binnewater Arts Center (BAC), a 100-year-old mercantile building that has been renovated to accommodate the specialized studios. The 5,000-square-feet of studio space is divided into areas for intaglio, papermaking, silkscreen, printshop, photo darkroom, and graphics darkroom. The hamlet of Binnewater, situated near Rosendale, is a small village in the foothills of the Catskill Mountains. A popular vacation area, it's 90 minutes north of New York City and an hour south of Albany.

Contact: Women's Studio Workshop, P.O. Box 489, Rosendale, NY 12472; (914) 658-9133.

WOODENBOAT SCHOOL
Brooklin, Maine
Five-day courses from June-October

The WoodenBoat School offers a four-month program of Sunday evening to Friday afternoon courses in seamanship, boatbuilding, woodworking, and related crafts. Students range from the novice to the seasoned professional and most classes are open to all levels with a few geared to those with woodworking experience.

The more than 20 boatbuilding, woodworking, and craft courses offered each summer include one and two-week sessions on Fundamentals of Boatbuilding, the classical theory and practice; Constant Camber Boatbuilding, an innovative design approach suited to mass production of diverse small craft, including a wood-epoxy trimaran; Wooden Boat Repair Methods, which covers a variety of repair problems; Building the Maine Guide Canoe, covering traditional techniques for the wood-and-canvas canoe; Basic Woodworking for Aspiring Boatbuilders, a beginners' course in using hand and power tools to build a toolbox; Marine Carvings, which covers the design and execution of decorative carvings; Pattern Making, in which students make their own cast-bronze hardware; and Lofting, Wooden Boat Repair Methods, Loft & Build a Canoe Mold, Joinerwork, and Building Half Models. Crafts courses cover marine painting and varnishing, marine mechanics, rigging, sailmaking, drawing and painting of marine themes, and marine photography.

Specialties: Boatbuilding, woodworking, marine drawing and painting, and related crafts.

Faculty: The more than 30-member faculty of experienced, working professionals, headed by Director Ben Ellison, includes Taylor Allen, Tim Allen, Warren Barker, Jim Brown, Eric Dow, George Fatula, Skip Green, Rich Hilsinger, Robin Lincoln, John Marples, Joe Norton, Greg Rossel, Gordon Swift, Rollin Thurlow, Brion Toss, and Andy Willner.

Costs, Accommodations: Tuition ranges from $330 to $735 per week; material costs vary. Room and board is $195 per week and campsites are available for $65; campers can have board for $85. A 1/3 deposit of total tuition, room, and board fees must accompany application, with balance due on first day of class. Refund of deposit, less $45 fee, is granted cancellations more than 30 days prior; between 15 and 30 days, deposit may be used as a course credit; no refund or credit thereafter. Previous attendees receive a 10% tuition discount. Partial tuition scholarships are available. Accommodations are double rooms with shared bath and meals are taken in the dining hall.

Location: WoodenBoat School is approximately 250 miles from Boston by car, and 150 miles — Down East — by boat. Airline service is available to Bangor and arrangements for pick-up and transportation can be made with the school.

Contact: WoodenBoat School, P.O. Box 78, Naskeag Rd., Brooklin, ME 04616; (207) 359-4651, Fax (207) 359-8920.

WOODSTOCK SCHOOL OF ART (WSA)
Woodstock, New York

Weekend to four-week workshops year-round

Founded in 1968 and incorporated as a nonprofit educational institution in 1980, WSA offers year-round classes and summer workshops in drawing, painting, composition, sculpture, and printmaking, with emphasis on landscape painting. Class enrollment is limited to 20 students of all levels. The school year is divided into three sessions: winter-spring (January-June), summer (June-September), and fall (September-December). Six to eight courses are offered during each session with classes scheduled from one to five days each week during one or more time periods — morning (9 am to noon), afternoon (1 to 4 pm), and evening (7 to 10 pm). The minimum course registration is one three-hour class per week for four weeks, however, students may register for up to five daily three-hour classes per week for four weeks. Sixteen workshops are offered during the summer session. Most are scheduled from 9 am to 4 pm daily, Monday through Friday, for one or two weeks, and a couple are held on Saturday and Sunday. Students can enroll for one week (five days) or two weeks (ten days) for either half or full days. During July and August, a series of Saturday noon slide lectures by professional artists features their work, professional development, and approaches to problem-solving. A student exhibition is held in late summer.

Course titles include Painting in Oil, Life Drawing, Watercolor, Etching & Printmaking, Drawing & Painting, Landscape Watercolor, Young People's Class, and Pastel Painting. Summer workshop titles include Landscape Pastel, The Head in Clay, Monotype, Sculpture, Etching, Plein-Air Watercolor, and Fall Foliage Watercolor (a weekend workshop).

Specialties: Drawing, painting, composition, sculpture, and printmaking.

Faculty: Includes professional artists Robert Angeloch, Vladimir Bachinsky, Abigail Belknap, Peter Clapper, Anna Contes, Staats Fasoldt, Albert Handell, Mary James, Peter Jones, Deane Keller, Alfred Koschetzki, Richard McDaniel, Elizabeth Mowry, Karen O'Neil, Richard Pantell, Ric Pike, and Nancy Summers. All have had their work widely exhibited.

Costs, Accommodations: Course tuition ranges from $85 for one three-hour class per week for four weeks to $210 for five classes per week for four weeks. Workshop tuition is $110 for five half-days (one week), $200 for five full days (one week) or ten half-days (two weeks), and $350 for ten full days (two weeks). A nonrefundable $75 deposit and one-time matriculation fee of $10 must accompany registration with balance due prior to the first session. Tuition scholarships are available. A limited number of students can be housed in a converted barn on the premises for $60 per week and a list of nearby housing is provided.

Location, Facilities: The complex of bluestone and timber buildings, which formerly housed the Art Students League Summer School, contains large studios with north light, a graphics studio, and art gallery. The school, which is handicapped accessible, is in a rural setting approximately one mile from the village of Woodstock, a center for artistic and cultural activity.

Contact: Woodstock School of Art, Inc., Rte. 212, P.O. Box 338, Woodstock, NY 12498; (914) 679-2388.

ZEN MOUNTAIN MONASTERY
Mt. Tremper, New York
Three and five-day retreats June, October, and December

Zen Mountain Monastery, the mainhouse of the Mountains and Rivers Order of Zen Buddhist temples in the U.S. and abroad, offers year-round retreats in a variety of disciplines, including Zen brush, Zen arts, and wood carving and whittling. The Zen Brush, a three-day October retreat, involves learning the process of Oriental art. Students are taught the process, the way of holding the brush, the order of strokes, the application, and create one long brushstroke painting, passing the brush hand to hand. Introduction to Wood Carving and Whittling, a three-day December retreat, focuses on mountain lore and precision craftsmanship. Zen Arts Week, a five-day mid-summer retreat, is an introduction to the five Zen arts: Chado (tea ceremony), Sumi-e (brush painting), Ikebana (flower arranging), Noh (drama), and Haiku (poetry). Participants practice the ritual art of receiving tea, create single-stroke brush paintings, learn Noh dance and chants, express themselves through haiku, and compose simple flower arrangements. Daily lessons and practice time with instructors enables students to develop skills they can practice at home.

The Monastery offers a variety of seminars and retreats on topics such as Zen training, writing, religion and ethics. Participants enter into the on-going monastic training program and join the resident monks and lay students in the full schedule of activities. Retreats begin on Friday and conclude on Sunday after a Dharma Discourse by Daido Sensi and a picnic lunch.

Specialties: Zen arts and crafts.

Faculty: Writer, calligrapher, and painter Kazuaki Tanahashi was trained in Japan and has had his brushwork exhibited at the Issacs Gallery in Toronto, East-West Center in Honolulu, and at Harvard University. Woodcarver Albert Ciaccio is president of the Hudson Valley Wood Carvers and has demonstrated his craft at the Canadian National Exhibition in Toronto. Visual artist Hank Tusinski trained in Sumi-e with Chicuin Sensei in Japan and completed a series of brush paintings for a book by George Schaller.

Costs, Accommodations: Cost, which includes lodging and buffet-style meals, is $125 for the three-day retreats, $235 for the five-day retreat. A $25 nonrefundable deposit must accompany registration and credit cards (VISA, MasterCard) are accepted. Cancellations at least 30 days prior receive full refund minus deposit; cancellations 7 to 29 days prior receive credit for another retreat within one year, minus $25 deposit.

Location: The Monastery is on a 200-acre nature sanctuary in the Catskill Mountains, 120 miles north of New York City and 80 miles south of Albany.

Contact: Zen Mountain Monastery, Box 197, Mt. Tremper, NY 12457; (914) 688-2228.

ZOLTAN SZABO WATERCOLOR WORKSHOPS
Scenic locations throughout the U.S.

Five-day workshops from January-October

Watercolorist Zoltan Szabo has conducted on-location workshops at scenic locations in the U.S. and Canada since the late 1960's. Approximately seven workshops are scheduled annually with each limited to approximately 25 artists of all levels, who receive individual instruction. On the last day of class, students receive a certificate of completion and are eligible to participate in a drawing for an original watercolor painting by Zoltan.

Specialties: Watercolor.

Faculty: A native of Hungary, Zoltan Szabo emigrated to Canada in 1948 and moved to the U.S. in 1980. He was resident artist and faculty member at Sault College in Sault Ste. Marie, Canada and is author of five books, including *Painting Nature's Hidden Treasures, Landscape Painting In Watercolor,* and *Creative Watercolor Techniques.* His work is in the collections of the Prime Ministers of Canada and Jamaica as well as the Smithsonian Institution, the Hungarian National Art Gallery Archives in Budapest, and the Art Gallery of Algoma, Ontario.

Costs, Accommodations: Tuition for each workshop is $275 and a $100 deposit ($50 of which is nonrefundable) secures reservation. Accommodations, which vary in cost, are selected for their comfort and convenience.

Location: Locales, which are chosen for their scenic beauty, include Captiva Island, Florida; Jackson, Wyoming; Cannon Beach, Oregon; Bird-in-Hand, Pennsylvania; Gainesville, Georgia; Appleton, Wisconsin; Warm Springs, Virginia; and Chittenden, Vermont.

Contact: Willa McNeill, Director, Zoltan Szabo Watercolor Workshops, 5014 Coronado Dr., Charlotte, NC 28212; (704) 568-4306.

II

RESIDENCIES and
RETREATS

ACT I CREATIVITY CENTER
Lake of the Ozarks, Missouri
Year-round

Founded in 1984 by Char Plotsky as a project of the nonprofit ACTS ("a creative time space") Institute, Inc., the Center provides a setting in which serious artists, writers, scholars, and scientists can work on their creative projects without interruption. It's situated in an idyllic setting in the Lake of the Ozarks region and accommodates up to six persons at a time for periods ranging from one week to two months. The peak period is from March to November. Residents are provided with a private room, workspace, and food, based on ability to pay.

Admission Policies and Costs: Applicants must state how much they are able to pay (actual cost to ACTS is $52/day) and submit a small work sample, a brief description of the project, a resume, and a $10 nonrefundable processing fee. Some fellowships are available. Applications take a month or more (two months or more for the fellowship program) to process.

Location: The Center is near one of the world's largest man-made lakes, with over 1,300 miles of shoreline. Nearby are fishing, boating, golf, tennis, riding stables, two state parks, historical sites, art galleries, fairs and festivals, and craft and antique shops.

Contact: Admissions Office, ACTS, Box 10153, Kansas City, MO 64111; (816) 753-0383. Enclose self addressed stamped envelope.

ALDEN B. DOW CREATIVITY CENTER
The Northwood Institute
Midland, Michigan
June-August

Northwood Institute, a private, accredited, business management college committed to a partnership between business and the arts, was founded in 1959 by Drs. Arthur E. Turner and R. Gary Stauffer. The Creativity Center was founded in 1978 as an outgrowth of the association between the Institute's founders and Alden B. Dow, architect laureate of Michigan and the first recipient of the Frank Lloyd Wright Creativity Award. The Center awards four ten-week fellowships each summer, from mid-June to mid-August, to individuals in any field or profession who wish to pursue an innovative project or creative idea. Respected professionals in many fields are available for consultation to the Fellows during their residency. Upon completion, Fellows make oral presentations of their projects to a selected audience and special certification and recognition are awarded. Fellows live in large, individual, furnished apartments in a wooded environment and weekday lunches are provided at the Center.

Admission Policies and Costs: Applicants should submit a Project Idea Form (statement of idea, outline of project, specific goals), resume, budget for project expenses, and list of needed materials to the Center by December 31. Selection is based primarily on the inherent quality and uniqueness of the idea. All applicants are notified and those whose projects are being seriously considered are invited to Midland for an interview. Fellowships are awarded April 1st and include travel expenses to and from Midland (within the U.S.), living quarters, project expenses, a per diem allowance for board, and a weekly stipend for incidental expenses and a mid-residency holiday.

Location: Midland is a culturally rich and diverse community of 38,000 located in the Saginaw Valley area of central Michigan, about 125 miles north of Detroit. Within a 50 mile radius are a state univerity and three colleges, research centers, galleries and museums, natural history centers, libraries, indoor and outdoor recreational facilities, and a center for the performing and visual arts.

Contact: Northwood Institute, Alden B. Dow Creativity Center, Midland, MI 48640-2398; (517) 832-4478.

ANDERSON RANCH ARTS CENTER
Studio Residency Program
Snowmass, Colorado
October 1-May 15

This interdisciplinary visual arts center offers a Studio Residency Program to encourage the creative, intellectual, and personal growth of emerging and recognized artists through the making of art in a supportive studio atmosphere. Residencies are offered in ceramics, woodworking and furniture design, painting, and photography. The Ranch provides studio space and facilities, scheduled critiques, exhibition space, and consideration for summer assistantships. Residents are expected to work up to ten hours per week for the Ranch.

Admission Policies and Costs: Residents are chosen on the basis of a demonstrated commitment and the ability to function in a community setting. Application should be received by May 1 and must include up to 20 slides, a current resume, a cover letter describing applicant's interest, and three references. Each summer a limited number of individuals are offered room, board, and a small stipend in exchange for working six days a week at the Ranch assisting workshop instructors and students and assuming such general responsiblities as ground maintenance, tent set-up, and preparing for gallery openings.

Location: See page 11.

Contact: Anderson Ranch Arts Center, P.O. Box 5598, Snowmass Village, CO 81615; (303) 923-3191.

ARTISTS BOOK WORKS (page 20)

ARTS AT MENUCHA (page 21)

ATLANTIC CENTER FOR THE ARTS
New Smyrna Beach, Florida

This interdisciplinary arts facility, chartered in 1979, was created to bring mid-career artists, writers, musicians, and composers — Associates — together with Master Artists in an informal interdisciplinary residency, where they have the opportunity to experiment and develop new projects. Four or five 3-week residency periods are scheduled each year, with three Master Artists of different disciplines in residence during each period. Master Artists in Residence have included painters Frank Faulkner and Robert Natkin, sculptors Lynda Benglis and Stephen Antonakos, visual artist Carolee Schneemann, and paper artist Kathryn Clark. During the program, Master Artists participate with Associates in individual and group sessions, develop projects, critique works in progress, hold readings and performances, and share ideas. Collaborative projects may be developed within individual groups and may involve other Master Artists and their groups.

Admission Policies and Costs: Each Master Artist in Residence selects his or her own Associates and sets the application criteria. Applications should be submitted at least four months prior to residency. Tuition for a three-week session is $200. Associates provide their own transportation, lodging, and meals. Approximate housing cost is $500. Some scholarships are offered.

Location, Facilities: The air-conditioned and handicapped accessible Center includes an administration/gallery complex, a multi-purpose workshop, a fieldhouse/commons building, three cottages for the resident Master Artists and an outdoor amphitheatre. Originally a 10-acre site, the facility acquired the surrounding 57 acres, which is being developed to include on-site resident housing, an arts resource center, and additional work space. The Center is located on the east coast of Central Florida.

Contact: Atlantic Center for the Arts, 1414 Art Center Ave., New Smyrna Beach, FL 32168; (904) 427-6975.

AUGUSTA HERITAGE CENTER (page 25)

BAULINES CRAFT GUILD (page 30)

BLUE MOUNTAIN CENTER
Blue Mountain Lake, New York
June 15-October 15

A working community of established artists and writers who don't require exceptional facilities, the Center provides a peaceful and comfortable environment to work free of distractions and demands. For six weeks prior to and following the residency sessions, the Center hosts seminars and work groups concerned with social, economic, and environmental issues. The atmosphere is quiet and informal, and guests are lodged in individual bedrooms/studies. Breakfast and dinner are served in the dining room and lunch is picnic style to avoid interruption of the residents' work. Residencies are for four weeks, between June 15 and October 15.

Admission Policies and Costs: Residents are chosen by an admissions committee interested in creative artists and writers whose work addresses social concerns and is aimed at a general audience. Applications are due before March 1 and should include samples of work, copies of reviews, short biographical sketch, and three references. Applicants are notified just after March 31. There is no cost other than transportation. Residents are asked to contribute to a special needs fund, but this is voluntary.

Location: The facilities of the center, located in Blue Mountain Lake, include tennis courts, lake, boats, trails, and a recreation room.

Contact: Harriet Barlow, Director, Blue Mountain Center, Blue Mountain Lake, NY 12812; (518) 352-7391.

BYRDCLIFFE ARTS COLONY
Woodstock, New York
May 1-October 1

Listed on the National Register of Historic Places, Byrdcliffe Arts Colony was built in 1902 by philanthropist Ralph Whitehead as a utopian arts and crafts colony. Since then it has served as a residence to painters, philosophers, ambassadors, musicians, social reformers, and poets, including Eva Watson-Schutze, Clarence Darrow, Thomas Mann, Wallace Stevens, Milton Avery, John Burroughs, and John Dewey. Now administered by the Woodstock Guild, the Colony offers five month residencies to working artists and writers. Approximately 25 to 30 residents and their families are accommodated in 25 buildings, ranging from small cottages to five or six-bedroom dwellings.

Admission Policies and Costs: Application deadline is January 30 and residents are accepted on a first come, first served basis. The cost of the five-month residency ranges from $1,800 to $5,300, depending upon lodging. Residents are responsible for their own meals.

Location, Facilities: Byrdcliffe is situated on 600 acres on the slopes of Mount Guardian in the Catskills, a few miles from Woodstock. Byrdcliffe also offers a repertory theater, nature study and mountain hiking trails, summer education programs, and seminars and workshops.

Contact: Byrdcliffe Arts Colony, The Woodstock Guild, 34 Tinker St., Woodstock, NY 12498; (914) 679-2079.

THE CAMARGO FOUNDATION
Cassis, France

January-May, September-December

The Camargo Foundation, established in 1967 with an endowment by philanthropist Jerome Hill, maintains a center for study in France and offers fellowships for American scholars who wish to pursue projects in the humanities relative to France. Fellows are provided a furnished apartment and access to a reference library and are expected to participate in academic functions that take place during the year and also to provide a progress report and a written report at the end of the stay. Because of the limited number of studios, only one artist is accepted each semester — from early September to mid-December and from early January to May 31.

Admission Policies and Costs: The selection of fellows is based solely on evaluation of the proposed project and of the applicant's professional qualifications. Applicants may include visual artists, writers, musicians, members of university and college faculties, secondary school teachers, and graduate students. Applications, including a curriculum vitae, detailed description of project, and three letters of recommendation, must be received no later than March 1 and decisions are announced by mid-April.

Location: Camargo, an apartment complex of four buildings, including living quarters, library, music-conference room, and studios, is located on Hill's former estate in Cassis, France, about a half-hour from Marseille by train or bus. There is no organized entertainment. However, fellows meet several times each month to hear each fellow describe his or her project and there are also occasional visiting lecturers and concerts.

Contact: Documents should be sent to The Camargo Foundation, Jane M. Viggiani, 64 Main St., P.O. Box 32, East Haddam, CT 06423.

CHATEAU DE LESVAULT
Villapourcon, France

November through March

This French country residence, located in the national park "Le Morvan", accommodates five residents at a time in five large rooms with private baths, furnished and equipped for living and working. All facilities are at the disposal of residents, including the salon, library, and grounds.

Admission Policies and Costs: There are no application forms and residents are accepted on a first-come, first-served basis. Requests should be made at least two months in advance. The cost is 4,000 FF per month for room, board (five days a week), and utilities.

Location: The Chateau is located in western Burgundy, halfway between Autun and Nevers, surrounded by green hills and forests.

Contact: Bibbi Lee, Chateau de Lesvault, Onlay, 58370 Villapourcon, France; (33) 86-84-32-91.

COUNTRY WORKSHOPS (page 55)

CUMMINGTON COMMUNITY OF THE ARTS
Cummington, Massachusetts

April-November

The Cummington Community of the Arts was founded in 1923 by Katherine Frazier, a concert harpist and aesthetician, as a summer arts school for college-aged students. Since the late 1960s, it has served as a community of artists and writers who live and work together. Residencies range from two weeks to three months. During spring and fall, up to 15 residents are accepted, usually on a monthly basis. During June, July, and August, approximately 25 are in residence each month. Living/studio accommodations are in individual cabins or two main houses and every effort is made to provide each resident with the most appropriate space available. During July and August, Cummington sponsors the Summer Children's Program, unique in the U.S., for residents who do not want to be away from their children for an extended period. Children of ages 5 to 14 work and play together in a converted barn under supervision of counselors, leaving parents free during the day to pursue creative work. All community residents take part in working on one weekly chore for the upkeep of the Community, and all residents, in pairs, cook one evening meal. Generally, residents prepare their own breakfasts and lunches from food provided in the community kitchens.

Admission Policies and Costs: Admission is competitive and based on the applicant's demonstrated level of accomplishment and commitment plus a willingness to participate in the cooperative community structure. Cummington seeks risk takers — those who are experimenting with new concepts and striving to define their individual creative voice. Visual artists should submit a resume and a work sample of ten slides in a 9x11 plastic sheet. Application deadlines are: January 1 for April, May; March 1 for June, July, August; June 1 for September, October, November . The fee structure varies, depending upon the amount of community work (repair, maintenance, office work, child care, etc.) the resident is willing to contribute. At present, the maximum fee for those who do not contribute community work is $500 per month. The children's program is $350 per month per child.

Location: Cummington is located on the edge of the Berkshires on 100 acres of fields, hiking trails, swimming holes, and woodlands. Facilities include a concert shed, library, and organic vegetable garden.

Contact: Cummington Community of the Arts, Cummington, MA 01026; (413) 634-2172.

DJERASSI FOUNDATION RESIDENT ARTISTS PROGRAM
Woodside, California
March 1-November 30

The Djerassi Foundation was founded in memory of Pamela Djerassi, a 28-year old painter and poet, whose studio, home, and estate were left to the Foundation upon her death. Fifty to seventy artists a year are selected to spend one to three months working on independent projects in a remote, natural setting. Applications are sought from accomplished artists who are not yet well known as well as from those with established reputations who desire a change of scene for refreshment and inspiration. Living quarters are provided in an eight-bedroom Artists' House with five baths, living room, dining room, kitchen, outside deck, and balconies. Studio space for artists is located in a 12-sided barn within walking distance of the Artists' House. Residents are served dinner each weekday evening and are expected to prepare their own breakfasts, lunches, and weekend meals.

Admission Policies and Costs: Applicant must provide a curriculum vitae, documentation of recent work, two references, a description of the proposed project, and months available (competition is keener for the summer months). Application deadlines are June 1 and September 1 for the following year. The Foundation pays for all costs of the residency and there is no requirement to leave any portion of completed work. Previous residents may re-apply after a year.

Location: The 1,400-acre SMIP Ranch, 600 acres of which belong to the Djerassi Foundation, is a former cattle ranch set in redwood forest in the Santa Cruz mountains, overlooking the Pacific Ocean. It's an hour's drive south of downtown San Francisco, thirty minutes west of Stanford University.

Contact: Sally M. Stillman, Executive Director, Djerassi Foundation, 2325 Bear Gulch Rd., Woodside, CA 94062; (415) 851-8395.

DORLAND MOUNTAIN ARTS COLONY
Temecula, California
Year-round

Homesteaded in the 1930s by Ellen and Robert Dorland, this primitive retreat is set on a 300-acre nature preserve along a ridge overlooking the Temecula Valley. The colony and buildings occupy about 10 acres with the rest of the land left in its natural state. Noted concert pianist and teacher Ellen Babcock Dorland and her friend, dedicated environmentalist Barbara Horton, founded the colony, which accepts artists, writers, photographers, playwrights, and composers for residencies of two weeks to one month. Longer residencies are also available under the Working Fellows Program. Each resident has an individual cottage, which is heated by propane woodstoves and lit by kerosene or Coleman lamps. Residents are not disturbed in their cottages, but may share their work in progress at an open studio. The only organized social activities are occasional potluck dinners.

Admission Policies and Costs: Applications are reviewed twice a year by an independent panel of recognized artists, writers, editors, composers, and others. Application deadlines are September 1 and March 1. There is a modest charge to residents.

Location: Dorland is about 100 miles from Los Angeles, 60 miles from San Diego, and about 8 miles from Temecula.

Contact: Admissions Committee, Dorland Mountain Arts Colony, Box 6, Temecula, CA 92390; (714) 676-5039.

FINE ARTS WORK CENTER IN PROVINCETOWN
Provincetown, Massachusetts

October-May

The Center was founded in 1968 by a group of eminent artists, writers, and patrons who wanted to encourage and nurture talented young artists and writers at the outset of their careers. Each year, ten visual artists and ten writers are selected from more than 800 applicants to spend a seven month residency, from October 1 to May 1, in a community of their peers. Fellows are provided with a limited monthly stipend, living and studio space, and a resident staff of artists who are available for studio visits. Throughout the season there is an active series of public slide presentations, readings, and performances by visiting professional artists and writers who also meet with the Fellows on an informal basis. Several established artists are invited for extended residencies.

Admission Policies and Costs: This is the only residency in the country that focuses solely on emerging talent and Fellowship awards are based on the quality of the applicant's work. Though there is no age limit, the Center aims to aid those who demonstrate outstanding promise and who have completed their formal training and are working on their own. Detailed information on submission of work for consideration is included in the application form. Applications must be received by February 1 in order to be considered.

Location: The Center is housed in historic studios in the small fishing village of Provincetown, within walking distance of the dunes and the beach .

Contact: Fellowship Application, Fine Arts Work Center in Provincetown, 24 Pearl St., Box 565, Provincetown, MA 02657; (508) 487-9960.

GRAND MARAIS ART COLONY (page 84)

THE HAMBIDGE CENTER
Rabun Gap, Georgia

May-October

Founded in 1934 by textile designer Mary Hambidge in honor of her late husband, American artist Jay Hambidge, The Hambidge Center for Creative

Arts and Sciences strives "to provide an environment where a balanced living experience is possible for mature people who are engaged in creative work and/or research and who are seeking the highest levels of excellence in their field". Two-week to two-month Fellowship Residencies, for individuals engaged in the artistic, scientific, humanistic, and educational professions, are limited to five participants at a time. Each year fellowships are awarded to 20 to 25 of the more than 800 applicants. Fellows have a private cottage equipped with a kitchen, sleeping and bathing facilities, and studio area. The Center also has pottery/sculpture, weaving/textiles, painting/drawing, and photography studios and a concert hall. Fellows are expected to prepare their own breakfasts and lunches and the Center provides evening meals from Monday through Friday.

Admission Policies and Costs: In addition to application and $10 processing fee, applicants are required to submit samples of work, curriculum vitae, reviews, and three letters of recommendation. Notification takes approximately two months. Resident Fellows are asked to contribute a small portion of the $300 per week cost.

Location: The Center is located on 600 acres of wooded hills, fresh water streams, and fields of wildflowers in the northeastern mountains of Georgia, bordering southwestern North Carolina, off U.S. Highway 441. It's about three miles from Dillard, 120 miles from Atlanta, and 90 miles from Asheville, North Carolina.

Contact: The Hambidge Center for Creative Arts and Sciences, P.O. Box 339, Rabun Gap, GA 30568; (404) 746-5718.

THE HELENE WURLITZER FOUNDATION OF NEW MEXICO
Taos, New Mexico

April 1-September 30

Since 1954, the Foundation has provided 12 individual furnished studio residences to persons engaged in creative fields in all media. Grants are awarded without respect to age, sex, religion, or ethnic origin for varying time periods, normally three months, which is flexible. The Foundation is open from April 1 through September 30. Facilities are handicapped accessible.

Admission Policies and Costs: The Foundation has no printed brochures, data, program information, or application guidelines. All submitted work must include self-addressed, stamped envelope for return. Following receipt of inquiry letter, application forms and procedures and general information are forwarded. The residencies are offered rent and utility-free and no monetary grants or stipends for living expenses or supplies are awarded.

Location: The residences are located in Taos.

Contact: Henry A. Sauerwein, Jr., The Helene Wurlitzer Foundation of New Mexico, P.O. Box 545, Taos, NM 87571; (505) 758-2413.

HILAI
THE ISRAELI CENTER FOR THE CREATIVE ARTS
Tel-Aviv, Israel

Year-round

Founded in 1984 by Tel Aviv writer Corinna, this organization provides a common ground in which Jews, Arabs, Israelis, and foreign guests can meet through artistic endeavor. Hilai maintains two residential working facilities for published or talented visual artists, poets, fiction writers, playwrights, and composers. Each resident is housed in a studio apartment with kitchen and private bathroom. Residencies of two weeks to three months are offered to three artists at a time in each location, and spouses may accompany artists at Mitzpe Ramon, where 2-bedroom studios are available. Six studio apartments are available at Ma'alot. Residents are asked to participate three to four hours a week in such community cultural activities as lectures, workshops, or readings.

Admission Policies and Costs: There is no application deadline and notification of acceptance takes at least 10 weeks. The first two weeks are free of charge and artists who remain for a longer period are asked to contribute according to their ability to defray costs.

Location: Facilities are located at Ma'alot-Tarshiha, in the western Galilee, and at Mitzpe Ramon, in the northern Negev, about a two-hour drive from Tel Aviv or Jerusalem.

Contact: Corinna, Hilai, The Israeli Center for the Creative Arts, 212 B'nai Ephraim St., P.O.B. 53007, Tel-Aviv 61530; 03-478704 *or* Sue Pucker, Hilai International, 98 Clinton Rd., Brookline, MA 02146; (617) 731-3112.

KALANI HONUA
Kalapana, Hawaii

Year-round

This intercultural conference and retreat center provides comfortable lodging and studio space on a 20-acre site bordered by the ocean and forest. There are two 1,000-square foot studios and rooms with shared studio space (500 square feet) in the conference area. Throughout the year, eight selected applicants can stay at half the regular rate on a space available basis. Four rooms in each lodge have kitchen facilities and shared baths.

Admission Policies and Costs: Artists wishing consideration should submit samples of their work (seven to ten 35mm slides), a biographical page, and a statement of interest, goals, and any benefits for Kalani Honua. Regular daily rate for room with shared bath is $40 single, $24 double occupancy and room with private bath is $50 single, $30 double.

Location: The retreat is located on the Kalapana coast, near secluded black sand beaches and several state and national parks.

Contact: Richard Koob, Artistic Director, Kalani Honua, Box 4500, Kalapana, Hawaii 96778; (808) 965-7828.

LEIGHTON ARTIST COLONY
The Banff Centre
Banff, Alberta, Canada
Year-round

This working retreat for professional artists, writers, and musicians, situated in a secluded pine grove on the side of Tunnel Mountain, consists of eight studios, two of which are specially designed for visual art. The ceramic studio is situated in the School of Fine Arts Ceramic Department in Glyde Hall. Named after David Leighton, the former president of The Banff Centre, who inaugurated its construction, the first studios were opened in 1984 and the colony was officially opened by Prince Philip in 1985. All studios have washrooms, kitchenettes, and comfortable furnishings and are designed to provide maximum privacy and take advantage of a private view. The working day is uninterrupted and visitors to studios do so by appointment. Telephone messages are delivered only in the event of emergency and housekeeping service is provided. While the studios are open 24 hours daily, they are intended as worksites. Meals are served in the Centre's dining room and lunches can be taken in the studios.

Admission Policies and Costs: Residencies are open to established artists who can demonstrate a sustained contribution to their discipline and show evidence of significant achievement. All nationalities are encouraged to apply. Applications should be submitted at least nine months in advance of the proposed residency and include description of project planned, a curriculum vitae, and representative work. Residents are expected to contribute toward the $70 daily cost of room, board, studios, and housekeeping. Canadian citizens or landed immigrants who demonstrate need can qualify for a limited financial subsidy.

Location: The Banff Centre is frequently visited by distinguished faculty and offers theatres, recital halls, art galleries, and a well-equipped recreation complex. It is situated at an elevation of 4,500 feet in Canada's first national park and is 80 miles west of Calgary.

Contact: Coordinator, Leighton Artist Colony, P.O. Box 1020, The Banff Centre, Banff, AB, T0L 0C0, Canada; (403) 762-6100.

THE MACDOWELL COLONY
Peterborough, New Hampshire
Year-round

Founded in 1906 in honor of the composer, Edward MacDowell, The MacDowell Colony provides uninterrupted time and seclusion for established or promising visual artists, filmmakers, writers, and composers, who each receive room, board, and the exclusive use of a studio and stay an average of five to six weeks. Almost no studio is within sight of another and each is simply but comfortably furnished. Breakfast and dinner are served in the Colony Hall and lunches are brought to the studios. Presentations, open studios, and parties are held in the evenings. The Colony accommodates 31 residents in the summer and 19 to 25 during the other seasons.

Admission Policies and Costs: Admission is competitive and based only on talent. Ability to pay is not a factor. Artists should submit five color slides of their recent work or five unmatted original prints, a description of the proposed project, and two references (optional). Application deadlines are: Sept. 15 for winter-spring, Jan. 15 for summer, and April 15 for fall-winter. Residents are asked to pay what they can. The daily cost of the residency is $25 and the basic fee is $15.

Location: The Colony is situated on 450 acres and has a library, piano, stereo, and tape recorders. The graphics workshop contains equipment for etching, lithography, serigraphy, and aquatint.

Contact: Admissions Coordinator, MacDowell Colony, 100 High St., Peterborough, NH 03458; (603) 924-3886 *or* (212) 966-4860.

THE MILLAY COLONY FOR THE ARTS, INC.
Austerlitz, New York
Year-round

The Millay Colony, a nonprofit organization, gives one-month residencies to visual artists, writers, and composers, who usually stay from the 1st to the 28th of the month. Steepletop, the 600-acre estate of poet Edna St. Vincent Millay and now a national historic landmark, provides accommodations consisting of four bedrooms and separate 14 by 20-foot studios. The Ellis Studio, which was opened in 1974, is a year-round 400-square foot work and living space designed to accommodate one artist at a time. It has a large north-lit skylight placed into a twelve-foot high ceiling, adjustable artificial lights for painting at night, and is equipped with a studio easel and a large movable wall.

Admission Policies and Costs: There is no residence fee required and the colony provides meals at no cost. The organization does depend on gifts for its existence and welcomes contributions. Decisions on applications are made by committees of professional artists and, on Feb. 1, applicants are reviewed for the following June-Sept., on May 1 for the following Oct.-Jan., and on Sept. 1, for the following Feb.-May. Applicants should submit a letter of reference and several examples of their work.

Location: Approximately 2 1/2 hours from New York, 2 hours from Boston.

Contact: Ann-Ellen Lesser, Executive Director, *or* Gail Giles, Assistant Director, The Millay Colony for the Arts, Inc., Steepletop, P.O. Box 3, Austerlitz, NY 12017-0003; (518) 392-3103.

MISHKENOT SHA'ANANIM
Jerusalem, Israel
Year-round

Mishkenot Sha'ananim (Hebrew for "Peaceful Dwellings") was constructed in 1860 on the initiative of Sir Moses Montefiore as the first building outside the protective wall of the Old City. It was founded in 1973 as a retreat for the creative and as a means to help Jerusalem expand its cultural, artistic, and spiritual vistas as well as provide inspiration for eminent figures from the worlds of the arts and ideas. Residents, who stay from one week to months, have included Alexander Calder, Marc Chagall, and Robert Rauschenberg. Facilities include seven fully-equipped and furnished two-bedroom apartments and four one-bedroom apartments. The larger apartments have full kitchens while the smaller ones have modest cooking facilities. All units have refrigerators and hot plates and daily room service is provided.

Admission Policies and Costs: Residents are invited by the representative committee. The daily cost for the large apartments is $95 per day, single or double occupancy. Smaller accommodations are $20 to $80 per day, single or double, depending on the size of the apartment. An additional person is $10 per day and 20% discount is offered on a monthly basis. The studios are $10 per day or $200 per month. Breakfast can be provided for $4 daily per person.

Location: Mishkenot is situated near the center of town, with a view overlooking Mt. Zion and the walls of the Old City.

Contact: Dr. Yael Amzalak, Director, Mishkenot Sha'ananim, Ltd., P.O. Box 8215, Jerusalem, 91081, Israel; 02-224321.

MORAVIAN POTTERY AND TILE WORKS (page 126)

OREGON SCHOOL OF ARTS AND CRAFTS (page 139)

PALENVILLE INTERARTS COLONY
Palenville, New York
June 1-September 30

This retreat facility, founded in 1982, provides an unpressured, creative environment for recognized and emerging artists in the performing, visual, musical, and literary arts, with a major focus on interdisciplinary projects. The residency includes private or semiprivate room or cabin, all meals, and studio space as required. The Colony accommodates a maximum of 15 residents, between June 1 and September 30, who stay a minimum of one and a maximum of eight weeks. There is partial handicapped access.

Admission Policies and Costs: Applicants should have a minimum of three years of professional experience. Admission is competitive and selection is based on ability, need for the retreat environment, and creativity of the proposed project. Visual artists should submit eight color slides of recent work, as well as a biographical resume. Applications must be received by April 1 and notification is made within four weeks. A weekly fee of $175 is suggested.

Location: The Colony, set on a rustic 120-acre estate, is on the site of America's first colony established by the painters of the Hudson River School and writers such as James Fenimore Cooper and Washington Irving.

Contact: Joanna M. Sherman, Palenville Interarts Colony, 2 Bond Street, New York, NY 10012; (212) 254-4614.

PENLAND SCHOOL (page 146)

PETERS VALLEY CRAFTS CENTER (page 148)

PEWABIC POTTERY (page 150)

PILCHUCK GLASS SCHOOL (page 152)

PYRAMID ATLANTIC (page 157)

RAGDALE FOUNDATION
Lake Forest, Illinois
January 1-June 15, July 1-December 15

The Ragdale Foundation offers a peaceful place and uninterrupted time for twelve serious artists, writers, and scholars to do their work. Accommodations include a library, community rooms, and two private visual artist's studios on two adjoining estates designed by Howard Van Doren Shaw in 1897. Meals, linen, and laundry facilities are provided for up to twelve residents. Applicants may come for periods of two weeks to two months.

Admission Policies and Costs: Applicants are required to submit a sample of work, curriculum vitae, names of three professional references, and description of work-in-progress. The major criterion for acceptance is proof of commitment to a specific project. The residence fee is $70 per week. A limited number of waiver and fee reduction scholarships are available. For priority consideration, applications should be submitted four months before beginning of residency.

Location: Ragdale is in Lake Forest, 30 miles north of Chicago near Lake Michigan. The estate, which is on the National Register of Historic Places, has a country garden and borders on a 60-acre nature preserve.

Contact: Ragdale Foundation, 1260 N. Green Bay Rd. Lake Forest, IL 60045; (708) 234-1063.

ROCKPORT APPRENTICESHOP (page 162)

SASKATCHEWAN WRITERS/ARTISTS COLONIES AND INDIVIDUAL RETREATS
Saskatchewan, Canada
Colonies: February, July, and August; Retreats: Year-round

The three Saskatchewan Colonies were established in 1979 to provide a place where writers could write free from distractions. They were soon after expanded to include visual artists. Fort San, Echo Valley, site of the two-week February colony, provides residents with private accommodations in a pavilion with spacious verandahs and common rooms. Meals are served in the main building of the complex. The eight-week summer colony is held at St. Peter's College, a Benedictine Abbey, where guests stay in private rooms in the guest wing and dine in the college facility. Year-round individual retreats are also offered at St. Peter's Abbey, allowing individuals to choose their own time. Artists/writers are limited to a maximum of one month's retreat a year and no more than three residents can be accommodated at one time. Emma Lake offers a two-week August colony, where residents are housed in separate cabins or single rooms and two artists share a large studio space.

Admission Policies and Costs: Applications are welcomed from artists and writers anywhere, but priority is given to Saskatchewan residents. Applicants should submit sample work, a resume of past work and description of colony project, the names of two references, and a $50 fee. Deadline for applications to the Fort San Colony (February) is Dec. 1, and for the summer colonies is April 1. Artists who prefer an individual retreat (Abbey) should apply four weeks before desired date. Colony costs are subsidized by Sask Trust and room and board are $50/week.

Location: Fort San Echo Valley is located in the Qu'Appelle Valley near the town of Fort Qu'Appelle. St. Peter's College is just outside the village of Muenster. Emma Lake is situated in a forest region approximately 25 miles north of Prince Albert, a few miles from the town of Christopher Lake.

Contact: Saskatchewan Writers/Artists Colony, c/o Box 3986, Regina, Saskatchewan S4P 3R9, Canada; (306) 757-6310.

SITKA CENTER FOR ART AND ECOLOGY (page 174)

SOUTHWEST CRAFT CENTER (page 177)

THE TYRONE GUTHRIE CENTRE
Annaghmakerrig, Ireland
Year-round

This home of the late theatre director, Tyrone Guthrie, is open to practitioners of all the arts of any age, from Ireland and from abroad, and offers an environment conducive to creative work. Each resident has a private apartment within the Irish Big House, which also offers an extensive library collection. Residences range from three weeks to three months and couples or small groups may stay up to a year in a cottage on the estate.

Admission Policies and Costs: Admission is selective and based on level of achievement, the proposed project, and the number of residencies available. Application should include examples of works in progress and a brief resume of past work including exhibitions, and a description of work to be done at the colony. Once accepted, Irish artists are asked to contribute what they can afford. Overseas artists are expected to pay the whole cost of residency, 1,000 IR£ per month. The Centre provides an official letter of acceptance which the applicant can use to approach philanthropic organizations for funds.

Location: Set on a 400-acre wooded estate in County Monaghan, Republic of Ireland, the house overlooks a large lake and is surrounded by gardens and a working dairy farm.

Contact: Bernard Loughlin, Resident Director, The Tyrone Guthrie Centre, Anaghmakerrig, Newbliss, Co. Monaghan, Ireland; 353-047-54003.

UCROSS FOUNDATION
Ucross, Wyoming
January-May and August-December

The Ucross Foundation Residency Program provides individual workspace, living accommodations, and time to concentrate without distraction in a rural setting in northeastern Wyoming. Residencies in the visual arts, writing, and other disciplines run from two weeks to four months, with an average length of six weeks. Residents stay in the remodeled Ucross Schoolhouse, which houses four at any one time and has private bedrooms and living and dining areas. The four studios, each with private entrance, are housed in a separate building. There is handicapped access.

Admission Policies and Costs: Admission is competitive and based on quality of work. Applicants should submit work samples, biographical information, and three letters of reference. Two residency sessions are scheduled annually. Application deadline dates are March 1 for the fall session, Aug. through Dec., and Oct. 1 for the spring session, Jan. through May. There is no charge for room, board, or studio space and the Foundation does not expect services or products from its guests.

Location: The Ucross Foundation is located 27 miles southeast of Sheridan in a fertile valley among the foothills of the Big Horn Mountains, at the confluence of Piney and Clear Creeks.

Contact: Residency Program, Ucross Foundation, 2836 US Hwy 14-16 East, Clearmont, WY 82835; (307) 737-2291.

VILLA MONTALVO
Saratoga, California
Year-round

Built in 1912 by former San Francisco mayor James D. Phelan, who named it for Ordoñez de Montalvo, the 16th century Spanish writer who coined the name California, Villa Montalvo was willed in 1930 to be used for the development of the arts and as a public park. The first residents were invited in 1942 and since then over 400 artists, writers, and composers have stayed there. Out of the 350 who apply each year, 16 to 18 are invited for a residency. The purpose of a Montalvo residency is to allow the artist to concentrate fully on a creative project with a minimum of distraction in a setting of natural beauty, yet easily accessible to urban resources. It's best suited to those with a focused, clear project which can be accomplished in a brief, intense burst of work. Applicants should have completed formal training and be engaged in their endeavor on a professional level. Five residents at a time can be accommodated in individual private apartments for a period of three months. Requests for shorter residencies (a minimum of one month) are considered as well as extensions (up to six months maximum), and applications from former residents are accepted one year after completion of the prior residency. Because Montalvo is also an active art center with two theatres, gallery, a public arboretum, and wedding facilities, and apartments are not totally secluded, complete solitude and quiet sometimes are not possible.

Admission Policies and Costs: Applications should be submitted eight months in advance of the desired period of residence (14 months in advance for the summer months) and be accompanied by a resume, three professional recommendations, a statement of the proposed project, a sample of recent work, and a financial assistance form, if appropriate. A refundable $50 security deposit is required and a fee of $100/month is charged to offset part of the cost. Actual cost for each apartment is about $1,000/month. Those who demonstrate financial need may be granted a waiver of the residence fee.

Location: Montalvo is located on 175 acres in the eastern foothills of the Santa Cruz Mountains at the edge of Silicon Valley. It's a mile and a half from Saratoga, four miles from Los Gatos, and about an hour's drive from San

Francisco and Berkeley. Most of the estate has been made into an arboretum and bird sanctuary, with miles of nature trails, numerous small creeks, and formal gardens containing many rare plants.

Contact: Villa Montalvo, Box 158, Saratoga, CA 95071; (408) 741-3421.

VIRGINIA CENTER FOR THE CREATIVE ARTS (VCCA)
Mt. San Angelo, Sweet Briar, Virginia
Year-round

A working retreat for visual artists, writers, and composers, the Virginia Center for the Creative Arts provides residential Fellowships of one to three months in a rural setting, free from distractions and responsibilities. Fellows have private bedrooms in a modern building and separate studios in the Studio Barn, which accommodates seven visual artists at a time. Breakfast and dinner are served in the dining room and lunches are delivered to the studios. Bedrooms and studio complexes are fully handicapped accessible.

Admission Policies and Costs: Admission is competitive and selective, based on a review of the applicant's submitted work. A nonrefundable $15 fee must accompany application, which should include a description of the proposed project and names of two references. Applications for residencies during Jan. to May are due Sept. 25, from May to Sept. are due Jan. 25, and from Sept. to Jan. are due May 25. Notification of status is made two months after deadline. Although the actual daily cost of the residency is more than $60, the standard suggested daily fee is $20.

Location: The VCCA is located at Mt. San Angelo, a 450-acre estate in Amherst County, about 160 miles southwest of Washington, DC. Facilities include a library, gallery, and swimming pool. The VCCA is affiliated with nearby Sweet Briar College, which has a lake, indoor pool, and tennis courts, and offers movies, lectures, plays, and use of the college library.

Contact: Admissions Committee, Box VCCA, Sweet Briar, VA 24595; (804) 946-7236.

THE WILLIAM FLANAGAN MEMORIAL CREATIVE PERSONS CENTER
The Edward F. Albee Foundation
Montauk, New York
May 1-October 1

The Foundation maintains the William Flanagan Memorial Creative Persons Center ("The Barn") as a one-month residence for six painters, sculptors, writers, and composers. The standards for admission are talent and need, the environment is simple and communal, and all are expected to help maintain the condition of the residence. Visual artists are offered studio space and a room. Handicapped persons can be accommodated.

Admission Policies and Costs: Applications are accepted between January 1 and April 1 for the up-coming season and should include six to twelve slides of work, a resume, two letters of recommendation, and a letter of intent outlining the proposed project. Residents pay board and transportation only. Applicants are free to request specific months but the Foundation often must offer alternate dates.

Location: Situated in a secluded area approximately two miles from the center of Montauk and the Atlantic Ocean, "The Barn" offers privacy and a peaceful atmosphere.

Contact: The Edward F. Albee Foundation, Inc., 14 Harrison St., New York, NY 10013; (212) 226-2020.

YADDO
Saratoga Springs, New York
Year-round

This 400-acre retreat, endowed by Spencer and Katrina Trask, provides room, board, and studio space for 30 visual artists, writers, and composers in the summer and 12 the other months. Invitations, issued without respect to age, sex, or race, offer one to two months and guests are expected to be at the professional level of achievement in their fields. Preference is given to poets, fiction writers, and playwrights.

Admission Policies and Costs: Applicants should submit resume, sample work, and letters of reference with $10 filing fee. The sole criterion for acceptance is talent, as judged by a committee of authorities in the applicant's discipline. Deadlines are Aug. 1 for winter-spring and Jan. 15 for "the large season" (mid-May through Labor Day). Notification is within three months. While there is no fixed charge for a guest-stay, contributions are accepted to help defray the cost of the program and can be made at the time of visit or later in the year in response to fund-raising appeals.

Location: Besides a mansion, a garage building with offices, three smaller houses, and several studios, the estate contains four small lakes, a famous rose garden open to the public, and hundreds of acres of woodland, including a pine and oak grove. Since Yaddo is a working community, it has no formal social activities. Ponds and numerous walking trails are located on the property, as well as a tennis court, swimming pool, croquet, bicycling and fishing.

Contact: Myra Sklarew, President, The Corporation of Yaddo, P.O. Box 395, Saratoga Springs, NY 12866; (518) 584-0746.

III

APPENDIX

GEOGRAPHIC INDEX

SPECIALTY INDEX

FOLK, NATIVE, AND REGIONAL ARTS & CRAFTS

SCULPTURE

WOOD

WORKSHOPS FOR YOUNG PEOPLE

IV

MASTER INDEX